P9-DCV-386

Praise for *Pathways to the Common Core*

While acknowledging the ambivalence swirling around the Common Core State Standards, *Pathways to the Common Core* takes a proactive stance, encouraging us to scrutinize the standards carefully and accept the challenge to raise expectations for all children's literacy learning. It reminds us that it is up to schools and districts to decide how to implement the standards and choose our own way forward.

—**Ellin Keene**, consultant and author of *Talk About Understanding*

I began reading *Pathways to the Common Core* in my favorite chair, music playing, dinner cooking on the stove. "I'll just read a couple of chapters," I thought. I finished the book hours later, sitting at my desk, a legal pad filled with notes of all I had learned, and hungry for conversation with colleagues (and for dinner that had long-ago burned). *Pathways to the Common Core* sets you on a path for thinking more deeply about the standards, for teaching more inventively with the standards, and for helping students achieve the goals of the standards.

—**Kylene Beers**, consultant and author of *When Kids Can't Read*

The success of the Common Core State Standards will depend largely on how teachers implement them and whether they are able to resist narrow interpretations that could lead to increased failure rates and achievement gaps. In the hands of informed teachers the standards could promote deeper thinking and higher classroom performance. Read *Pathways to the Common Core* and be informed.

—**Tom Corcoran**, Co-director of CPRE, Teachers College

The Common Core State Standards are here and, as with any new initiative, there are the inevitable questions and concerns, debate and discontent. *Pathways to the Common Core* does not take sides; rather, the authors acknowledge the range of opinions swarming around the CCSS and wisely focus their energy on making sense of the standards. They provide a clear examination of what *is* and *isn't* stated and then invite us to seize this opportunity to reflect on our practice and to become "co-constructors of the future of instruction and curriculum." Let's take up that challenge.

—**Lester L. Laminack**, author, educator, consultant

Calkins, Ehrenworth, and Lehman have taken up the challenge of the Common Core standards in a most valuable way. *Pathways to the Common Core* provides a context for teachers and administrators to advance productive instructional strategies while offering the critical language and logic needed to stand up to unfortunate interpretations and nonsense.

—**Peter Johnston**, Professor, The University at Albany

I love it when I sit down to view a table of contents and end up reading the whole book. *Pathways to the Common Core* is the most useful unpacking of the Common Core State Standards available to date. Lucy, Mary, and Chris help us understand what the standards emphasize and how this emphasis might lead us down different paths of instruction than we've taken before. With generous wisdom and experience, they help us keep one eye on rigor and the other on meaningful reading and writing.

—**Gretchen Owocki**, Ph.D., Director,
Reading and Writing Clinic, Saginaw Valley State University

Some of our most valuable resources in supporting a child's journey toward college and career readiness are the teachers who propel that journey. If the standards specify what every child needs to know and be able to do to be college or career ready, then *Pathways to the Common Core* specifies what every educator needs to know and be able to do to implement the ELA standards effectively.

— **Meghan Berry**, CPS, K–5 Writing Content Lead,
Office of Reading and Language Arts, Chicago

While the standards may be daunting and technical, I am inspired by the way *Pathways to the Common Core* eases the reader through the concerns we all feel and supports us as we come together to take an honest look at our instructional practices and create systems that will accelerate student achievement. This book is encouraging and supportive; I feel prepared to roll up my sleeves and get to work alongside my staff.

— **Liz Tetreault**, Principal, Port Salerno Elementary School, FL

Pathways to the Common Core

Accelerating Achievement

LUCY CALKINS ◆ MARY EHRENWORTH

CHRISTOPHER LEHMAN

HEINEMANN ◆ Portsmouth, NH

Heinemann
361 Hanover Street
Portsmouth, NH 03801–3912
www.heinemann.com

Offices and agents throughout the world

© 2012 by Lucy Calkins, Mary Ehrenworth, and Christopher Lehman

All rights reserved. No part of this book may be reproduced in any form or by any electronic or mechanical means, including information storage and retrieval systems, without permission in writing from the publisher, except by a reviewer, who may quote brief passages in a review.

"Dedicated to Teachers" is a trademark of Greenwood Publishing Group, Inc.

The authors and publisher wish to thank those who have generously given permission to reprint borrowed material:

Excerpts from the *Common Core State Standards* © Copyright 2010. National Governors Association Center for Best Practices and Council of Chief State School Officers. All rights reserved.

Excerpts of "Shoot-Out" in Chapter 5: Copyright © 2009 Condé Nast. All rights reserved. Originally published in *The New Yorker*. Reprinted by permission.

Library of Congress Cataloging-in-Publication Data

Calkins, Lucy.
    Pathways to the common core : accelerating achievement / Lucy Calkins, Mary Ehrenworth, Christopher Lehman.
       p. cm.
    Includes bibliographical references.
    ISBN-13: 978-0-325-04355-5
    ISBN-10: 0-325-04355-8
    1. Education—Standards—United States. 2. Academic achievement—United States. 3. Reading—United States. 4. Language arts—United States. I. Ehrenworth, Mary. II. Lehman, Christopher. III. Title.

LB3060.83.C36 2012
371.26—dc23   2012000322

Editors: *Kate Montgomery* and *Teva Blair*
Production: *Vicki Kasabian*
Cover design: *Jenny Jensen Greenleaf*
Cover art: © *veer.com/ImageZoo*
Typesetter: *Kim Arney*
Manufacturing: *Steve Bernier*

Printed in the United States of America on acid-free paper
16 15 14 13 12 VP 4 5

Contents

CHAPTER ONE

An INTRODUCTION to the COMMON CORE STATE STANDARDS

Pathways to the Common Core will help you and your colleagues teach in ways that will bring your students to the Common Core State Standards' level of work in literacy. This book will illuminate both the standards themselves and the pathways you can take to achieve those ambitious expectations. It will help you understand what is written and implied in the standards and help you grasp the coherence and central messages of them. Above all, *Pathways to the Common Core* has been written to help you tap into the standards as a source for energetic and beautiful reforms in your literacy instruction and in your work with colleagues.

The Common Core State Standards (CCSS) are a big deal. Adopted by forty-five states so far, the standards represent the most sweeping reform of the K–12 curriculum that has ever occurred in this country. It is safe to say that across the entire history of American education, no single document will have played a more influential role over what is taught in our schools. The standards are already affecting what is published, mandated, and tested in schools—and also what is marginalized and neglected. Any educator who wants to play a role in shaping what happens in schools, therefore, needs a deep understanding of these standards. That understanding is necessary for anyone wanting to be a co-constructor of the future of instruction and curriculum and, indeed, of public education across America.

Pathways to the Common Core is written for teachers, literacy coaches, and school leaders who want to grasp what the standards say and imply—as well as what they do not say—deeply enough that they can join in the work of interpreting the standards for the classroom and in questioning interpretations others may make. The Common Core State Standards are clear that the responsibility for interpreting and implementing these expectations rests on the shoulders of teachers and principals (as well as those of state leaders). The standards say, "The Standards leave room for teachers, curriculum developers, and states to determine how those goals should be reached and what additional topics should be addressed. . . . Teachers are thus free to provide students with whatever tools and knowledge their professional judgment and experience identify as most helpful for meeting the goals set out in the Standards" (2010a, 4). *Pathways to the Common Core* expects that you will take the standards at their word and see it as your responsibility—individually and as a member of a school community—to study the expectations for end-of-grade results outlined by the CCSS and to use the Common Core as a lens for reflecting on your practice and for planning ways to support deeper and further learning. *Pathways* aims to help you embrace this role in shaping the future. It will allow you to listen critically to other people's understandings of what it means to align curriculum to the Common Core and to either say yes or to say no. Most of all, it will allow you to make your own interpretations.

This book, then, is written for educators who are eager to embrace the responsibilities of implementing the Common Core, who see schools as centers of professional study, and who believe that teaching well means engaging in a continual process of studying students and their work in order to strengthen teaching and learning. The book will especially help you implement the CCSS in ways that strengthen student-centered, deeply interactive approaches to literacy, approaches that invite students to live richly literate lives, using reading and writing to pursue goals of personal and social significance. The rhetoric around the CCSS changes rapidly as new documents and assessments emerge. Rather than attempt to have the last word on the standards, we've chosen to help you with some implementation on the front end of the curve. We hope this decision helps with your immediate needs as well as your developing discernment and judgment, which will be brought to bear on future mandates.

We do not expect that you, our readers, will be wholehearted fans of every part of the Common Core, nor do we expect *Pathways* will erase your feelings of ambivalence about the standards. We are convinced, however, that ambivalence cannot be an excuse for not responding to the call for reform that is implicit in the standards.

You Can View the Standards as a Curmudgeon—or as if They Are Gold

Often, when we talk with teachers and principals about the standards, we begin by pointing out that each one of us can choose how we regard the standards. We often tell them about a minilesson in which we ask a class of young readers, "Do you know what a *curmudgeon* is?" and then tell the children that on Halloween, they probably circle past the neighborhood curmudgeon's house, not trick-or-treating at his door lest he rush out, snarling and waving an angry stick. In the minilesson, we tell children, "You have a choice as readers. You can read like a curmudgeon," and we illustrate by reading a line or two of the class' read-aloud book as if it were duller than dishwater. But then we quickly reverse our tone and energy and we point out, "But you can, instead, read as if the text is gold." Then we reread the passage, this time reading with heart and soul.

Reading the Common Core State Standards as Curmudgeons

Educators, like those young readers, have a choice. We can regard the Common Core State Standards as the worst thing in the world. Frankly, it can be fun to gripe about them. Sometimes, we say to the educators who convene at our Common Core conferences, "Right now, make your face into a curmudgeon's face. As a curmudgeon, think about those standards—the timing, the way they arrived on the scene, their effect on your school. Now turn and, as a curmudgeon, whine and complain about the Common Core."

If you do this with your colleagues, you will find the room quickly erupting into heated conversation. After just a few minutes, you can reconvene the group. If people share complaints, they'll probably mention some of the following, as well as others.

If we really want to tackle the achievement gap, shouldn't we be tackling poverty first and then standards? Why is *now* a good time to raise the stakes for our kids, when a huge percentage are living in poverty and when the safety nets have been torn apart and there is no funding to improve education? The percent of children growing up poor in this country continues to rise, from 16% in 2000 up to 21% in 2009 (National Center for Children in

Poverty 2009). Of all industrialized nations, the United States ranks second highest, only slightly behind Mexico, for the percentage of children living in extreme poverty (UNICEF 2005). Not surprisingly, the countries that most often outrank the United States in international education measures have child poverty rates less than half of our own.

How can we possibly raise standards when conditions that support teaching and learning keep getting worse? School budgets have been cut to the bone. In Hawaii in 2010, students lost nearly a month of teaching because of excruciatingly thin budgets. In California's Orange County, Fremont and San Jose have pushed the cap for kindergarten from twenty up to thirty students in a class. In some Oregon districts, middle school teachers are squeezing more than thirty-six students into classrooms.

Underlying the CCSS is the questionable concept that skills that are essential at the college level should be combed backward throughout all the grades. The entire design of the standards is based on the argument that the purpose of K–12 education is to prepare K–12 students for college (the rhetoric touts preparation for career as well, but this is not reflected in the standards). Because the standards were written by taking the skills that college students need and distilling those down through every single grade, kindergarten children, for example, are expected to "use a combination of drawing, dictating and writing to compose opinion pieces in which they tell a reader the topic or the name of the book they are writing about and state an opinion or preference about the topic or book" (CCSS 2010a, 19). The very premise that decisions about kindergarten curriculum should be based on a study of what college students do is questionable. For example, what research supports that kindergartners should spend their time writing pint-size literary essays rather than writing about firsthand experiences and observations? Whatever happened to the idea that curriculum reflects children's development?

While the gridlike design of the document makes it easier to comprehend, this design also leads to questionable content. For example, because the informational reading and literature standards are both grounded in the same ten anchor standards and because each grade level's standard for informational reading has a mirror image in a standard for literature reading, every skill that is important to readers of informational texts must also be spotlighted in the literature reading standards. While it makes sense that readers of *informational* texts must gather and read several texts on a topic, comparing and contrasting the points of view of those texts and noting the different ways authors accentuate their claims, it is less clear that this is important work for readers of literature. Is it really the case that in real life, fiction readers collect books by a single predetermined theme and then compare and contrast the points of view and craft moves in those books?

Who wrote the standards anyway? One can search all 399 pages of the document and its appendices and find no trace of an author's name, and yet now that the CCSS have been ratified, two people, David Coleman and Sue Pimentel, have emerged referring to themselves as "the" authors in their own documents. If this is the case, why was their identity kept secret while states considered the standards? Was the goal to make it *look* like a large number of people (such as the Council of Chief State School Officers themselves) wrote the standards and thereby prevent questions about the specific authors' credentials from derailing ratification?

Some documents published after the CCSS were ratified add guidelines for evaluating methods of implementation, contradicting the intention of the standards. Since the CCSS were ratified, Coleman and Pimentel (and even others claiming to have some connection to the CCSS) have continued writing addenda to and interpretations of the CCSS that are hailed as "written by the authors of the CCSS," as if this gives these addenda and interpretations the same authority as the CCSS themselves. These new documents spell out methods of implementation in a fashion that directly contradict the CCSS's explicit premise that implementation decisions be left in the hands of teachers and school leaders. The document that was reviewed and ratified by states explicitly says, "the Standards define what all students are expected to know and be able to do, not how teachers should teach" (2010a, 6). Yet now, after states have agreed to take on these standards, some people are spelling out implications and specifying what they wish the Common Core had said, doing so without approval from all of the subcommittees that worked on the CCSS or from the states that have already signed on. One can argue, then, that it is problematic. Thomas Jefferson couldn't rewrite the Constitution that the states agreed to, nor was he (or any other one person) appointed as the Designated Interpreter of the Constitution. The full weight of these documents is not yet felt. At the time of this publication, Coleman, as co-founder and CEO of Student Achievement Partners, received a four-year 18 million dollar grant from the GE Foundation to develop materials and do teacher training around the CCSS. There will certainly be additional materials and documents that emerge following this new round of money, with the potential to make similar curricular claims as the *Publishers' Criteria for the Common Core State Standards in English Language Arts and Literacy, Grades 3–12* (Coleman and Pimentel 2011) and the *Rubrics for Evaluating Open Education Resource (OER) Objects* (Achieve 2011). When documents such as these are presented as if they've gone through the process of review and been ratified by the states on the subcommittees, it is troubling. Without that endorsement, these materials should not be regarded as having the authority of the CCSS.

The CCSS will be expensive. We hear the tests will be taken on computers. Many schools have so few computers that it would be impossible to put every kid onto one of them on the same day, or even the same week. Plus, in any school, half the computers or the server are not functioning at any one time. Spending every new dollar on the technology to support a massive testing program is problematic as compliance with the CCSS requires other expenses as well. The CCSS will cost money that could have supported smaller classes, professional development, even access to books, Kindles, and iPads.

If we assessed America's students now, only 15% would perform at the level suggested by the standards. How will it be a good thing to label 85% of kids as failures? Who will pay for the remedial education after everyone fails?

We do not have enough successes to declare with confidence that we have a research-based One Best Way for K–12 teachers to prepare students for college and career success. The CCSS claim to be research based, but the vast majority of the research cited supports the fact that all is not well in America's schools; the deficits in U.S. education are well documented in the Common Core. Granted, some of the particular solutions set forth do draw on some practices that are research based (e.g., writing across the curriculum). But on the whole, the image of curriculum implicit in the CCSS (and explicit especially in the new documents attempting to spell out implications for instruction) is not visibly research based; it is not based on large-scale reforms that have demonstrated a method for bringing high-needs students to the levels of the Common Core. If that were the case, then the nation would be invited to observe otherwise typical high-needs schools where most of the graduates are flourishing at their colleges. The CCSS represent an important hypothesis, but the *problems* are far better researched than the pathway forward.

■   ■   ■

After a few minutes of inviting people to share their qualms about the standards, we quell that conversation. We say to the principals, coaches, and teachers who have joined us to learn about the CCSS, "Like readers who need to decide if they will approach a book like they are curmudgeons or as if the book is gold, we also need to decide how we will approach the standards."

Reading the Common Core State Standards as if They Are Gold

Cory Booker, the mayor of Newark, New Jersey, has, through his approach to his city, helped us think about the need to read the standards or any initiative as if they are full of potential, to see them with eyes of hope. In a recent commencement speech at Williams College (2011), Booker told the story of how, as a young Yale law student, he decided to become a community organizer and thought the best place to start was Newark, the city that *Time* magazine had called "the most dangerous city in the nation." People in Newark said to him, "If you want to help this city, you don't need to learn from all those Yale professors. You need to learn from the Queen Mother."

"The Queen Mother?" he asked. He said that it was suggested that he visit a woman who lived on the fifth floor of Brick Towers, one of Newark's most notorious developments.

Cory Booker climbed the stairs and knocked on the door of Virginia Jones' apartment. A seventy-something-year-old woman came to the door. Retelling this story, he recalled saying, "Ma'am, I am Cory Booker. I am from Yale Law School, Ma'am. I am here to help you out."

The Queen Mother, unimpressed, responded, "Well, if you really want to help, follow me." They walked down five flights, through a courtyard, past a group of drug dealers, and into the middle of the street. "Tell me what you see around you," she instructed Cory.

In his speech, Cory began to describe the scene around him: "I see an abandoned building filled with people doing nefarious activities, I see graffiti. . . ."

The Queen Mother stopped him. "Boy, you can't help this city," she said and stormed off.

Cory ran behind her, stunned. "Ma'am? Ma'am?" he asked. "What just happened?"

Virginia Jones wheeled around and said to Cory, "You need to understand something, boy. The world you see outside of you is a reflection of what you have inside of you. If you are one of those people who only sees problems and darkness and despair, then that is all there is ever going to be for you. But if you are one of those people who sees hope, opportunity, and love, then you can make a difference."

Cory Booker learned this lesson as he stood in the intersection of a busy street. We, in this country, stand at the intersection not of a busy city but of educational history. The field of American education is changing in ways that are more dramatic and more far-reaching than anything any of us could have imagined. If we are going to play a role in shaping the future, then we need to take the Queen Mother's advice to heart. We need to see hope and opportunity. As part of this, we need to embrace what is good about the Common Core State Standards—and roll up our sleeves and work to make those standards into a force that lifts our teaching and our schools. For there is good in them. We would be pleased indeed if students in all our classrooms could do this level of work independently.

So let's look back to the standards, this time reading them as if they are gold. While concerns and questions are valid and important, we believe there is a lot to celebrate in the Common Core State Standards as well. We are convinced that if we can get about the business of embracing what is good in this document, we can use it to support dramatic improvements in our schools. Equally important, seeing the good in the standards can position us all to talk back to the not-so-good aspects.

So, what is good about the standards?

The CCSS provide an urgently needed wake-up call. America has gone from providing our children with a world-class education to scoring far below other countries on international assessments, landing in fourteenth place on the most recent PISA (Program for International Student Assessment) test for reading (OECD 2010).

Meanwhile, the world has changed. Whereas twenty-five years ago, 95% of jobs required low skills, today low-skills jobs constitute only 10% of our entire economy (Darling-Hammond et al. 2008). New levels of literacy are required in the information economy of today. Consider this statistic: During the four years between 1997 and 2002, the amount of new information produced in the world *was equal to the amount produced over the entire previous history of the world* (Darling-Hammond et al. 2008)! The old mission for America's schools—providing universal access to basic education and then providing a small elite with access to university education—may have fit the world of yesterday, where most jobs required low literacy skills, but children who leave school today without strong literacy skills will not find a job. It is no longer okay to provide the vast majority of America's children with a fill-in-the-blank, answer-the-questions, read-the-paragraph curriculum that equips them to take their place on the assembly line. The assembly lines have closed down. Instead of continuing to provide the vast majority of students with a skill-and-drill education, the United States needs to provide all students with a thinking curriculum, with writing workshops, reading clubs, research projects, debates, think tanks, Model UN, and the like. The Common Core State Standards offer an absolutely crucial wake-up call.

The CCSS emphasize much higher-level comprehension skills than previous standards. Although some may question a few particular priorities of the Common Core, the document becomes more admirable when one considers what it replaces. It was just a few years ago when No Child Left Behind (NCLB) required educators to focus on the expectations of the National Reading Panel. Back then, the whole big world of comprehension was compacted into one small item in a list of five priorities—phonemic awareness, phonics, fluency, vocabulary, and comprehension—with all of comprehension being equal in emphasis to phonemic awareness. One glance at the Common Core's expectations reveals that today's document places a much stronger emphasis on higher-level comprehension skills. Even young children are asked to analyze multiple accounts of an event, noting similarities and differences in the points of view presented, assessing the warrant behind people's ideas. Readers of today are asked to integrate information from several texts, to explain the relationships between ideas and author's craft. Whereas the nation's last attempt to lift the level of literacy instruction defined literacy in a fashion that fit easily into basal reading programs, with their emphasis on seatwork and on little reading groups convened under the teacher's thumb, this new call for reform forwards an image of literacy instruction that involves students in reading lots of books and documents of all sorts, meeting in small groups to engage in heady, provocative conversations about what they have read, taking stances for and against the views they find in books, and engaging in accountable-talk interactions. Surely this represents an important step ahead.

The CCSS place equal weight on reading and on writing. When NCLB expectations became the law of the land, there was zero emphasis on writing. Writing was not even mentioned in those mandates. What a reversal! Now, in these new standards, the emphasis on writing standards is parallel to and equal to the emphasis on reading, and furthermore, one can't help but think that reading will be assessed through writing, making writing even more critical.

Face it. People across our nation do not agree on much. This is a nation in which people are divided between Fox News and CNN, between the Tea Party and Occupy Wall Street movements. It is huge, then, that a nation as divided as ours has come together to say that higher-level comprehension matters, that critical reading and analytic thinking matter. It is even more remarkable to think that the whole nation has agreed that writing needs to take its place alongside reading.

The CCSS stress the importance of critical citizenship. The adoption of the Common Core suggests that America's image of what it means to be educated will change. The Common Core document asks us to bring up a generation of young people who listen to or read a claim and ask, "Who is making this claim? What is that person's evidence? What other positions are being promulgated? How can I compare and contrast these different views, think about the biases and assumptions behind them, weigh their warrants, and come to an evidence-based, well-reasoned stance?" It is hard not to celebrate any effort to move our nation toward this sort of critical citizenship.

The CCSS emphasize reading complex texts. Then, too, most of us agree with the Common Core's emphasis on the importance of students learning to handle texts of increasing complexity, and have been engaged in this work for years. It is a relief to see that the makers of tests and standards are coming around, belatedly, to understanding that the level of text complexity a student can read is a big deal. For years, we have heard that when a student got this or that question wrong on a high-stakes test, it showed this or that skill deficit—he couldn't infer, she couldn't handle cause-and-effect questions—and for years, we have known that the issue was more likely to be that the particular passage was either a challenging one or one that came late in the test.

The CCSS has a clear design, with central goals and high standards. Also, when one reads the standards like they are gold, it is hard not to admire the clean, coherent design of the document. The Common Core text repeatedly says that the aim should be for standards that are high, clear, and few. These standards accomplish this goal. The design is admirable, with ten anchor standards in reading and ten in writing, for example, which capture the ultimate goals. Then each of the ten reading anchor standards is rolled out across grades K–12, with corresponding, parallel work being expected in fiction and nonfiction. For educators who are accustomed to state standards that can't be contained within a huge bulging notebook and that ramble on endlessly, the design of the CCSS is impressive.

The CCSS convey that intellectual growth occurs through time, across years, and across disciplines. Another strength of the Common Core document is that it articulates grade level benchmarks and a trajectory of skill development. For example, reading anchor standard 2 is *determining central ideas of texts and analyzing their development*. The grade level standards create a progression of this anchor standard by expecting students to be able to retell stories in a way that includes details in grade 1, to determine a central message, meaning, or moral of a story in grade 3, to determine a central theme or idea and to show its development in the text in grade 8, and to analyze how themes develop and interact with each other across a text in grade 12. This kind of specification is helpful for grade level curriculum planning and for designing assessments. When one can see the spread of work across the grades, it can be a wake-up call, showing you that what seemed to be challenging eighth-grade work is in fact work that should be taught in the fifth grade. Then, a teacher can ascertain where her students are in the trajectory of skill development and then begin there, ramping up their proficiencies.

The CCSS design is also one of strongest features of the standards because it sends a message loud and clear: Growth takes time; it can't be the job of the fourth-grade teacher, or the tenth-grade teacher, to be sure students reach the expectations for that grade level. Instead, students need to be supported by a spiral curriculum within which teachers across the K–12 spectrum share responsibility for students' progress along trajectories of skill development.

The CCSS call for proficiency, complexity, and independence. It is important to note (and celebrate) that the emphasis in the Common Core is on students learning to read and write complex texts *independently* at high levels of proficiency and at a rapid enough rate to be effective. That is, it doesn't do a student a lot of good if she can handle college-level work only with her classmates and her teacher in tow. The Common Core State Standards focus on proficiency and complexity, yes, but also on independence. The Common Core want to be sure kids graduate from high school able to do quick, on-the-run research when needed, to express their thinking verbally and in writing, and to summarize, synthesize, analyze, and design without needing teachers to insert the key questions along the way or to walk students through a step-by-step approach.

The CCSS support cross-curricular literacy teaching. These standards embrace the notion that literacy is everyone's work. Social studies, science, and math teachers are all expected to support literacy. The same rich, provocative, critical reading and writing work that happens in ELA needs to be present across the curriculum.

The CCSS emphasize that every student needs to be given access to this work. Students with IEPs (individualized education programs) still need to be taught to question an author's bias, to argue for a claim, to synthesize information across texts. Teachers are invited to use assisted technology or other scaffolds to be sure that every learner has access to the thinking curriculum that is at the heart of the CCSS.

The CCSS aim to put every state on the same measuring stick. It is a big deal that forty-five states have signed on to the CCSS. For years, each state has commissioned its own state test and has, year after year, made the test easier or more predictable to make it seem that students across the state have been steadily improving. Meanwhile, however, on the one and only test that has been given consistently across every state for decades, the National

Assessment of Educational Progress (NAEP), kids' scores across the same interval have flatlined.* The Common Core aims to put all of us alongside the same measuring stick, creating a basis for credible judgments as well as encouraging states to learn from one another in ways that move the nation toward higher levels of accountability for student achievement.

The CCSS respect the professional judgment of classroom teachers. Also impressive is the humility with which the standards writers introduce their document, taking several pages to outline not only what *is* in the standards, but also what the standards *do not* intend to do. Limitation 1 even begins: "The Standards define what all students are expected to know and be able to do, not how teachers should teach" (2010a, 6). It is important to celebrate that the standards acknowledge that teachers need to draw upon the knowledge of our field in order to bring students to these ambitious levels. Embedded in the document, then, is the right for the teachers across a school or a district to make decisions. This document does not support mandates that say, "Your standards-based classroom must look like X, Y, Z."

IMPLEMENTING THE COMMON CORE

In the end, the most important aspect of the Common Core State Standards is the part that has yet to be figured out: the implementation. As challenging as it must have been to write and to finesse the adoption of this document, that work is nothing compared with the work of teaching in ways that bring all students to these ambitious expectations. The Common Core State Standards have been written, but the plan for implementing them has not. The goal is clear. The pathway is not.

We trust that once you have read this book, you will be poised to think between your existing approach to literacy and the goals outlined in the Common Core. In order to determine a pathway for implementing the Common Core, it helps to know the standards inside out, but it is even more important to know the resources you can draw upon in your own

---

* NAEP scores for fourth and eighth grades have essentially remained flat since 1992, the first year the test was given, with only slight improvements at grade 8 and no change at grade 4 since 2007 (National Center for Education Statistics 2011).

classroom, school, and district. In developing a plan for implementation, you will need to consider initiatives that are already under way in your school, the resources and assets you will (and will not) be able to draw upon, the pressures that your students, teachers, and parents most want addressed, the nature of your student body and of your existing curriculum, and of course, the knowledge base and the beliefs of the professionals who will be involved. That is, you and the others who know your school well will, in the end, need to be the ones to determine your particular pathway to implementing the Common Core.

Having said this, it is also true that teacher educators at the Teachers College Reading and Writing Project have now helped hundreds of principals and teacher leaders design plans for adopting the Common Core. As we've worked together to study school after school, in each instance engaging in data analysis and strategic planning, a few principles have emerged that are broadly applicable across many different settings. Because some of our advice could influence the way in which you read this book, we will summarize a few especially important recommendations in this first chapter and return to the recommendations in the final chapter, at which point our discussion of schoolwide standards-based reform will be well grounded in the details of the document.

The first thing we want to stress to anyone who is interested in standards-based reform is that the Common Core is, above all, a call for accelerating students' literacy development. The most important message centers on lifting the level of student achievement, not on course coverage and compliance. The most important reforms that a school system can make will be those that involve creating systems that support continuous improvement of instruction and increased personal and shared accountability for raising levels of student achievement.

It is tempting to interpret the mandate for reform as requiring a school to add some new little thing to your school day. But it will be a missed opportunity if the call to align curriculum to the Common Core is seen as a call for curricular compliance that leads a school to add this or that to the curriculum so that teachers can say, "Sure, we do the Common Core—we do it from 11:15 to 11:35." The real work on Common Core reform needs instead to revolve around creating systems of continuous improvement that result in teachers teaching toward clearer and higher expectations and doing this work in more transparent, collegial, and accountable ways, with teachers working together within and between grade levels to be sure that students make observable progress along trajectories of skill development. We discuss this in more detail in our final chapter.

For now, let's just say that if you are going to adopt the Common Core State Standards, it will be important for teachers across your school to work together to ratchet up the level of instruction and, in so doing, to develop stances and systems for engaging in continuous improvement. It also won't be possible to tackle this work across the board, all at one time, so you will need to decide the best place to start.

First, look at your current literacy initiatives and set goals for how to improve them.

We strongly recommend that in order to determine a starting place for Common Core reforms, you look at literacy initiatives already under way in your district and ask whether any one of them is already aligned to the Common Core. And then instead of checking that one facet of your literacy work off, declaring it a done deal, and moving on to address your deficits and gaps, we suggest you consider strengthening teaching and learning within that one area in ways that will allow your school to develop systems and habits of continuous improvement that can eventually be used more broadly.

If you feel as though one of your school's newer initiatives is already aligned to the Common Core, then we suggest that after taking a few minutes to pat yourselves on the back, you reread the standards, this time looking closely and critically at your students' work and at your own teaching. If your school is truly teaching this particular subject in ways that bring all students to the level of the CCSS, then examine the systems that are working well and consider ways to use those same systems to support other aspects of your curriculum. But chances are good that when you said, "Yes! We do this!" you meant, "Yes! We are *on the way toward doing that.*" And if that is the case, your yes should be a beginning, not an ending, of your reform work.

If you and a group of colleagues do a schoolwide walk-through to look honestly between the CCSS and an area of actual classroom practice and then do some reflective observations within your own classroom, chances are good that you'll see opportunities for growth. For example, you'll see instances when the promising initiative has not been implemented with fidelity. You'll see instances when people are implementing the initiative in a rote, mechanical fashion, without any real personal commitment to these methods. You'll see instances when teachers continue to teach and teach and teach, without noticing that the student work is not improving as it should, without stopping to let students' work function as feedback to the teachers, prompting them to revise the instruction so that it actually supports observable progress. Addressing these underdeveloped initiatives is one of the most important things you can do to implement the Common Core, and to raise levels of student achievement.

Next, look at gaps in your curriculum and develop a long-term plan for reform.

Having said that we do not recommend that a school rush around adding this or that to the school day in order to be "Common Core compliant," we do think that a school needs to reflect on the gaps that exist between what the school is already doing and what the Common Core requires, looking especially at the biggest and most fundamental mandates of the CCSS. Then the school needs to begin to plan and engage in at least one and perhaps more than one new area of long-term, systemic, and deep school improvement work. In weighing the decision over areas of priority, educators should know that there are a few emphases in the Common Core, and any one of these could lead to critically important changes. We suspect, however, that some areas of reform will be easier and less expensive to implement and will lead to more obvious, dramatic changes. Others seem to us to be options for schools that already support high levels of comprehension and composition and are ready to tackle new terrain.

Implement a spiral, cross-curricular K–12 writing workshop curriculum. Certainly for many school districts, we recommend a district-wide effort to improve writing instruction. There are many advantages to making writing instruction a priority. First, it's inexpensive. A school needn't purchase costly supplies for every student. The only expense is that of providing teachers with the professional development and the teaching resources they need to become knowledgeable in this area, both of which are important, as this is an area where few teachers have received any training at all.

Another advantage of instituting a district-wide writing initiative is that the way forward in the teaching of writing is very clear. In the field of writing, there are no substantial debates over how best to proceed. Even the very conservative and old-fashioned textbook Warriner's supports a writing process approach to the teaching of writing, as do the standards. The CCSS are exactly aligned to the work that experts in the teaching of writing have been doing for years (although there are a few new priorities in the Common Core). We suggest, then, that a district implement a K–12 spiral curriculum, allowing students to spend considerable time working within informational, opinion, and narrative writing units of study, producing work that matches the work described in the Common Core.

An additional advantage to spotlighting the teaching of writing is that when students are actually taught writing and given opportunities to write an hour a day within a writing workshop, their skills develop in a very visible fashion. By teaching a genre-based writing workshop with an attentiveness to skill development along trajectories of skills, teachers can learn a great deal about the relationship between teaching well and student progress. By helping teachers plan and teach writing together and by helping them collect student work, teachers can learn a lot about working within systems of continuous improvement. The final advantage to supporting ELA writing instruction is that once students become fluent, fast, structured, and proficient writers across a range of genres, it is easy to take those skills on the road, using writing as a tool for thinking across all the disciplines. When students write across the curriculum, it not only escalates their engagement in other subjects but also makes teachers more accountable and more responsive. When students write about their fledgling understandings, teachers can't help but take students' ideas into account and to adapt instruction so that it has real traction. Supporting writing instruction and then using writing across the curriculum may be one of the most potent ways to help teachers across the entire school become more student focused and accountable.

Move students up levels of text complexity by providing them with lots of just-right high-interest texts and the time to read them. Then, too, we recommend a focus on moving students up the levels of text difficulty in reading. As we discuss later, the standards in reading place special emphasis on this. Research and experience both have shown that often when students do higher-level thinking, the challenge is not that they do not have skills enough to compare and contrast, for example, but rather that they can't handle the texts in the first place. As Allington states, "You can't learn much from books you can't read" (2002). We recommend, then, that teachers across a K–5 school, and across some middle schools as well, be asked to conduct running records of students' work with texts at a gradient of text levels, ascertaining the level of text complexity that the students can handle, and to track students' progress up the ladder of text complexity. Of course, in order for students to make the necessary progress, they need at least forty-five minutes in school and more time at home to read books that they can read with 96% accuracy, fluency, and comprehension. The challenge here is that students need access to lots and lots of high-interest, accessible books that have been leveled. This reform, then, is not an easy one to put into place, but if schools begin to divert monies from expensive textbooks and toward single copies of trade books, it will make an important difference. Teachers will also want to collect data not only about the volume of reading students are doing and their progress up the gradient of text difficulties, but also about the actual eyes-on-print time they have in which to read. Chances are good that students who are not making optimal progress as readers do not have time in school each day for forty-five minutes of eyes-on-print reading (not talking about books, not writing about books) and similar time at home.

■　　■　　■

These first two priorities are urgent. Students need to become strong writers, and to do that, they need expert instruction, time to write, and meaningful opportunities for writing a wide range of informational, argument, and narrative texts. They also must become proficient readers of more complex texts, and that means they need expert instruction and opportunities to read a wide range and very deep volume of texts. A school simply must get these two literacy cornerstones in place. Assuming that these initiatives are in place and that you have already invested considerable energy in lifting the level of teaching and learning within these areas, then your school will probably want to consider how to support higher levels of reading and writing.

Prioritize argument and informational writing. You may decide that your school has a strong approach to writing but that you need to prioritize argument and informational writing. To start with this work, you'll need to recognize that writers generally refer to those kinds of writing differently.

Instead of saying he or she is writing an argument, a writer is apt to say he or she is writing a review, a persuasive letter, an op-ed column, an editorial, or an essay. Instead of saying he or she is writing an informational text, a writer is apt to label the work as an all-about book, an article (or feature article), or literary nonfiction.

Focus on higher-order comprehension instruction. You may think that if you have students moving up levels of text difficulty, you already have in place the higher-order comprehension instruction that is one of the hallmarks of the Common Core. You may. But it's very possible that your readers are mostly reading for plot, grasping the gist of what they read, moving rapidly across books, but not really working on their reading. And it may be that the comprehension work that second-grade readers are doing is not all that different than the work that sixth graders are doing. You and your colleagues might do a shared walk-through, noticing, for example, the way second graders and sixth graders grow theories about characters. If seven-year-olds are writing on sticky notes, "Poppleton is a good friend because . . . ," and sixth graders are writing, "Abe Lincoln is humble because . . . ," you and your colleagues may decide that it would be helpful to detail the intellectual work that students are doing at different grade levels in order to make sure that the same strategies are not being recycled year after year. This shouldn't be the case in a school that takes Common Core expectations for comprehension seriously. When you look at the standards for reading, you may find that even the adults in the building want to work on their reading in order to meet the high expectations of the CCSS. That is, the standards focus on a certain kind of close textual analysis. If you are familiar with Webb's depth-of-knowledge work, you'll see right away that the Common Core wants readers to be doing the intellectual work that is at levels two and three of Webb's hierarchy. That is, the Common Core State Standards expect students to sort and categorize, compare and contrast, evaluate, analyze, and reason. You'll see when you read Chapter Four of this book that the level of fiction reading demanded by the CCSS is very high—and the height comes not just from the level of text complexity that students can handle but also from the nature of their reading. If your students are already reading a lot and moving up levels of text difficulty, you'll find that the reading chapters in this book will provide you with pathways you can take to raise the level of work your students are doing *as* they read.

Increase cross-curricular, analytical nonfiction reading. For many schools, the Common Core State Standards are a wake-up call, reminding people that students need to read more nonfiction texts across the curriculum as well as to receive focused ELA instruction in nonfiction reading. It is a mistake, however, to interpret the CCSS as simply a call for more non-fiction reading. The standards also call for students to move away from simply reading for information, toward reading with a much more analytical stance. The standards suggest that at very young ages, readers be taught to compare authors' perspectives and points of view. If the sum total of discipline-based reading that occurs within your school is textbook reading, you will want to consider making some social studies and science units into reading-rich domains, and to do so you will need many primary source materials, trade books, and digital texts related to those topics of study. The Common Core emphasizes the importance of reading several texts about a topic, with readers determining the central ideas, issues, and disputes in those topics, and anticipating the arguments around a topic. That means that instead of reading a summary of the American Revolution, fifth graders in a CCSS–aligned classroom will read speeches made by Patriots, look at propaganda on the part of Loyalists and Patriots, weigh the reasons people took sides in that war, and imagine themselves in the shoes of people who hold different views on this topic.

Finally, wherever you decide to begin your Common Core work, you'll find that you'll need to focus on assessment as well as instruction.

In writing, you'll need assessments that will let you see the visible progress students are making as writers along the way, so that you'll be able to track the success of your teaching. You'll need the same in reading. Most schools already have formative assessments that let teachers see how students are moving up levels of text difficulty in fiction (though some secondary schools may find these assessments new and helpful as well). Many schools, though, have struggled to track meaningful progress in nonfiction reading and in upper-level interpretation and analytical skills across any kind of text. So as you focus your initiatives and decide on priorities, remember that assessment is a crucial part of that decision making. Chapter Eleven provides some help with looking at the assessments that are currently available and with designing assessments to give you insight into students' and teachers' progress.

How the Book Is Structured and How You May Use Individual Chapters

We've organized the book so that you can read the whole text at one time, or you may dive into individual chapters according to your priorities. If you are a school leader, you'll want to read across the whole text, as the parts of the Common Core work are interlocking puzzle parts, and each piece is affected by other work. The reading and the writing work build on each other. The speaking and listening work can help students with the reading and writing work, and so on. Also, we tuck research and tips into each chapter where each seems most appropriate and don't repeat that research and those tips in other chapters. We have, however, designed the chapters so that you might choose one chapter at a time to read as a study group for a faculty meeting, a think tank, or a grade level or department level study. The one caveat is this: if you choose a reading or a writing chapter, you'll want to quickly read the overview chapter to reading or writing to give you some background before you get started.

In each chapter, we made decisions about how to best understand the Common Core State Standards and how to use them to raise achievement. We made these decisions after working with teachers and school leaders in workshops, in think tanks, and across yearlong studies. You'll see, therefore, that each chapter begins by unpacking the most significant aspect of the standards themselves. Then there is a section on implementation, where we have made practical suggestions for pathways toward achieving the standards. Where we thought it would be helpful, we have described some activities that teachers might want to try, in order to come to a closer understanding of the implications of the Common Core. We've tried to write those activities in such a way that you could duplicate them in a study group.

We wish you all the best as you embark on your Common Core studies. We've found this work to be illuminating. We've found that it has helped us raise the level of work students are doing in our schools. And we've found it can be a unifying force to help teachers think and work together. We hope it is the same for you.

CHAPTER TWO

OVERVIEW of the READING STANDARDS

What Do They Say and What Does This Mean for Us?

The Common Core reading standards are unusually efficient in the way they organize reading skills into a kind of grid. It is a grid that offers a set of skills for readers of every age, and for both fiction and informational texts. Whether you read the anchor standards, or the standards for reading literature, or those for reading informational texts, you'll encounter the same skill set. As you read across the grades, you'll note that the specific expectations for skills grow. These skill progressions—represented in the anchor standards—are the same whether the reader is reading fiction or informational texts.

To appreciate the elegance of this grid, simply glance at one page of the reading standards. For instance, let's look at the standards for reading informational text for grades 3–5 (CCSS 2010a, 14):

Grade 3 students:		Grade 4 students:		Grade 5 students:
Key Ideas and Details				
1. Ask and answer questions to demonstrate understanding of a text, referring explicitly to the text as the basis for the answers.	1.	Refer to details and examples in a text when explaining what the text says explicitly and when drawing inferences from the text.	1.	Quote accurately from a text when explaining what the text says explicitly and when drawing inferences from the text.
2. Determine the main idea of a text; recount the key details and explain how they support the main idea.	2.	Determine the main idea of a text and explain how it is supported by key details; summarize the text.	2.	Determine two or more main ideas of a text and explain how they are supported by key details; summarize the text.
3. Describe the relationship between a series of historical events, scientific ideas or concepts, or steps in technical procedures in a text, using language that pertains to time, sequence, and cause/effect.	3.	Explain events, procedures, ideas, or concepts in a historical, scientific, or technical text, including what happened and why, based on specific information in the text.	3.	Explain the relationships or interactions between two or more individuals, events, ideas, or concepts in a historical, scientific, or technical text based on specific information in the text.

Grade 3 students:	Grade 4 students:	Grade 5 students:
Craft and Structure		
4. Determine the meaning of general academic and domain-specific words and phrases in a text relevant to a *grade 3 topic or subject area.*	4. Determine the meaning of general academic and domain-specific words or phrases in a text relevant to a *grade 4 topic or subject area.*	4. Determine the meaning of general academic and domain-specific words or phrases in a text relevant to a *grade 5 topic or subject area.*
5. Use text features and search tools (e.g., key words, sidebars, hyperlinks) to locate information relevant to a given topic efficiently.	5. Describe the overall structure (e.g., chronology, comparison, cause/effect, problem/solution) of events, ideas, concepts, or information in a text or part of a text.	5. Compare and contrast the overall structure (e.g., chronology, comparison, cause/effect, problem/solution) of events, ideas, concepts, or information in two or more texts.
6. Distinguish their own point of view from that of the author of a text.	6. Compare and contrast a firsthand and secondhand account of the same event or topic; describe the differences in focus and the information provided.	6. Analyze multiple accounts of the same event or topic, noting important similarities and differences in the point of view they represent.
Integration of Knowledge and Ideas		
7. Use information gained from illustrations (e.g., maps, photographs) and the words in a text to demonstrate understanding of the text (e.g., where, when, why, and how key events occur).	7. Interpret information presented visually, orally, or quantitatively (e.g., in charts, graphs, diagrams, timelines, animations, or interactive elements on Web pages) and explain how the information contributes to an understanding of the text in which it appears.	7. Draw on information from multiple print or digital sources, demonstrating the ability to locate an answer to a question quickly or to solve a problem efficiently.
8. Describe the logical connection between particular sentences and paragraphs in a text (e.g., comparison, cause/effect, first/second/third in a sequence).	8. Explain how an author uses reasons and evidence to support particular points in a text.	8. Explain how an author uses reasons and evidence to support particular points in a text, identifying which reasons and evidence support which point(s).
9. Compare and contrast the most important points and key details presented in two texts on the same topic.	9. Integrate information from two texts on the same topic in order to write or speak about the subject knowledgeably.	9. Integrate information from several texts on the same topic in order to write or speak about the subject knowledgeably.
Range of Reading and Level of Text Complexity		
10. By the end of the year, read and comprehend informational texts, including history/social studies, science, and technical texts, at the high end of the grades 2–3 text complexity band independently and proficiently.	10. By the end of year, read and comprehend informational texts, including history/social studies, science, and technical texts, in the grades 4–5 text complexity band proficiently, with scaffolding as needed at the high end of the range.	10. By the end of the year, read and comprehend informational texts, including history/social studies, science, and technical texts, at the high end of the grades 4–5 text complexity band independently and proficiently.

© Copyright 2010. National Governors Association Center for Best Practices and Council of Chief State School Officers. All rights reserved.

For a moment, look at third grade, on the far left, and move your eyes down the page from top to bottom, from standards 1 to 10. Then run your eyes down fourth grade, and then fifth grade. You'll immediately notice the same ten skills are present, whether you read grade 3, grade 4, or grade 5. Then too, the skills required up and down the grade levels of a standard are cohesive (there isn't a laundry list of assorted subskills subsumed under any one skill). Then choose one of those skills, such as that described by standard 1, which is reading closely to determine what the text says. Look horizontally across the page, and you can notice how this skill changes as readers progress from third to fourth to fifth grade.

Chances are, you've done this before. You've looked across the reading standards, and thought to yourself that it's convenient how they are organized. It's more than convenient, though. The remarkable aspect of the Common Core standards is the way they create a unified statement about what is important in reading. Most standards try to be all things to all people. Often they end up with so many criteria there is no way to figure out what is important. The Common Core, though, has decided that there are a small number of enduring skills that constitute reading for readers at any age, no matter what kind of text a reader holds. You may agree or disagree with the values that are embedded in the CCSS, but in any case, these standards make a coherent and clear statement about reading. The Common Core conveys this statement in ten standards—which are really nine skills, because standard 10 simply calls for the ability to perform standards 1 through 9 on grade level texts. So, the first notable achievement of the Common Core reading standards is that they distill reading to a single set of nine reading skills that readers can carry across texts and up grade levels.

The second notable aspect of the Common Core reading standards is that these nine skills all require deep comprehension and high-level thinking. If we turn back one page in the standards document, we'll see that the first skills that the youngest readers, kindergartners, are asked to work toward when reading informational texts, for instance, are "ask and answer questions about key details in the text" (standard 1), and "identify the main topic and retell key details of a text" (standard 2). The low-level literacy work of sound-letter correspondence and so on—work that dominated the National Reading Panel report (2000) that has undergirded NCLB for years—has been, thankfully, marginalized in its own separate section of the CCSS. That work doesn't even qualify as part of the reading and writing standards. Reading, in the Common Core, is making meaning. To confirm this focus, look at the reading skills for the lowest grades. You'll notice that kindergartners and first graders are asked to compare and contrast, categorize, identify key details, and demonstrate understanding of the main topic or central message of any kind of text. All readers, therefore, from the youngest age, are expected to attend to meaning, according to the Common Core.

In this chapter, we look at

- what the standards do and don't value in reading comprehension
- how the same skills are applied to reading literature and informational texts
- implementation implications of the reading standards

What the Standards Do and Don't Value in Reading Comprehension

It is important to notice what the standards value and devalue in reading comprehension. We have seen that they value deep comprehension and high-level thinking skills—but which skills in particular? We can judge what the standards value by looking at what they give repeated attention to and what they leave out. For instance, these are some of the phrases that are repeated in the descriptive text leading into the reading standards: "close, attentive reading" (CCSS 2010a, 3), "critical reading" (3), "reasoning and use of evidence" (3), "comprehend, evaluate, synthesize" (4), "comprehend and evaluate" (7), "understand precisely . . . question . . . assess the veracity" (7), "cite specific evidence" (7), "evaluate other points of view critically" (7), and "reading independently and closely" (10).

These are phrases repeated in the grade level specifics (grades K–12): "demonstrate understanding of a text, referring explicitly to the text" (12), "refer to details and examples in a text" (12), "quote accurately from a text" (12) "objective summary" (36), "determine . . . describe . . . explain . . . compare and contrast . . . analyze" (12).

These phrases are *not* in the Common Core: make text-to-self connections, access prior knowledge, explore personal response, and relate to your own life. In short, the Common Core deemphasizes reading as a personal act and emphasizes textual analysis.

To educators who have followed reading schools of thought for many years, the Common Core marks a return to the kind of reading that was promoted in the thirties and forties through New Criticism. New Criticism put the text at the center and equated reading with close analysis of the text. It's a kind of highly academic reading that can be particularly effective on very complex texts that reward poring over language and structure and deciphering internal meanings—you can see why seminars on New Critical approaches proliferated at Ivy League institutions and at the Sorbonne. Perhaps because the Common Core authors worked backward from these elite college skills and imagined a progression of reading skills that would lead to this sort of reading of university-level texts, the standards reside in this territory of academic reading. Objective, close, analytical reading is what is valued as deep comprehension and interpretation by the Common Core.

In focusing on textual analysis as the primary means of comprehending and interpreting texts, the Common Core puts aside theories of reader response. To return to the historical view, the notion that all meaning resided solely in the text was rejected by Louise Rosenblatt. In *Literature as Exploration*, Rosenblatt (1938/1968/1976/1995) argued that the meaning of texts resides in the interaction of the reader with the text. The logical consequence of Rosenblatt's definition of reading is that when two readers read *Charlotte's Web*, they can't and won't see the same things in it because their own experience partially shapes their interpretation. Even the same reader at different ages will see different things in the text. The reader as a third grader may particularly notice Fern's friendship with Wilbur, while that same child, twenty or thirty years later as a mother, may reread *Charlotte's Web* and see more clearly a theme of the willingness to sacrifice oneself for a loved one. Reader response approaches to reading suggest that even if you claim that themes reside within the corners of the text, the variation in the readers' experience and preoccupation releases meanings differently. Louise Rosenblatt, Peter Johnston, many reading researchers, and we posit that reading, like any activity, is never subjective. As Robert Scholes remarks, reading remains "incomplete unless it is absorbed and transformed in the thoughts and deeds of readers" (1989, x).

You may want to assess your students to see if they need more support with academic, text-based responses. If you want to assess adults' or children's current reading practices, ask them to discuss a poem or story with a familiar plot or issue. Do they veer off into discussions of their own experiences? They'll need nudging to move to CCSS work.

How the Same Skills Are Applied to Reading Literature and Informational Texts

As mentioned previously, the skills for reading literature and the skills for reading informational texts are the same in the Common Core. That is, they share the same ten anchor standards. The Common Core does, though, provide individual grade level skills for reading literature and for reading informational texts. Sometimes the grade level skill for a standard is exactly the same for reading literature and for reading informational texts. Other times, there are subtle differences in the skill as it is described for reading literature and for reading informational texts. For example, if you look at the sixth-grade version of anchor standard 1, it describes the skill of restating a text in a way that is applicable for all genres:

> Cite textual evidence to support analysis of what the text says explicitly as well as inferences drawn from the text. (2010a, 36)

Because this skill is appropriate for narrative as well as expository text, it is worded identically in both sets of standards, for literature and informational texts, at sixth grade.

However, this is not the case for the sixth-grade version of anchor standard 3 (analyzing how various elements develop over the course of a text). The literature standard reads:

> Describe how a particular story's or drama's plot unfolds in a series of episodes as well as how the characters respond or change as the plot moves toward a resolution. (36)

Obviously describing narrative structure and pivotal moments of change makes for sharp analytical work in literature but may not pay off in a science text. For reading informational texts, this same standard reads:

> Analyze in detail how a key individual, event, or idea is introduced, illustrated, and elaborated in a text (e.g., through examples or anecdotes). (39)

You can see that these iterations of anchor standard 3 are two sides of the same coin. Both versions push readers to look closely at how parts, problems, characters, and ideas are introduced and connected, but they do it differently.

Generally, then, the Common Core works to unify reading so that readers bring the same skills to various texts. Within the grade level specifics, you will, as noted, find small variations in how the anchor skill is described for literature versus informational texts, and these differences relate both to the particular challenges different types of texts pose for readers and to the different purposes that readers often have when reading the different kinds of texts. Readers usually turn to informational texts to be informed and persuaded, and so the Common Core informational skills emphasize reading to determine central ideas and analyze authors' viewpoints. These same readers, when reading literature, usually expect to encounter vivid characterizations, thematic connections, and expressive language, and so the Common Core literature skills emphasize reading to determine themes, to elucidate figurative language and allusions, to trace narrative elements.

The Common Core does not give more weight to fiction than nonfiction or vice versa. However, in weighing these types of reading experiences equally, and requiring deep comprehension and interpretive skills for each, there is an implicit sharpening of focus on nonfiction, as reading instruction in most schools, until now, has happened exclusively in ELA classrooms.

You'll find recommended distribution charts for literary versus informational reading in the first few pages of the standards. There, the Common Core recommends following the NAEP (National Assessment of Educational Progress) distribution, which is

- 50% literary texts and 50% informational texts at fourth grade
- 45% literary texts and 55% informational texts at eighth grade
- 30% literary texts and 70% informational texts at twelfth grade

This distribution does not mean that the CCSS call for dramatically more nonfiction reading within the ELA classroom. To the contrary, the standards make it clear that the call is for literacy to be a shared responsibility in *content-area classrooms* as well as in ELA classrooms. The CCSS say, "because ELA classrooms must focus on literature (stories, drama, and poetry) as well as literary nonfiction, a great deal of information reading in grades 6–12 must take place in other classes" (5).

Implementation Implications of the Reading Standards: Some Essentials

The Common Core's emphasis on high-level comprehension skills calls for a reversal of NCLB's focus on decoding and low-level literacy skills. Even for the youngest readers, the Common Core pushes for reading for meaning. This shift in focus means a few things. One is that classrooms (or states) that have coasted on low-level reading skills need to quickly get on board with high-level reading skills. You might try the activity with *Charlotte's Web* that we offer in Chapter Four to illuminate the higher-level reading skills called for in the Common Core. You might watch videos of students engaged in high-level partnership or book club conversations (there are many such videos available on the Teachers College Reading and Writing Project website: www.readingandwritingproject.com/), and ask whether your students are conversing in equally analytic, text-based ways. You might consider how your school can recommit itself to teaching high-level comprehension skills through read-aloud and accountable talk.

As you embrace high-level comprehension and analytical reading skills, you may need to acknowledge that many teachers never received any training or practice with these skills in their education or own reading lives. Some of the CCSS skills, such as analyzing texts for craft and structure (more on that in upcoming chapters), do feel very much like university skills. You'll need to study and practice these skills as a community, probably through some shared reading of texts. We think of the National Writing Project, for instance, and how it brought generations of teachers to shared, insider knowledge of writing. That same urge to work on our reading and become mentor readers will be needed here.

In order for students to do Common Core reading work, they'll need explicit instruction in the skills and strategies of high-level comprehension. Undoubtedly students will need explicit instruction in high-level comprehension. They'll need a repertoire of strategies that undergird these reading skills. They'll need the skills broken down into manageable steps, and they'll need to practice these steps and get expert feedback along the way. They'll need lots of repeated practice, on a variety of texts. As they do this practice, teachers will need assessments that will allow them to carefully calibrate their teaching, to move kids up levels of skill and text difficulty. They'll also need structures that will make reading work visible—structures such as reading partners and clubs, which give students opportunities to have the rich literary conversations about fiction and nonfiction that the standards call for. Teachers will also need to focus on methods of giving feedback while kids are practicing these skills, with gradual release and decreasing scaffolds, to lead students to internalize these skills.

Teachers will need to assess the texts the kids are holding, and ensure they are texts on which they can actually practice synthesizing and critical reading. Classrooms that have depended on excerpts, anthologies, and textbooks will find themselves needing to extend their libraries with literature and, for older students, primary and secondary sources. Students don't have to hold *Black Beauty*, as fifth graders, or *The Odyssey* as ninth graders. They can do this work on *The Tiger Rising* or *The Absolutely True Diary of a Part-Time Indian*. But if they're holding an anthology of texts that are short, modified, or excerpted, they can't truly analyze craft, structure, symbolism, or thematic development except in the most rudimentary way. If they're holding a textbook, they can't really analyze the warrant and reasoning that back up authors' claims, or compare craft, structure, and perspective; everything is already a summary.

Because reading will no longer be the domain solely of ELA teachers, as it has been in most schools, science and social studies teachers will need to participate in professional development on reading instruction. Teachers who have been proven effective at improving reading outcomes for students will be called on to offer support across the content areas. School leaders will need to arrange ways to share strategies and methods across classrooms so that students can carry reading skills to every text they encounter—and content teachers can help kids carry their literacy learning across the disciplines. Teachers who share teaching charts, look at student assessments together, organize collaborative teaching of nonfiction reading, and create shared language in a building will help the teaching of reading become systemized in a school.

We consistently see teachers underestimate how much reading kids get done when they read. Third graders who read Magic Tree House books, for instance (level M, about eighty to ninety pages with pictures), often read two of these texts every three days. If they read for extended periods at home, or you extend their protected reading time in school, they'll read more. That means you'll need somewhere between five and seven books for them for each week.

In *Outliers*, his study of conditions that lead to extraordinary success, Malcolm Gladwell (2008) talks about the theory that expertise requires an investment of ten thousand hours. This research looks at piano players, programmers, NBA players, and so on. The unifying factor that led to their greatness? Hours of practice. Hours and hours. Ten thousand hours. Readers, too, become great when they have many hours of practice.

CHAPTER THREE

LITERAL UNDERSTANDING and TEXT COMPLEXITY

STANDARDS 1 AND 10

In many respects, text complexity is the hallmark of the Common Core State Standards. Read the document, visit the official CCSS website, or listen to the rhetoric of those who have come to be closely associated with the Common Core, and you'll hear over and over the grave concern that students need to be able to read more complex texts. This emphasis is contained within reading anchor standard 10, which asks readers to "read and comprehend complex literary and informational texts independently and proficiently" (2010a, 10). The grade-specific iterations call, more specifically, for students to read what the CCSS refer to as grade level complex texts and to do so with independence. Doug Reeves, who leads institutes across the country on the Common Core State Standards, included a post on his website that begins, "Just as the Aorta carries blood from the heart, Common Core State Standard number 10 carries increasing levels of text complexity up from Grade 2 through Grade 12 and into College and Career Readiness" (Piercy 2011). The standards do not lay out a pathway for moving readers toward this goal, as they are not a curriculum, but they do shine a bright spotlight on the fact that currently, millions of students in schools across the country can't comprehend grade level texts and therefore can't access the information carried in those texts.

The Common Core's discussion of text complexity leans heavily on *Reading Between the Lines*, a 2006 report released by ACT that explains that when students didn't achieve benchmark on the ACT, their struggles stemmed more from the levels of text complexity in the passages than from deficits in the specific skills called for by the questions. The CCSS sum up the results of the report:

> *Surprisingly*, what chiefly distinguished the performance of those students who had earned the benchmark score or better from those who had not

was not their relative ability in making inferences while reading or answering questions related to particular cognitive processes, such as determining main ideas or determining the meaning of words and phrases in context. Instead, the clearest differentiator was students' ability to answer questions associated with complex texts. . . . The most important implication of this study was that a pedagogy focused only on "higher-order" or "critical" thinking was insufficient to ensure that students were ready for college and careers: what students could read, in terms of its complexity, was at least as important as what they could do with what they read. (emphasis added; CCSS 2010b, 2)

As we mentioned in the first chapter, this focus on text complexity and skill is a relief. For years, teachers have received computerized spreadsheets detailing the specific reading skills students do and do not demonstrate, based on an analysis of which particular questions they got right and wrong. A student answers the last four questions on the test incorrectly, and the teacher is told that because three of those four questions were "main idea questions," more skill and drill on main ideas is required. The astute teacher has always thought, "But what if those questions followed a particularly difficult passage, so that the trouble wasn't determining main idea but rather the student's reading level? What if the student was progressing through the test too slowly and never read the passage in the first place?" Although documents claiming that the student has trouble with this or that skill have always looked very official, teachers have known that these data are far from infallible because the data ignore the varying text complexity of the passages. It is a good thing, then, that the Common Core recognizes that it is important for students to progress toward being able to read grade level complex texts.

However, in order to understand reading standard 10 of the Common Core, it is important to also understand standard 1, the literal comprehension standard. Standard 1 asks readers to "[r]ead closely to determine what the text says explicitly and to make logical inferences from it" (CCSS 2010a, 10). Some people who are close to the Common Core have likened the reading standards to a ladder, with standards 1 and 10 as the crucial struts that form the two sides of the ladder, and the other reading standards as the rungs of the ladder. The two standards, combined, have sometimes been referred to as the running records standards, as the work involved in meeting these standards has, in many K–8 schools, revolved around teachers conducting running records to track students' ability to progress up the gradient of text complexity while continuing to read with fluency, accuracy, and basic comprehension. The link between the two standards is important because it suggests that although it is crucial for students to be able to handle increasingly complex texts, reading must never be mere word calling; accuracy without strong literal comprehension is not reading.

Text complexity, in connection with literal comprehension, turns out to be a complicated topic, however. There are four disputes within this area, three of which are central to the Common Core standards, and one which lies outside the domain of the Common Core. The first area of dispute is how to measure text complexity; the second is what the standards mean exactly when they say that students should read at a grade level's "text complexity band"; the third is what the CCSS expectations are for literal comprehension; and finally, the fourth is what the Common Core's emphasis on text complexity means for curriculum and instruction. Must fifth graders, for example, read fifth-grade complex texts if they cannot yet do so with comprehension? We provide evidence from the document suggesting that this final dispute should be addressed within the walls of a school, for the Common Core standards put the responsibility for resolving this final issue squarely into the hands of teachers and school leaders.

This chapter, then, looks at standards 1 and 10 together to address the following:

- How do the CCSS suggest educators determine a text's level of complexity?
- What are the standards' suggestions for grade-level-appropriate texts?
- What are the CCSS' expectations for literal comprehension?
- What does the CCSS say about the implications for instruction?

How Do the CCSS Suggest Educators Determine a Text's Level of Complexity?

The Common Core provides a lot of detail about the standards' definition of text complexity. The details may not be important to you; in the end, they can be summed up by saying that the standards do not claim that one system of measurement is sufficient in and of itself. If someone has told you that the Common Core requires that you level books by this or that system, the truth is that the standards recognize the limitations of all existing leveling systems and call for additional research in this area. Meanwhile, they do stress that teachers need to do everything possible to move students toward increasingly complex texts.

If you are interested in reading in more detail about methods for leveling texts, then you will want to turn to Appendix A of the Common Core ELA document (CCSS 2010b), which is divided by the three measures the standards regard as most important for determining text complexity: qualitative measures, quantitative measures, and reader and task consideration measures.

Qualitative Measures

The qualitative measures the Common Core puts forward include levels of meaning, structure, language conventionality and clarity, and knowledge demands. The discussion includes a chart, adapted from the ACT study mentioned earlier, *Reading Between the Lines*. The chart gives us useful lenses for determining the complexity of a literary or informational text. Are the meanings explicit or implicit? Is the structure conventional or unconventional? Is the language literal, figurative, or domain specific? Are the knowledge demands everyday or highly specialized? These are helpful lenses, and the message implicit in the chart is especially helpful. The chart seems to suggest that teachers can judge text complexity for themselves, not needing to always rush to some database or another in order to ascertain the level of difficulty posed by a particular text.

Quantitative Measures

The Common Core standards suggest that in addition to qualitative factors, educators should also take into account quantitative measures. Quantitative measures are ones that can be calculated by computer software, such as word length, frequency, sentence length, and text cohesion. The appendix overviews several systems and tools that are used to measure these factors, including the Flesch-Kincaid test, the Dale-Chall Readability Formula, and the Lexile Framework for Reading. Although the CCSS seem to settle, for now, upon using Lexile ranges rather than the other systems, it suggests using Lexile in concert with qualitative measures. In fact, the standards include a grid suggesting that complex texts for grades 2 and 3 will be those that fall within the 450–790 range, for example. Then, too, the CCSS include many caveats about Lexile levels, pointing out that the extremely complex Pulitzer Prize–winning novel *The Grapes of Wrath* includes so much dialogue and colloquial language that it is ranked by Lexile as a text that is appropriate for second- and third-grade readers (which is far from the case). The standards conclude, then, "Until widely available quantitative tools can better account for factors recognized as making such texts challenging, including multiple levels of meaning and mature themes, preference should likely be given to qualitative measures of text complexity when evaluating narrative fiction for students in grades 6 and above" (8).

Reader and Task Consideration Measures

Reader and task consideration is the third measure the CCSS take into account when determining text complexity. This measure is underdeveloped in the CCSS discussion, but it is significant that the standards give a nod to the role that prior knowledge and motivation play, positioning text complexity as situational. Sentence and word length are only part of what counts; the familiarity the reader has to the language and content of the text as well as the reader's motivation to comprehend the text play a role as well. Hence, the CCSS have the "expectation that educators will employ professional judgment to match texts to particular students and tasks" (CCSS 2010b, 7).

■　■　■

These lenses, of course, are not new. Educators who know Fountas and Pinnell's guide to leveled texts recognize that their system for measuring texts involves measuring almost exactly what the Common Core takes into account—meaning, content, structure, vocabulary. It may, then, be puzzling to teachers why the CCSS do not mention Fountas and Pinnell's system for leveling text. When we met with Sue Pimentel, who has been referred to as one of the lead writers for the CCSS, we asked why they ignored such a widely used leveling system. Pimentel explained that the standards were written in a top-down fashion. The first step involved specifying the levels of text complexity that students need to be able to handle in order to be "college and career ready." Fountas and Pinnell's scale cannot be used to measure the text complexity of IRS documents or of economics and physics textbooks. Their system wasn't designed to be applicable to such high levels of text complexity.

The question still remains, then, whether Fountas and Pinnell's leveling system can be used by K–8 teachers wanting to move kids along the gradient of text difficulty. Because the criteria used by the CCSS to assess text complexity are similar to the criteria used by Fountas and Pinnell, it seems clear that a school that is already assessing students according to Fountas and Pinnell levels should continue doing so.

What Are the Standards' Suggestions for Grade-Level-Appropriate Texts?

Of course, some of the most pressing questions that a teacher will ask about text complexity are, How high am I expected to take my readers? and What level of text complexity is considered grade level appropriate for my students? Many people find it hard to discern the Common Core's answer to these questions, and one is left to wonder whether the confused message was intentional, contributing to the states being willing to adopt this document, or whether it was unintentional.

Look at the Grade Band Exemplar Texts in Appendix B for Help

One of the best sources of information to help a teacher answer the question, How high is high enough? is the list of exemplar texts representing approximate levels of text difficulty that the standards regard as sufficient, provided in Appendix B of the CCSS ELA document (2010c). It is challenging to decipher the directives that are implicit in these lists, however, because the lists include books that are appropriate for a range of grade levels. For example, the list for grades 2 and 3 contains *Poppleton* (which, as a level J text, is often considered on target for the end of first grade) as well as *Sarah, Plain and Tall* (which, as a level R text, is generally considered appropriate for the end of third grade). If a third-grade teacher interprets this list to be suggesting that she is doing well if all her third graders end the year reading within the range of books that fall between *Poppleton* and *Sarah, Plain and Tall*, that teacher will probably feel that these expectations are not overly challenging. Of course, it is unlikely that the authors of the Common Core standards meant to send a message that students who are reading *Poppleton* at the end of third grade are doing standards-level work. In fact, if one reads the standards closely, they explicitly say that third graders should end the year reading texts at the high end of the list of exemplar texts deemed appropriate for grades 2 and 3.

The answer to the question, How high is high enough? is equally muffled at other grade levels, where again, the lists of exemplar texts represent widely divergent levels of text complexity. The Common Core's message is diffused also because most of the books cited are not books like *Poppleton* and *Sarah, Plain and Tall*—that is, most are not well-known books that are emblematic of a whole host of other books commonly found on school bookshelves. Instead, the Common Core's lists are filled primarily with classics: for example, *Black Beauty*, with its formal, archaic language, is included in the grades 4–5 list, as is *Alice's Adventures in Wonderland*. Just glance, for example, at the publishing dates of this portion of the 4–5 list:

- *Alice's Adventures in Wonderland*, by Lewis Carroll (1866)
- *The Secret Garden*, by Frances Hodgson Burnett (1910)
- *The Little Prince*, by Antoine de Saint-Exupéry (1943)
- *The Black Stallion*, by Walter Farley (1941)
- "Zlateh the Goat," by Isaac Bashevis Singer (1984)

Contemporary children's literature clearly takes a backseat to classics here, reflecting perhaps the preferences or the knowledge base of the CCSS authors.

Look at the Lexile Levels Chart for Help

The Common Core standards do provide in Appendix A a chart of recommended Lexile levels to help teachers understand the expectations for grade-appropriate texts (8). (Although, remember that the CCSS widely advise readers to regard Lexile as just one measurement system among many others.) This chart suggests that in fact, the expectations embedded in the Common Core standards are just slightly more rigorous than the expectations embedded in Fountas and Pinnell's lists and closely match the recommendations of the Teachers College Reading and Writing Project (but remember that the Common Core places special emphasis on readers reading with independence, i.e., without text introductions and without the support of a small group). For example, Fountas and

Pinnell's materials suggest that fifth-grade readers should be able to read level V texts (*Number the Stars, Holes, Mrs. Frisby and the Rats of NIMH*), which Fountas and Pinnell claim belong in the Lexile level 800–899. *Alice's Adventures in Wonderland* is on the high end of the Common Core's grades 4–5 list, and it is leveled as a V, implying a rough alignment. A separate chart lists a Lexile level of 980 (a bit higher than Fountas and Pinnell's current suggestions) as the high end for the end of fifth grade.

WHAT ARE THE COMMON CORE'S EXPECTATIONS FOR LITERAL COMPREHENSION?

The Common Core State Standards insist that the absolute first order of business is that students need to be able to grasp what a text actually says and suggests. The Common Core argues that if students don't understand what a text says explicitly, they won't have a clue about doing textual analysis. Documents written since the Common Core was released amplify this expectation, emphasizing that readers need to "read within the four corners of the text" (Coleman 2011), a phrase the CCSS authors have since used frequently when talking and writing about the standards. Looking closely at anchor standard 1 for reading enabled us to see that the goal of this standard is not just to quote accurately but to comprehend literally, including being able to infer the import of details.

If we think back to the ACT study that suggested students suffer on standardized tests when they cannot read complex texts well, this standard seems to say that it is necessary for readers to *get* the text. Readers need to get their mental arms around the text, to be able to retell it, to cite it, to ground anything they have to say about the text with textual references, to talk and think in ways that are confined within what you might call "the four corners of the text."

The message, we think, is that the authors of this document are intent on correcting what they feel has been an overemphasis on personal response, on text-to-self connections. They seem to be reacting against book talks in which there are lots of comments like "I remember the time when . . ." and "The same thing happened to me . . ." and "I can connect with this because one time . . ." and not a lot of talk about repeated images, structure decisions, connotative language, implicit metaphor, and so forth. For a long time, the TCRWP has worked on behalf of a similar emphasis, feeling something is amiss when readers merely glance at a text and then talk off from it, leaving the specifics of the text behind.

Literal Comprehension Demands a Sharp Rise in Expectations as You Move Up the Grade Levels

To understand the work of anchor standard 1, you might want to turn to the grade level specifics for reading literature and then for reading informational texts. What you'll find is that the challenge involved in grasping what the text says increases as texts become more complex.

In first grade, for example, students are asked to "[a]sk and answer questions about key details in a text" (CCSS 2010a, 11). You can imagine a first grader, reading a simple Clifford the Big Red Dog book, asking herself about what kind of trouble Clifford will get into today. By the end of the book, she'll be able to answer that question by saying that today, Clifford chased a truck and got in trouble. By third grade, though, standard 1 asks readers to "[a]sk and answer questions to demonstrate understanding of a text, referring explicitly to the text as the basis for the answers" (12). And in fifth grade, standard 1 asks the reader to include two new subsets of skills as part of demonstrating literal understanding—inferring across the text and quoting explicitly when explaining the story: "Quote accurately from a text when explaining what the text says explicitly and when drawing inferences from the text" (12).

Notice the growth in skill level: now students need to do everything that came before (those skills are prerequisites for understanding more complex texts), and they also need to sort through and cite several places of the text, clarifying what they know for sure and what they are inferring. So, a fifth grader reading *Number the Stars*, for example, could quote the ending of the book, when Annemarie gives Ellen's necklace to her father and asks, "Can you fix this? I have kept it all this long time" (132), and point to the fact that Annemarie wishes to wear the necklace until Ellen returns, as evidence to support the inference that Ellen's necklace is more than just a piece of jewelry; it has become a symbol of her identity. The reader who can do this work, quoting from the text and using the text to make inferences, is meeting the rising expectations of the CCSS.

Literal understanding of informational texts in the CCSS also demands a sharp rise in expectations. These standards are not talking about merely decoding a text. This is not about reading the words and letters and saying those accurately, nor about restating the headings and subheadings.

Let's look at what qualifies as literal comprehension for informational texts as you move up the grade levels. In grade 2, standard 1 asks students to "[a]sk and answer such questions as *who, what, where, when, why,* and *how* to demonstrate understanding of key details in a text" (CCSS 2010a, 13). Imagine a seven-year-old reading the level J text *The Life Cycle of a Butterfly,* by Lisa Trumbauer. As she reads this informational book, she knows that she needs to ask herself, "What have I learned about butterflies?" And then, a bit later, "What else have I learned now?" Essentially, she will be asking what butterflies are, where they live, how and when they change from a caterpillar into a butterfly, and so on. The CCSS share that these are predictable questions nonfiction readers ask and carry in their minds whenever they read. By third grade, readers are expected to refer explicitly to the text, to point to specific pages to support their explanations. And by fifth grade, just as in the literature standards, students are expected to "[q]uote accurately from a text when explaining what the text says explicitly and when drawing inferences from the text" (14).

So the Common Core now expects students to cite textual evidence as they explain what the text teaches. The important thing to realize is that each grade lays essential groundwork for the next. If you had the work in place in grades 2 and 3 so that students were able to demonstrate an accurate understanding of what they read, then this high-level fifth-grade work would be a continuation of those skills. When this same child was in eleventh grade she must be sure to "cite strong and thorough textual evidence" as well as be able to determine "where the text leaves matters uncertain" (38)—all as part of demonstrating literal comprehension.

Of course, as students progress up the grades, they are not only referring to texts in increasingly complex ways. They are also progressing up a trajectory of inference work. By grade 5, for example, whether students are reading literature or nonfiction, they are expected to infer. Just as literary texts begin to rely on a reader to notice implicit connections across parts of the text, nonfiction texts demand this same close reading.

If you want to try this work with colleagues, you might examine *Shark Attack!,* a level R/S book by Cathy East Dubowski that many fifth graders read, to demonstrate these Common Core expectations. What can you infer from the title, from the headings, from the anecdotes in the book? One might cite the exclamation point and word choice in the title ("*Attack!*"), the descriptions of "deadly sharks," and the anecdote about the boy being attacked even in fresh water, putting them all together as evidence to support the inference that sharks can be dangerous—perhaps more dangerous than the average reader had been thinking. To understand what this text says, both explicitly and implicitly, the reader needs to compile information across the text and to draw inferences based on patterns found in the details, connecting them to the whole of the text. This is exactly what the CCSS specify for fifth grade.

You'll notice, we hope, that as we moved up the grade levels, the skills involved in literal understanding became more challenging because the texts themselves became more complex. There is intellectual work involved in constructing literal comprehension as texts become denser and more complex, and the Common Core argues that this intellectual work is the most important work a reader needs to achieve, before all else.

What Does the Common Core Say About the Implications for Instruction?

If you decide to implement the CCSS, then you will want to think about your current efforts to help students move up the ladder of text complexity. If you and your colleagues want to teach in ways that are accountable to the standards—that is, if you are not going to cherry-pick a few especially appealing standards to implement but are instead going to align your reforms to the emphases in the standards—then you have no choice but to take seriously the implications of reading standards 1 and 10. This discussion of the implications of those standards, then, does not provide a menu of possibilities so much as a road map, organized in a step-by-step sequence, designed to help you and your school assess, decide, plan, and initiate reforms.

1. Take stock of your school's current efforts to move students up the ladder of text complexity.

You will want to begin by taking stock of where your current students are in relation to the standards' levels for text complexity. If your kids read high-level texts rapidly and speak knowledgeably about them, you can move on. If not, though, you need to find out what level of text they *do* comprehend. The best way we know to do this in a K–5 school, or a secondary school where many students read below grade level and will therefore still benefit from being assessed as readers, is to be sure that each teacher has been trained to use running records to assess readers. These can be done using the DRA, the QRI, Fountas and Pinnell's assessments, or the assessments that are open access on the Teachers College Reading and Writing Project's website (http://readingandwritingproject.com/). The choice of one assessment system over another is relatively inconsequential. Each of these systems provides the teacher with a series of increasingly difficult texts that, taken together, constitute a ladder of leveled texts.

Other tasks could function as needs assessments. Use a text you are including in the curriculum, or print one of the texts on the high end of the Common Core's list of recommendations, and move among your students, asking one, then another, then another to read that selection aloud. Start by listening for fluency alone, as you'll be able to gauge that within even just a minute of listening. If the student reads in phrases with intonation, the text may well be appropriate for that reader (although you'd need to study the reader's comprehension to be sure). If the reader reads in phrases and lacks appropriate intonation or reads mostly word by word, the text is probably too hard. Tim Rasinski notes that fluency is one of the strongest indicators of comprehension (2010). Of course, before you can say that a text is just right for a reader, you'll need to also confirm that the reader understands what he or she is reading, but often a check of fluency alone can reveal problems.

In order to gauge how closely your students' abilities match the expectations of the Common Core, you will need a clear answer to the question, How good is good enough? On the TCRWP website, you'll find a chart of benchmark levels across the year for grades K–8. These levels have been aligned with the New York State English Language Arts standardized test, and have helped teachers assess how close to grade level individual students are at various points in the year.

Chances are good that a fair percentage of students will not be reading texts that match the CCSS levels of expectation with accuracy, fluency, and comprehension. After all, these standards are ambitious. The question, then, will be how best to go forward. The upcoming section will help you respond to this question.

2. Accelerate students' progress up the ladder of text difficulty.

Of course, you will not only want to create the conditions that allow you to match readers to books and to provide students with opportunities to read extensively. You will also want to accelerate their progress up the ladder of text complexity so that over time, they read increasingly complex books.

We have found that it helps if classroom teachers have a hypothetical plan for how each student will advance, and it helps if that plan is written (perhaps onto a calendar) and shared with the student and is public so that each student (and sometimes the student's parents, too) can work with resolve toward those clear goals. You might share such a goal with a reader by saying something like, "On the first of October, let's give the Amber Brown (level N/O) books a try because if you read up a storm between now and then and if you really turn your mind on high to *think* about these books, I bet you might just be ready to tackle that level of book by then. Look at them. You see how . . . ? So, are you game for working toward that goal?" Or, "If you read these shark books first, this Seymour Simon book is going to make a lot more sense."

You may feel uneasy about reducing reading to a ladder of text levels. We have squirmed when students have talked about their reading lives in a "move up levels" kind of way, or when they've talked about reading with an "accruing points" mentality ("I've read ten books so far, I hope I'm going to get to an S by Thanksgiving"). But a large body of research by John Hattie (2009), among others, that reviewed fifty thousand studies of twenty to thirty million learners on the factors that make for achievement has shown that when the goal is to maximize achievement, it helps for the learner to have a crystal-clear target in mind and to be given concrete instructional feedback about his or her progress toward that target.

Remember, though, that in the effort to move students up levels, it is not helpful for students to "read" texts that are too hard for them, because they're not really reading. Also, it is important for students to access complex texts not just for reading reasons but also because those texts give students access to more knowledge. We must get kids up to the reading levels that will let them access content knowledge as well as read more complex literature. As the Common Core explains,

> A turning away from complex texts is likely to lead to a general impoverishment of knowledge, which, because knowledge is intimately linked with reading comprehension ability, will accelerate the decline in the ability to comprehend complex texts and the decline in the richness of text itself. This bodes ill for the ability of Americans to meet the demands placed upon them by citizenship in a democratic republic and the challenges of a highly competitive global marketplace of goods, services, and ideas. (2010b, 4)

Of course, it is important to reassess often. All too frequently, we have seen teachers conducting running records or other assessments just at one or two points during the school year, and not dreaming of accelerating progress save at those intervals. If readers are advancing on course, they are probably moving up three text levels a year during many years, and readers who enter the school year well below level might progress as many as five or six levels in a single year. For this to stand a chance of happening, teachers need to assess and reconsider the level of text difficulty a reader is reading at many junctures during the year.

In the elementary schools we know best, teachers enter the data about their students' levels of text difficulty into our web-based software system, Assessment Pro, and both the teachers and others who care about the classrooms are able to view readers' progress through a range of analytic lenses. A principal can ask, for example, "How many readers in each of my four fourth grades are now reading at or above the expected benchmark level for fourth grade?" and, if more children in one room seem off course, that principal can ask, "What's been the rate of acceleration in each of my four fourth grades?" In this way, a school leader has a bird's-eye view of progress—and lack thereof—across the school and is able to send extra resources into identified places of need. In middle and high schools, teachers and students keep statistics on their reading using online systems such as Goodreads, or apps on their smartphones, or paper records, so that teachers and readers can reflect on how students are ranging across levels, authors, and genres as they move through young adult novels and into classic and contemporary literature.

A word of caution: Implicit in this entire discussion is the idea that a reader's recorded progress up the ladder of text complexity reflects growth in reading. This may not always be the case. In some classrooms, the reader's climb up the ladder of text difficulty may instead reflect the teacher's increasing awareness that he or she will appear to be teaching well if students appear to be able to handle texts of increasing complexity. Time and again, we have seen that in instances when school leaders evaluate teachers by noting their students' progress up the ladder of text difficulties, and especially when principals come down hard on teachers whose students are not making expected growth, it is extremely common for teachers to simply move kids up to harder texts whether or not they are ready for those texts. The CCSS' emphasis on grade level text complexity will only increase this pressure. While it is important to move students along levels of text difficulty, Elfrieda Hiebert (2012) reminds us that doing so at the expense of student comprehension is not a practice supported by research. She makes the case that there is no evidence to suggest that raising the bar of text complexity in the primary grades will get students to the level of college and career readiness at the end of high school, especially since texts in K–3 core reading programs have become increasingly harder—not easier—since the 1980s. As a result, students end up holding books they cannot read, and all hope that they'll make real, lasting progress vanishes. It is critically important for a school leader to support rather than to punish teachers when their students do not make the expected progress, and it is equally important for the principal to come right out and say, repeatedly and firmly, that it would be utterly unacceptable for teachers to move readers up to books that they cannot read with 95% accuracy, fluency, and comprehension. And it will be important to sometimes spot-check to see that students within a class tend to be accurately matched to books.

You and your colleagues will want to have a repertoire of strategies for scaffolding a reader's work with a text that is just a mite hard for her.

+ You might *read aloud the first chapter of a book* and discuss it with readers. Within that first chapter, usually the characters are introduced, the protagonist's motivations are revealed, the setting is established, and the reader becomes accustomed to the voice of the text. Helping readers with just this one chapter, and then using this chapter to establish expectations for upcoming chapters, is a wonderful and easy way to support readers.

+ You might *set readers up with a same-book partnership* and help the partners establish habits that will support each other. One habit would be to read silently, but to still progress through the text in sync; another would be to regularly spend time recalling the chapter that they've just read, linking any aspects of that chapter to earlier information. Partners can also help each other with confusing parts of the narrative and with challenging vocabulary.

+ You might *support readers who are new to a text level by giving a book introduction* and sometimes expanding this into a text introduction. So if you are introducing *Sarah, Plain and Tall*, you might say, "This book is set in the prairie and as you read, you are not just supposed to learn about the character of Sarah and about the other people in her family. You are also supposed to learn about the place of the prairie, as it plays a symbolic role in this book and in its sequels."

✦ You might *encourage a reader to listen to an audio version of a book that is a notch too hard* and to then read that book for himself or herself. If the book has a sequel, the work with the first volume might provide enough support for the reader to have a satisfying experience while reading the next volume on his or her own.

✦ You might *allow a reader to have a go at a too-hard book when you note the reader's high motivation.* Teachers generally find that it is important to set a deadline for this reading. "You want to read this? That's okay with me if you are sure, but let's say that by next Wednesday, you need to be done this book." Of course, the best thing would be to then provide the reader with some of the supports described above.

3. Devise a plan for altering curriculum to support your students' progress toward reading more complex texts.

There are differences of opinion over the best way to move readers to the levels of text difficulty espoused by the Common Core. Although PARCC (Partnership for Assessment of Readiness for College and Careers) offers their suggestions for implementing the Common Core, it is important to stress that these are optional, and they are distinct from the actual Common Core. The standards themselves are clear that the job of developing teaching plans is outside their province. The document that was ratified by forty-five states says repeatedly and in no uncertain terms that decisions about teaching are to be left in the hands of the professionals—of you, the teachers, and of other literacy experts. For example, the CCSS document opens with the statement that the standards focus on results rather than means. "By emphasizing required achievements, the Standards leave room for teachers, curriculum developers, and states to determine how those goals should be reached. . . . Teachers are thus free to provide students with whatever tools and knowledge their professional judgment and experience identify as most helpful for meeting the goals set out in the Standards" (2010a, 4). First on the list of what is not covered by the standards is this statement: "The Standards define what all students are expected to know and be able to do, not how teachers should teach" (4).

So, the Common Core State Standards—in the document that was ratified—explicitly leave decisions about teaching up to the professionals. As we mentioned at the start of this discussion, you and your school will need to determine the path that you will take in order to help your students advance through the levels of text complexity. You are held responsible for achieving the goals of the CCSS, and the decision over how to reach those goals is clearly left in the hands of you and your colleagues. In *Publishers' Criteria for the Common Core State Standards in English Language Arts and Literacy* (2011), Coleman, the CEO of the Grow Report, and Pimentel, an architect of the Diploma Project (which studied what college students need in order to do well) diverge from this stance and lay out their plan for bringing students to the standards' levels of achievement. That plan is formalized also in documents written by PARCC, in which Pimental and Coleman play influential roles. Those plans include their interpretations of the CCSS document, interpretations that are illuminating and noteworthy but are, nevertheless, personal interpretations and not ratified consensus. We would like to see more research to substantiate the effectiveness of their plan.

In *Publishers' Criteria for the Common Core State Standards in English Language Arts and Literacy*, Coleman and Pimentel suggest that if you assess your students and find they are not successful when reading texts that the CCSS regard as complex for those students' grade levels, the answer is nevertheless to keep providing those students with texts that are aligned to the CCSS. They write, "All students, including those who are behind, [must] have extensive opportunities to encounter and comprehend grade-level complex text as required by the standards. Far too often, students who have fallen behind are given only less complex texts rather than the support they need to read texts at the appropriate level of complexity" (2011, 3 and 11). The scaffolding that they envision includes instruction on grade level texts and fluency practice. They claim, "Students who need additional assistance, however, must not miss out on essential practice and instruction their classmates are receiving" (3). They also say, "Instructional materials should also offer advanced texts to provide students at every grade level with the opportunity to read texts beyond their current grade level to prepare them for the challenges of more complex texts" (3). These recommendations are laid out in much more detail in a draft of model content frameworks released in October 2011 by PARCC. PARCC is one of two consortia that have been charged with the job of designing new assessments aligned to the CCSS, which will be unrolled in 2014.

It is clear from the guidelines to publishers and the model frameworks that these individuals believe the best way to help students move up the ladder of text difficulty is for teachers to select a small number of "Common Core complex texts" and for the entire class of students to read in unison, with teachers generating text-dependent questions for students to answer through conversation and required writing exercises. PARCC's draft frameworks recommend that the class devote two to three weeks to close study of one novel—reading, rereading, discussing, rereading again, and writing about it—and that the class then devotes four to five weeks to close study of six to seven shorter texts, again selected by the teacher, with pieces such as the Declaration of Independence and King's "Letter from a Birmingham Jail" as suggested texts. The PARCC draft even makes this bold assertion: "A significant body of research links the close reading of complex text—regardless if the student is a struggling reader or advanced—to significant gains in reading proficiency, and finds close reading to be a key component of college and career readiness" (5). And yet of the few footnoted studies it cites as the "significant body of research," nearly all took place in college or high school; one involved adolescents, one was a paper discussing the debate over the pros and cons of constructivist teaching, and another, "The Role of Deliberate Practice in the Acquisition of Expert Performance" (Ericsson, Krampe, and Tesch-Römer 1993, 367), was a discussion of developing expertise in all fields including physical fitness, which, it turns out, never mentioned close reading at all and even contained this quote: "Hence mere repetition of an activity will not automatically lead to improvement in, especially, accuracy of performance (Trowbridge and Cason 1932)" (Ericsson, Krampe, and Tesch-Römer 1993, 367). None drew from the far larger body of research on children's literacy development, a surprising point as half of the assessments PARCC is designing are aimed at elementary school students.

PARCC anticipates that teachers will ask, "What about the students who cannot read this level of text?" and the authors write, "Flexibility is built in for educators to build progressions of more complex texts within grade bands (e.g., grades 4–5, 6–8, 9–12) that overlap to a limited degree with earlier bands, but reading texts from the appropriate band lies at the core of the Model Content Frameworks" (2011, 6).

4. Implement your plan.

When designing an approach that will accelerate your students' progress up the ladder of text difficulty, research strongly supports that you conduct running records or use some other means to determine the level of text difficulty that each reader can handle with 95% accuracy, fluency, and comprehension, and then match readers to appropriate texts, and teach in ways that keep readers progressing toward texts that are just one notch beyond those they can read with total ease. Provisioning students with an extensive collection of high-interest accessible books is a critical part of this work. Some people suggest the minimum number of books in a classroom library is twenty books per student; most schools agree that over time, it will be important to provision students with more books than that. Guthrie and Humenick (2004) report a meta-analysis of twenty-two experimental or quasi-experimental studies of reading motivation and achievement and found that of the four classroom factors that were strongly related to success in reading, the most influential factor was ensuring the students had easy access to high-interest texts, and the second most influential factor was providing students with choice over what they would read. Michael Pressley and his colleagues (2003) conducted a similar meta-analysis and found high-motivation and high-performing classrooms were, above all, filled with books at different levels of text difficulty. Conversely, on their list of the characteristics of classroom practices that undermine motivation and achievement is: "The teacher does not give students opportunities to have power over their own learning. Students do not have choice in their work" (46). This underscores the importance of the decisions that you and your colleagues will need to make.

If your goal is to accelerate readers' ability to comprehend increasingly complex texts, matching readers to books is necessary, but not sufficient. The engine that motors readers' development is the time spent in engaged reading and in talking and writing about that reading. It will be important, therefore, for you to organize the school day so that students have long blocks of time for reading.

Although one can rely on common sense when concluding that in order to progress up the levels of text complexity, students need to read a lot, this is actually the one conclusion that is most supported by research. Krashen (2004), for example, explains that 94% of the tests on reading comprehension that collect data on volume of reading show that kids who are given more time to read do better than kids who have little time to read. Guthrie (2004) has shown that reading volume predicted reading comprehension and that dramatic increases in reading volume are important for thoughtful literacy proficiencies. The *NAEP 1998 Reading Report Card for the Nation and the States* (Donahue et al. 1999) showed that at every level, reading more pages at home and at school was associated with higher reading scores. Students in the classrooms of more effective teachers read ten times as much as students in classrooms of less effective teachers (Allington and Johnston 2002). After reviewing the overwhelming research on this important topic, Allington concludes, "So how much daily in-school reading might we plan for? I would suggest one and a half hours of daily in-school reading would seem to be a minimum goal given the data provided by these studies. . . . However my ninety-minute recommendation is for time actually reading" (2005, 44).

Resources Available on the RWP Website

The following is a list of resources that are open access that will be helpful in matching readers to books and setting up classroom libraries. To access these resources, visit http://readingandwritingproject.com/. No password is needed.

- Independent Reading Benchmarks: a chart of benchmark *independent* reading levels that has been calibrated to students' success on state and NAEP exams

- Book lists: extensive lists of leveled texts in a variety of genres, useful for purchasing new books or determining the level of existing books

- Classroom libraries: leveled texts grouped by category, useful for classrooms undertaking genre or unit of study work

- Assessments: informal reading inventories correlated to the Fountas and Pinnell leveling system, designed to repidly assess comprehension, miscues, and fluency; also, an "in-book" assessment for middle and high school that allows teachers to assess students in the books they are reading

CHAPTER FOUR

READING LITERATURE
STANDARDS 2—9

One of the beauties of the Common Core reading anchor standards 2–9 is that they assume that works of literature are about more than the plots they unfold. The standards suggest that even young readers are ready to read for meaning. Reading literature involves learning from the characters in stories and looking to books for lessons in courage, determination, and integrity. As students investigate language, delve into themes, and analyze possible morals and meanings of stories, they'll develop insight into the text, which is the goal of the Common Core, and insight into themselves and the lives of others, which is one of the purposes for reading at all.

Thank goodness. For too long, the focus of NCLB and concurrent high-stakes testing has been on decoding and on readers demonstrating low-level inferences with small chunks of texts. Perhaps it was this preoccupation with basic skills alone that explains why, even with billions of dollars being channeled into NCLB's version of reading instruction, reading flatlined during the years of NCLB. How could it not? If you empty reading of meaning and purpose, young people won't step up to the hard work it takes to become more powerful readers. As long as there is a reward for their work, children and teens are game to work hard. But a higher score on a Scantron sheet won't rally a young person to read with engagement. Entering the wondrous lives of others—that will fascinate a reader. Developing a sympathetic imagination for those who dwell in villages, forests, farms, and cities—that will engage a reader. Learning how to live your life—that will sustain a reader.

We spoke in the last chapter about the emphasis the Common Core places on developing literal understandings of complex texts with reading anchor standards 1 and 10. Students have to comprehend what they're reading or the rest of this work will be out of their reach. We're assuming, therefore, that you have the work of anchor standards 1 and 10 in place, and you're ready to raise the analytical skills of your readers. This chapter will help you harness the reading standards that support higher levels of intellectual work with literature. In order to understand reading literature standards 2–9, you'll want to grasp the big reading moves described in the anchor standards, as well as understand the grade level progressions toward those larger reading goals. The anchor standards capture the Common Core State Standards' vision of analytical, engaged reading more than the specific grade level standards do. The anchors are the overarching goals; they provide the benchmarks that you should aim toward in your teaching and your curriculum development.

This emphasis on the anchor standards does not mean the grade level specifics won't be valuable to you—they will be. They may not, though, always provide you with a full understanding of your goal, especially if you look at your grade level in isolation. It is when you look along a trajectory of grade level specifics that you will see the standards' vision for a learning progression that can take your students toward the goals of the anchor standards. You'll particularly want to note the trajectory that is implied in the grade level specifics that come before and after the grade in which you teach. If you read the standards horizontally, seeing what comes before and after the grade-specific standards for the students you teach, you can assess your readers along timelines of development, ascertaining where the bulk of your class seems to be in its journey toward the goal of the CCSS. Then you can tailor your whole class so that you move the majority of your students in a way that has real traction, and then tailor small-group teaching to support students who are earlier or more advanced in their level of skill development.

In order to help you understand both the goals set forth in the anchor standards and the grade level progressions the CCSS provide toward those goals for literature, we'll walk you through not just the main categories but also the reading work of literature standards 2–9, using a sample text, *Charlotte's Web*, to focus on the reading practices each of those groupings spotlights. Then, in the implementation section of this chapter, we think about broader implications for literature instruction. In this chapter, then, we offer an overview of

- reading literature for key ideas and details
- reading literature for craft and structure
- reading literature to integrate knowledge and ideas

We end the chapter by offering pathways for implementing the literature standards in your school and classroom.

Reading for Key Ideas and Details: Ensuring Students Read for Meaning Across a Story

Anchor standards 2 and 3 ask readers to summarize the text, to connect parts of the text, to infer central ideas and themes, and to trace their development across the text. The standards specifically say:

Key Ideas and Details

2. Determine central ideas or themes of a text and analyze their development; summarize the key supporting details and ideas.

3. Analyze how and why individuals, events, and ideas develop and interact over the course of a text. (10)

This work requires that readers who may be accustomed to approaching texts with blinders on, focused just on the words on the page before them, must develop the ability to carry meaning across the whole story, seeing what happens on one page as being part of a thread of meaning that weaves through the text. Readers who can do the work of standards 2 and 3 can carry their understandings across a story. These readers are not constantly caught off guard by what happens; instead, these readers infer a logic of cause and effect, synthesizing character traits and motivations and analyzing the logical consequence of events.

All of this work becomes more important as books get more complex, but as the Common Core standards convey, the thinking work begins early. Imagine a second grader reading "Neighbors," a story in *Poppleton*. In that story, Poppleton gets tired of his neighbor Cherry Sue coming over constantly to offer him food. He maintains a polite silence through several visits (which happen across several pages). Finally, Cherry Sue makes another visit, sings out her "Yoo-hoo!" and Poppleton simply can't stand it anymore and he soaks her with a hose. To understand why events unfold the way they do, the second grader needs to carry Poppleton's growing frustration from each visit to the next. The final event is then a culmination. By teaching anchor standards 2 and 3, you help readers of texts as simple as the Poppleton books consider events in the stories as related, one to the next.

Reading for key ideas and details involves more than synthesizing events. If you incorporate this category of standards into your literature reading work, you will push your readers to infer character motivation and to see cause-and-effect relationships. You will teach them to ask, "Why?"

and to see that the answers lie within the specific details and the language of the stories. Poppleton, after all, has reasons for his behavior. To a reader who focuses only on the page where Poppleton soaks Cherry Sue, Poppleton's actions seem shocking—and uncharacteristic of how kind Poppleton is in other stories. But for the young reader who has learned to *expect* that events are related and has noticed Poppleton's motivation grow across pages, this climax is a logical consequence of earlier pressures.

Earlier, we mentioned that some standards will seem more important to readers at higher levels of proficiency. This grouping of reading literature standards will pay off especially once students are reading true narratives, which usually means they are reading texts at levels G or above. Texts below this level of text difficulty may not contain stories that are coherent and detailed enough to support this work fully, although of course very young readers can do this thinking with stories they experience through read-aloud and shared reading, or in response to digital texts.

Let's look more closely at anchor standard 2, determining central ideas or themes. To unpack this standard, let's go back to "Neighbors" for a moment. The second-grade version of this anchor standard for literature reads, "Recount stories, including fables and folktales from diverse cultures, and determine their central message, lesson or moral" (11). The second grader who has been taught to think about the central message, moral, and lesson conveyed through a story will probably chat about how Poppleton has learned a lesson about keeping his temper. For this second grader, the moral of the story might be as simple as "don't go to neighbors if you are not invited" or as sophisticated as that "it is helpful to use your words before you blow up." The goal, of course, would not be to teach students *the* moral or meaning of a story, but rather to teach them the habit of thinking, "What might the main character have learned that I, too, could learn?" As children progress through the school year and beyond, it will be important for them to learn to initiate this sort of thinking, and to bring more skills and knowledge to this interpretative work over time.

An Activity to Familiarize Teachers with the Literature Reading Standards: Trying Out Reading for Key Ideas and Details with *Charlotte's Web*

To lead students toward the high level of reading work described in the anchor standards, it may be helpful for you and your colleagues to try this reading work together. We've found that sometimes when you are with colleagues, just staring at the academic jargon of the standards, you may think that all your students have to begin doing college-level work on their third-grade stories. We recommend, therefore, to be sure that you have firsthand experience with the reading work that the standards ask you to teach. By devoting even just a bit of time to trying the standards on for size, you and your colleagues will develop some common language and under-standings, some shared expertise, and a wellspring of experience that you can draw upon when you invite students to try this same work.

To try reading in ways that the Common Core standards describe, take a story—a favorite read-aloud text, for example—and talk about the text using the reading literature standards to guide your discussion. For instance, let's imagine revisiting just the first few pages of the childhood favorite, *Charlotte's Web*, a text that is often read aloud in third grade (and which you can find online easily if you don't have the book at hand) as a way to get to know the reading literature standards. Imagine that you and your colleagues read the first chapter, in which you meet Fern's family, find out that the runt of the newly born piglet litter is about to be killed, and watch Fern save Wilbur from this fate. Now imagine trying out the first anchor standard, the one discussed in the previous chapter, which asks readers to "[r]ead closely to determine what the text says explicitly and to make logical inferences from it; cite specific textual evidence when writing or speaking to support conclusions drawn from the text" (10). The work of anchor standard 1 for literature, then, asks you to recount the story, citing specifically from the text.

So perhaps you explain that this is a story about a girl who lives on a farm with her mother, father, and brother. Her name is Fern. The story begins with Fern's father, Mr. Arable, setting out with an ax, and Fern ask-ing: "Where's Papa going with that ax?" The story goes on to show that Fern is terribly upset that her father is going to kill a piglet because it is a runt and, as he says, "a weakling makes trouble." Fern calls this event a terrible injustice and persuades her father to give her the piglet instead.

As you recount the story, you and your colleagues will want to work to add in details that seem important, reminding one another of the spe-cific parts or even words that seem important, like Fern's words about injustice. Your goal is to show that you have read *closely* and that you are citing *specific* textual evidence. This means that you will remind each other to draw details right from the text. When you notice that your retell-ing is proceeding in a global fashion, bypassing detail, one of you might say, "Wait, we left out an important part." Working collaboratively in this fashion, you might add in that Fern names the piglet Wilbur. Someone might add that the chapter ends with Fern nursing Wilbur from a bottle. Someone else might quote Fern. If this feels very heady, it sounds like what readers actually do when they first talk about what they've read—they say things like "I think the part where _____ is important . . ." or "We also found out. . . ."

The first anchor standard, with its emphasis on literal comprehension, is critical for readers. If the CCSS are known for anything, they are known for an emphasis on text-centered discussion and thinking. If anyone tries a "This reminds me of . . ." detour and you want your work to be aligned to the Common Core, steer the discussion right back to the text. Similarly, if someone says, "This makes me think . . . ," try staying focused on the text just a bit longer. Linger on the literal details of the text before jumping to ideas. If someone skips right to an idea, one of you might say, "Wait, let's just make sure we've really put onto the table what actually happens before we jump to big ideas. Just to make sure we've really captured what we've learned so far."

Once you've recounted what happens in the chapter, move on to anchor standards 2 and 3, which invite you to talk about central ideas and themes, paying attention to the interaction of characters and to events. The work of standard 2 is to determine central ideas and themes, and the work of standard 3 invites students to determine how events, characters, and ideas are connected across the text. As part of this work, you will want to think about central ideas that are beginning to emerge. You might ask, "What is this story beginning to be about?" That is the crucial work of moving from literal comprehension to deeper understanding of embedded meanings. We realize that literature is about more than the plot, and we begin to ask: "What is this story starting to be about?" As we do this work, we remind ourselves that the standards acknowledge that stories are about more than one idea, so we push ourselves to think of a few different ideas the story is beginning to explore.

Someone in the group might reasonably suggest that maybe this story is starting to be about a struggle for justice. Whatever the idea might be that a colleague puts forward, invite each other to give some examples from the text as evidence. Say to each other, "What in the story makes you say that?" This invitation might push the conversation to go from the proposition that the book is starting to be about a struggle for justice to the supporting evidence that when Fern tries to wrestle the ax from her father's hand, she says things such as "This is the most terrible case of injustice I've ever heard of." The standards, of course, want you to notice how themes and ideas are developed across the text, and in a discussion of just Chapter One, you won't be able to do much of that work, but you could agree to carry ideas about justice forward as you read. Or, you might read just a bit further to see what this feels like. Someone might add that the story is also evolving into one about a girl's relationship with her father, and how it's unusual the way Fern seems to be teaching Mr. Arable. You might gather up some details from the text that support that idea. Other colleagues are sure to have different ideas about characters, and you might, for example, agree to investigate Fern's character as a particularly compassionate child. After just twenty minutes of talk, then, you and your colleagues will have forged a closer relationship to the key ideas and details anchor standards for literature.

READING FOR CRAFT AND STRUCTURE: HELPING STUDENTS SEE THAT CRAFT, STRUCTURE, AND MEANING ARE INTERCONNECTED

If you think of the first grouping of reading standards as reading for *meaning*, think of the second grouping of anchor standards as reading for *craft*. If you think of the first category as focused on *what* the text says, think of the second as focused on *how* it says it. The two categories are not as distinct as they seem, however, because the point of the second grouping of standards is, in the end, to deepen the reader's understanding of meaning. Following are the anchor standards in the "Craft and Structure" category:

Craft and Structure

4. Interpret words and phrases as they are used in a text, including determining technical, connotative, and figurative meanings, and analyze how specific word choices shape meaning or tone.

5. Analyze the structure of texts, including how specific sentences, paragraphs, and larger portions of the text (e.g., a section, chapter, scene, or stanza) relate to each other and the whole.

6. Assess how point of view or purpose shapes the content and style of a text. (10)

Essentially, these anchor standards ask readers to investigate the effect of authors' decisions—about language, structure, point of view, voice, style—on the meaning of texts. To understand the rationale for this emphasis in the CCSS, it helps to remember that the standards were constructed through a process of backward planning. The first question was, What is it that young people need to know and be able to do to be successful in college and careers? Those proficiencies were then combed backward through all the grades. This puts the work that is highlighted in this second grouping of standards into context. Clearly, understanding how texts work and reading with an alertness to perspective, point of view, and craft are critical reading skills for high school and college students. It is essential work, actually, for anyone who wants to be a knowledgeable citizen. Every time we vote, we sift through candidates' stories. Often as we read the news, we ask ourselves, Who wasn't included in this story? Readers who have many years of practice will be even more adept at close reading.

Surely it is the case that the skills supported by these standards *can* be adapted so they are relevant to very young readers. You can see the early signs of this work in the teacher who, during read-aloud, poses questions such as "How do you know that Poppleton is getting so angry?" Or, when this teacher poses questions like "I wonder what led Cherry Sue to issue so many invitations?," she is really asking her young readers to ponder point of view, and she is introducing the notion that characters have different perspectives on events in a narrative—the work of standard 6. Readers don't have to wait, therefore, until they are analyzing *The Scarlet Letter* to be alert to how craft affects meaning. Jerome Bruner has often been quoted in this regard, for his declaration that "the foundations of any subject may be taught to anybody at any age in some form" (Bruner 1963, 76). The question is one of priority—and it is an entirely reasonable question. When implementing the standards, you will not be able to address every standard at once, and some will seem especially important for particular grade levels. Or, some will seem to apply most prominently to nonfiction as opposed to fiction. For now, our goal is to help you understand the work of reading standards 2–9. Later, we explore implications for instruction.

In order to understand what reading for craft and structure looks like when the text is a children's story or novel, let's think for a minute about the intellectual work, or what Bruner might term the *foundational work*, involved in reading the *Poppleton* story "Neighbors." In this story, it is the repeated language that grabs every child reader's attention. "Yoo-hoo!

Poppleton!" Cherry Sue yells again and again across the story, as she invites him for oatmeal, toasted cheese, spaghetti. Listen to a first or second grader read this book, and you can hear their voice rise each time, as they intuitively grasp how the refrain makes Poppleton crazy. Those same children will talk about how it was lucky Poppleton found the hose, as he might otherwise have picked up a tennis racket and really hurt Cherry Sue. They may not have the literary language yet to name symbolism, but these children are realizing the hose is more than just a hose—it's an everyday object used as a weapon, something children are familiar with from the schoolyard or the backyard. Of course, you can read "Neighbors" and not talk about what words make Poppleton crazy, or which parts seem connected, or if there are any objects that are kind of important. It's a great story, on plot alone. But if children are led to this work gracefully and naturally, they'll begin to see more in the stories they read.

As texts become more complex and more carefully wrought, thinking about the craft moves that an author has made and looking between the structure and the meaning of the text moves from being interesting enrichment work to being work that is essential to understanding. You can, of course, delve into symbolism in the Poppleton books or in the Nate the Great series, but to do so, you need to be a very high-level reader—arguably, higher than the plot of the text would fascinate. And frankly, one might well suggest that if young readers do the work of the first three anchor standards well—comprehending, inferring, synthesizing—then they'll move rapidly up levels to the kinds of stories where paying attention to craft, structure, and language will become an essential part of their everyday reading work. For example, in the novels students are reading in the upper grades, like *Tiger Rising* or *The Hunger Games*, craft and structure emerge more prominently. Symbols such as the suitcase or the tiger are pretty inescapable in *Tiger Rising*, as is the mockingjay in *The Hunger Games*. By the time readers are reading *The Giver*, comprehension will not be possible without an attention to craft and structure. Readers who attempt to read this book for its plot alone, who read without trying to unlock the secrets of this story, will never grasp the story at all, for Jonas' quest to disentangle the multiple meanings of phrases, events, images, and objects is also the reader's quest.

You'll also find, as students get older and embark on classic and adult novels, that many works of literature embed their meaning in symbolism more than in plot, and that literal understanding of the plot is only partial understanding of a novel. Think of *The Scarlet Letter*, a classic text in high school. Nothing actually happens; the plot unfolds before Chapter One. There is an adulterous love affair, an illicit child, a shunning, and a public act of humiliation, but that all happens before the book begins. From then on, the book is all about *repressed* desires of love and vengeance, and all the language is metaphoric. Reading this kind of novel would be pretty daunting for an unprepared reader. But for a reader who has gradually built up a repertoire of increasingly sophisticated reading skills, practiced (as appropriate) on the stories read as a child, the move into classic, highly metaphoric literature will be a reasonable next step.

Trying Out Reading for Craft and Structure with *Charlotte's Web*

Let's return to the earlier work that you and your colleagues were doing with *Charlotte's Web*. So far, you have applied the first three anchor standards to your reading of Chapter One. You will not want to pause before bringing standards 4 through 6 to your work with this book. When one is reading a book as engaging as E. B. White's classic, the craft and structure standards will especially pay off, helping you find even more in the text. These standards invite you to first pay attention to language, so you may want to start by pushing yourself and your colleagues to consider the word choices in the portion of the story that you have read. Ask yourself whether some words matter more than others. Look back over the story, and perhaps do some jotting in the margins or put your finger on words that seem significant and talk to a partner about those word choices. Become accustomed to asking, "Which words really call our attention here? What do we notice as we reread them?"

If you return to the first scene in the story, for example, where Fern has rushed upstairs to change, and Mr. Arable has brought the piglet into the kitchen in a carton, you might notice the sentence "The kitchen table was set for breakfast, and the room smelled of coffee, bacon, and wood smoke from the stove." Perhaps you'll notice how the words *kitchen table*, *wood smoke*, *stove*, *coffee*, and *bacon* all combine to create a sense of security, family, and prosperity. This is not a starving home. This is one where families settle in by the stove, where they sit together at the breakfast table, where food is plentiful. And yet there is something ominous about the implications of bacon. Bacon. You can almost feel E. B. White laughing as he inserts this portentous detail. All is not well for pigs in this home.

Other colleagues might notice how the light shines through the pig's ears as he sits in his carton, creating a kind of miraculous glow—and of course, for those of you who already know the story well, the pig does turn out to be miraculous! Someone else might notice how Mr. Arable washes his hands as he gives Fern the pig, as if he is washing his hands of the whole matter. The delightful aspect of this Common Core reading work is that it doesn't take a lot of extra work to see more in the text—all it really takes is pausing for a moment to notice what is there already. And you don't need to be reading really hard texts to do this work—this is a children's story.

Reading to Integrate Knowledge and Ideas: Helping Students Develop Lenses and Tools to Think Across Text Sets

The final anchor standards will help you mobilize your readers to read texts (books as well as other sorts of texts) that "go together" and to think across those texts, making connections and comparisons. Anchor standards 7–9 fit under the category of "Integration of Knowledge and Ideas." The anchor standards are as follows:

Integration of Knowledge and Ideas

7. Integrate and evaluate content presented in diverse media and formats, including visually and quantitatively, as well as in words.

8. Delineate and evaluate the argument and specific claims in a text, including the validity of the reasoning as well as the relevance and sufficiency of the evidence. (Not applicable to literature)

9. Analyze how two or more texts address similar themes or topics in order to build knowledge or to compare the approaches the authors take. (10)

When we think about doing this reading work, of relating ideas across stories, it doesn't necessarily mean that someone has gathered for us a collection of books around one obvious theme. This is often the case with nonfiction—but remember, the standards for literature are the same as the standards for informational texts. Nonfiction readers definitely want to read more than one text on a topic, to compare authors' ideas, information, perspectives, and *reasoning*, which is why standard 8 is reserved for informational texts. For literature, readers might compare the book to the movie (as many young readers have done with *Charlotte's Web*), or we might compare and contrast how different books treat themes that we have noticed are similar across books. Readers do this work all the time— we hold onto books after we've read them. We do not just read and think about one text, and then put that text behind us, as if we had never read it.

When you are asking yourself how much of this work is appropriate for young readers, it is not a big stretch to channel fiction readers into other genres, authors, and topics of special interest and to have them think between texts. This is what these standards do at the younger grade levels, inviting readers to conceive of their reading lives as small projects. First graders, for example, are asked to "compare and contrast the adventures and experiences of characters in stories" (11). After reading "Neighbors," the young reader who does this work will find the Poppleton basket (if you wisely set this up) and read all the Poppleton books. With some guidance from you, presumably, she'll learn that readers who love a series find more books by the same author or about the same topics. Perhaps this reader soon goes from the Poppleton books to other books by Cynthia Rylant. Then again, maybe she has noticed that the Poppleton stories are often about friendship, and so later, when you see that she is reading in the Henry and Mudge series or the Mr. Putter and Tabby series, you can help her think and talk about how the friendships in those books are the same and different from those in Poppleton books. Soon you'll be using the story of this one reader to help all your students see that readers benefit from becoming engaged with authors, themes, and genres, and then thinking across all the related texts. This work will make a difference in this young reader's reading life, opening her up to more meaning as she compares characters within and across series. She'll be not just reading but developing passions as a reader, projects that will guide her as she continues to read. For young readers, this work will depend on your scaffolding, your guidance—at least at first.

Later, your more experienced readers will graduate to comparing not just characters but themes and even the treatment of themes. Although it is rare for young readers to independently initiate reading projects that lead them to compare and contrast themes, noting how the treatment of a theme occurs differently in different literary texts, once you have taught readers to read interpretively, this is exactly what you will see them beginning to do. They'll see the same themes popping up everywhere. They will come to realize that one book teaches the lesson that one person can make a world of difference, and all of a sudden, as they think back over other literature they know well, they'll start saying, "Hey, that book teaches the same thing!" Certainly, when teachers select texts to read aloud to the whole class, it is usual to think of those selections as creating a text set that readers can later think across . . . but once readers know one book really well, they'll find that they see echoes of that book everywhere. And in fact it is true that once a reader begins to think about ways two books develop the same theme differently, the reader will suddenly be engaged in close analytic reading. What matters in terms of ensuring high-level reading work is that the Common Core asks readers to not only name themes and subjects that can be found in more than one text, but also *trace the development* of these themes.

Interestingly, as readers pursue the work of anchors 7 and 9, they end up finding themselves becoming more skilled at analyzing craft and structure, the work of anchors 4–6. This makes sense when you think about it, as it's easier to *see* craft and structure when you are already comparing two texts that develop similar themes, through different craft decisions. Even young readers will, on their own, talk about the movie versions of *Charlotte's Web* or *101 Dalmations*, and which one they like better. It's not a huge leap to teach them to also talk about *why* one version is more pleasing—and you'll begin to hear them say, "This one is more scary," "That one makes the rat mean." That's the work of standard 7, which right now teens are pursuing as they compare *The Hunger Games* and *Twilight* films to the novels.

We've emphasized the Common Core's focus on comparing and contrasting texts that address the same theme differently, and the standards actually ask for a wider range of comparison work. The CCSS, for example, recognize the potential opportunities for analysis that are embedded in any instance when one reads or otherwise experiences different versions of something. How many of us have compared the latest Harry Potter movie with the book? That's Common Core work. How many of us have compared historical and fictional interpretations of the same events? Anchors 7 and 9 invite students to compare versions of a narrative, to read nonfiction texts that are related to fiction stories, and to explore the literary traditions from which some stories spring. That is, the Common Core asks readers (and teachers) to choose texts purposefully to take advantage of the fascinating intellectual work that is available to those who "read around" a text.

Trying Out Reading to Integrate Knowledge and Ideas with *Charlotte's Web*

Finally, you might glance from *Charlotte's Web* to reading anchor standards 7 and 9, and now you'll notice that they invite you to consider what texts you could lay alongside the one you are talking about, to deepen your understanding and extend your thinking. You don't have to actually go to the library; you can, for now, simply imagine what you might want to read. You might want to compare the book *Charlotte's Web* with a film version. You might want to think about E. B. White's *Stuart Little*, another childhood favorite, and another tale of talking animals. You may be interested in reading more about raising pigs. What you are doing, as you imagine laying any of this reading alongside this story, is imagining the Common Core work of integrating knowledge and ideas.

PATHWAYS FOR IMPLEMENTING THE LITERATURE STANDARDS

In the vast majority of America's classrooms where kids have opportunities to read a lot of children's and young adult literature, students are poised to do the work that is described in the reading literature standards. The standards will help you issue an invitation. That students are eager to do this work is evidenced in classrooms where you see children putting their fingers or Post-it notes in places they think are important in Poppleton books or in *Tiger Rising*, and where you hear teenagers debating hotly about the Hunger Games trilogy in the hallways. As long as kids are reading, they are bound to be ready to read more closely.

Where you may run into some trouble getting ready to implement the literature standards is if your students are not reading children's and young adult books. If you have a reading program that focuses only on working with text excerpts (anthologies) or basals, for instance, you may need to insert some read-aloud and book club work into your curriculum. Students will need meaningful opportunities to practice the close reading of literature.

Whether you are providing opportunities for students to do this work on independent books, read-aloud texts, book club books, or a combination of these, your first step will be to make sure that readers actually comprehend the texts they are reading. We said more about assessing reading levels and literal comprehension in Chapter Three, and if you are worried about whether kids are holding books they can read, the implementation section of Chapter Three should help you.

Assuming that your students can read their books, then we recommend a couple pathways to getting to the standards. The first is to do a needs assessment—one that lets you see what students are doing as they read. The second is to align teaching methods and the content of reading instruction so that teachers do, in fact, teach students the skills of close reading, and so that students are able to practice these skills regularly.

1. Take stock of where your students are with a needs assessment.

If you and your school are going to undergo the reforms necessary to meet the high standards of the Common Core, you may want to begin with a quick needs assessment. Whereas it is easy to contrast the writing done by typical students today with the writing examples in the CCSS document, current levels of reading comprehension are not as visible, nor do the CCSS include examples against which to compare what students are currently able to do with their reading and what the standards ask them to do. So people are not apt to look up from the reading literature standards and say, "We need to totally ramp up our emphasis on higher-level comprehension of literature!" But that, in fact, is probably the case.

Colleagues in our schools did a needs assessment in the fall of 2011. We selected a few short books at levels N, R, and Z to become our assessment texts, deciding as we did so that running records of two-hundred-word passages wouldn't suffice for assessing higher-level comprehension skills. We selected *Amber Brown Is Not a Crayon*, *Skylark*, and *Night*, but we could have selected any other books of short length.

We read those books ourselves, noting places in the books where it seemed to us almost essential that any reader of the texts would be doing some of the intellectual work described in the reading standards. And in those places, we embedded text-dependent questions to prompt students to reveal the thinking work they were doing. We gave the books only to students who could demonstrate literal understanding. Our goal, though, was to move beyond literal understanding. For example, there is one place in *Skylark* when Sarah, the new bride who struggles with homesickness for her family in Maine and the sea, watches while her friend Maggie finds her well bone-dry and then loads all her family's worldly belongings onto a stagecoach and drives off, the dust billowing behind her. At this point in the text, we inserted the question, What is Sarah thinking as she watches Maggie drive off? We inserted a follow-up question as well so as to elicit more from students; we found a way to follow each student's first answer to the question with the prompt, What *else* might Sarah be thinking? We asked this question because anyone who had been tracking the theme of Sarah's loneliness and the family's worry that she would leave them for her home in Maine would have responded to the question with something to the effect of "Sarah is wondering if she, too, should leave the prairie and head to Maine," or "Sarah is thinking about how she can stay on the prairie with no water, no neighbors." Then we asked several hundred students who could easily read the book to read it to themselves and, as part of an assessment, to answer the questions when they came upon them in the novels. We found that astonishingly few students were doing that intellectual work independently; you will probably find the same. And that was a level R text. As texts get more complex, it's crucial that students have become inculcated in seeing beyond the surface of the plot.

If you'd like to do a needs assessment, you could mark up some leveled texts, as we did, and collect students' responses. Or you could gather students' Post-it notes or reading notebooks if they keep them. Or you could film a few partner conversations—anything to let you *see* what students are doing as they read. Then you'll be better ready to lay your course.

2. Ensure your instructional practices are moving your students forward by aligning teaching methods and content.

Once you have come to the realization that implementing the Common Core State Standards means putting a new emphasis on teaching higher-level comprehension skills in literature, the question becomes how to go forward. Start by realizing that the methods most schools in America have used to teach reading have not produced readers who demonstrate the skills of the CCSS—that's why the Common Core standards have been put in place. Almost two-thirds of American elementary schools have been teaching reading through "core reading programs," or basals. In these programs, what generally happens is that every student reads the same text (selected by the teacher) in unison (either silently, in round-robin fashion, or chorally) one day, and then the class may or may not discuss the text the next day, and then each reader answers teacher-developed questions the next day, and does various extensions the following day, before reading yet one more selection and repeating the process. Sometimes the questions can be answered in blanks on workbook pages, and sometimes they may require open-ended responses ("List five words to describe the setting in *Skylark*." "How do changes in the setting influence Sarah?" "How do changes in the setting influence Pa?").

Teachers in secondary schools have taught an extension of this sort of instruction, sometimes relying on textbooks and more often on whole-class novels. We caution that it is not enough to simply do this work in shared experiences such as through read-aloud or whole-class novel discussions—too many kids hide during that work, and you don't know if they can really do the high-level work on their own, in their independent reading. In the spring of 2011, when we were working with Doug Reeves to study what most affects student achievement in schools, he cautioned us that teachers demonstrating or orchestrating high-level work do not necessarily achieve transference. You'll want to make sure, therefore, that instruction moves immediately from demonstrating reading skills to coaching students to do this work on their own and giving them feedback as they try it, whether it is in book clubs or independent texts. The approach of sidestepping independent reading work—and we are lumping the elementary and secondary variations together because they are, in fact, similar—has not worked well for America's students. It doesn't ask the kids to do enough intellectual work. They look as if they are reading and thinking, but really, they are looking for little parts of the text that can answer questions someone else has posed.

Although it is clear that doing more of the same is not the way to go, it is less clear what pathway will lead to whole schools full of students—including high-needs students—achieving at the levels set by the Common Core reading standards. Different thought collaboratives of educators recommend different pathways for trying to move readers forward in elementary, middle, and high schools. That is appropriate because schools and students can differ widely from neighborhood to region. Whereas national *standards* are arguably helpful, our country is by no means ready for a national *curriculum*. In education, there is no gigantic list of amazing success stories, especially in high-needs schools, that provides a body of evidence conclusive enough to warrant deciding that there is one clear pathway to take. And if there were accumulated evidence of success, that success would be determined by current standardized tests, and those tests, with their little paragraph-long passages and multiple-choice questions, do not come close to assessing the standards of the Common Core. Then, too, time and again the schools that are cited as success stories one year turn out to not be so successful the next year. Others, upon closer inspection, are found to work with a special population of students or teachers, or to be flush with money from hedge fund leaders and philanthropists who adopt schools, or have unusual schedules, outside of union regulations. As Dick Allington often warns, if someone tells you the data are clear or research shows clearly that this or that is *the* way to proceed, be skeptical. Do we know some practices that seem to have been established as effective? Absolutely. Is there one way that has been proven to always work and can be considered the best way to put those practices together into a coherent approach to teaching the reading of fiction (or nonfiction)? No.

So, while the pathway you choose will depend on the needs of your student and teacher population, in the following sections we lay out a handful of principles that we (and the larger thought collaborative known as balanced literacy) believe are important in any effort to accelerate reading achievement.

Students should be doing lots and lots of in-school reading. In elementary schools, there has been a lot of research about dedicating time to independent reading, to moving kids as rapidly as possible up levels of texts, and to teaching higher-level reading skills within the books they are each reading. Thousands of schools have done that work and shown tremendous reading progress. What happens at the middle school and high school, though, is that reading time is cut. For readers to actually move up levels, they have to read a lot. And they need instruction and, more importantly, feedback—and those both take time. Some middle schools have made ninety minutes for literacy or even double that when leveled reading is inserted in content areas, and students in those schools have surged ahead, but it takes educators wrestling with the schedule to make sure kids get time to read in school. In highly literate, usually highly affluent, communities, where kids encounter texts across their days and their lives outside of school, it's less crucial, perhaps, to make time for reading in school. But for the kids for whom school is the site where they will move their literacy skills forward, it's essential that they actually get extended time to read many pages of text each day. Peter Johnston has been researching a high-needs middle school in Virginia. In this school, they instituted independent reading, without any other instruction. Kids were mostly reading novels, and they began to devour them. Even though their state test focuses mostly on nonfiction, and kids were reading fiction, their test scores began to climb immediately. The kids hadn't been reading, and now they were. So one lens you'll want to look through immediately is: *Are students in your school actually reading a lot?*

Students learn to read by reading. This is true whether they are learning to word solve and think on the run as they proceed through simple text or they are learning to read with an eye toward the way essential themes undergird a beautifully crafted novel like *To Kill a Mockingbird*. Gentry has shown that if students are reading novels at levels T and above and are reading those novels with fluency, they can generally finish one a week. If they are reading books at level P, such as *Stone Fox*, they can read several a week, and if they are reading books on the level of Frog and Toad, they can read several a day! Students who read a lot score better on every imaginable test—the NAEP, the SAT, the ACT. Any standards-based reading instruction needs to build in the expectation that students will do a huge volume of reading, and they will spend a good portion of ELA time reading and getting feedback. The reading program in a school must support all students, and one of the best ways of doing this is to allow students to read habitually, and in ways that literate people the world over read. Watch your strong readers. One factor they have in common? They read a lot.

Readers should have opportunities to choose from a wide range of high-interest texts. There is a tremendous amount of high-quality young adult literature out there that will allow fascinated readers to move up ladders of text complexity and to delve into the higher-level reading skills, within stories they find intriguing. Teachers can ignite interest in books in a host of ways—by talking up a series, by reading a small bit during a minilesson, by simply carrying around a book and seeming obsessed by it. And once a reader is engaged with reading, teachers can extend and shape that reader's diet. But one of the surefire ways to throw cold water on a reader's willingness to read is to create an instructional program that relies on a steady diet of teacher-chosen whole-class novels. In her book *When Kids Can't Read*, Kylene Beers (2003) showed that the very teachers who most love literature, high school teachers, are too often the ones who kids report kill reading for them. It's unlikely that a seventeen-year-old is going to be insightful about a midlife crisis, or want to keep reading avidly, when he or she encounters *Death of a Salesman*. Give that kid *The Absolutely True Diary of a Part-Time Indian* or *My Sister's Keeper* or *The Things They Carried*, though, or any novel *with a kid in it*, and he or she will likely want to keep reading.

Readers need explicit instruction in the skills of effective reading. Explicit instruction will often involve a teacher or a more skilled peer demythologizing what it means to do serious reading work. So if the challenge is to determine the theme of a story, the teacher might tell young students about how her grandmother always used to turn any little event into a parable, with a little life lesson attached. "That always goes to show you that . . . ," she'd say. The teacher might then demonstrate specific strategies or step-by-step procedures she uses in order to determine themes of stories, detailing the steps she takes as she does so. "Now you try it," she might say, and coach students to try this work with assistance, perhaps by revisiting a read-aloud text that the class knows well. Then—and this is the most important part of this instruction—the teacher needs to channel students to try this same work repeatedly, in books that are appropriately complex for them to read with independence, and the teacher needs to watch and coach into that work. The same will hold true for older students as teachers show them the moves readers make to really see the secrets that are hiding in complicated novels. Students try the new skill they have learned repeatedly, and as they do so the teacher will up the ante, perhaps suggesting, "This time, try to . . . ." Students might apply instruction they have received in a skill such as interpretation to a whole sequence of books that they read. Most of this work will be done first in jotted responses to the reading (perhaps on sticky notes or in notebook entries, or in online journals) and then discussed in short conversations with another reader or a small group.

Students should have ownership over this intellectual work. We've found that the reading skills described in the Common Core standards are ones that students are completely pleased to tackle when they are invited to do this work with novels they enjoy. Too often, they just don't realize the payoff in the books they actually want to read. This is truly great reading work. So as you begin to implement these Common Core standards for higher-level reading, you may want to consider the overall tone and approach you'll use as a community. There is a way of talking about hard work as if it is a fascinating challenge, and there is an alternate tone that makes it seem as if hard work is put on us by outside forces, which is deadly. Here's what we found in doing this kind of reading work with literally thousands of readers of all ages: they love it. They don't know enough to initiate the work themselves, and they are perfectly content to go along, reading for plot, but when you interest them in hidden meanings, symbolism, and subtext, they are intrigued. It needs to sound something like this: "You know the books you are reading are becoming more complicated, and that means there is new and fascinating work we can do as readers that will pay off in these books. For instance. . . ." And then you let them in on secrets, of how characters are no longer trustworthy, how stories suggest many things, how the meanings of symbols grow and shift. We've found that if your initial tone is one that makes it sound like all this work is going to make their reading so much more interesting, students pretty much immediately take on the challenge.

So, while introducing this important reading work to your students is vital to their reading success, you also have to restrain yourself and ultimately turn it over to the kids. This means that you really allow students to determine meaning themselves. When fourth grader Maria says slowly, "You know, I think the star necklace in *Number the Stars* might be symbolic," you have to act surprised and curious. "What are your thoughts on that?" you might say, rather than "I was wondering when you would finally pick that up," or "I told you that as we began this chapter." Remember that the Common Core standards don't ask kids to simply supply provided supports for central ideas and themes that others give them. The standards ask kids to *determine* central ideas and themes, and to trace how those are developed across literature.

It's incredibly important, therefore, that you put this work into the hands of students. We've seen time and again that left to their own devices, students either obsess about the plot or halfheartedly support a teacher's ideas about a text with some evidence they find on their own. But teach them *how* to disentangle narrative threads, how to construct potential meanings and follow those across a narrative, how to compare scenes and characters, how to trace objects or phrases that might be symbolic, and you'll get kids who are truly doing the intellectual work of the CCSS—at pretty much any age. Don't let yourself be fooled when a few kids dominate a class discussion, or when they parrot back an idea they may have overheard in class about a shared text. Really ask kids to do this work in their independent books and book clubs. Look at their jottings along the way and give them feedback, teach them to use writing to deepen their engagement with their novels, and coach them to coauthor interpretations in partner conversations.

You'll undoubtedly find, as we have, that students love to do deeper interpretation. Want to know the most popular temporary tattoo for teens in New York City in 2010? The mockingjay from the Hunger Games trilogy—and this was before the movie was released. This complex dystopian trilogy created readers out of hundreds of thousands of kids in our city, almost overnight. Kids (and teachers!) wore the bird on their notebooks, on their arms, on their ankles, on their foreheads. They adorned themselves with the bird resting, and the bird in flight, and the bird in song. They discussed the way the metaphor of the mockingjay shifted across the trilogy, and whether they preferred the symbol of secret resistance or that of open defiance. Get great books into kids' hands, show them how to do higher-level reading work, and you'll find that adolescent readers who are taught how to delve deeper into texts come to love The Hunger Games, and Harry Potter, for the secrets that unfold as much as for what happens.

When you do find small groups of kids who are accelerating as readers, or whole classes, or grades, or schools, we invite you to do one more thing: study these readers and research the conditions that have led to their progress. If there's one thing this nation needs more of, it's research on what *is* working. We have to share practices across more communities, including the often overlooked details that surround curriculum, such as scheduling, pedagogy, and the culture of the school community. Kids don't just need good classrooms; they need good schools.

Teachers need support and professional development to help their students rise to this high-level reading work. The most important reason why the jury is still out on effective methods for accelerating students' skills at reading of literature is that in the end, given equal access to time and books, the one and only thing that has been shown repeatedly to make all the difference in the world is the presence of a good teacher. So one approach or another will work well, or less well, depending on whether it is in the hands of a good teacher. So actually, perhaps the best way to conclude that an approach will work well is to see if that approach attracts good teachers to the school and keeps those good teachers in the profession and in the classroom, and empowers those teachers to go from good to great. Then, too, it is important that an approach to teaching reading be one that helps only somewhat effective teachers become good teachers. So keep that in mind: when you and your school make the decisions about a way to teach students, you are also thinking about a way to recruit and retain teachers.

CHAPTER FIVE

READING INFORMATIONAL TEXTS

STANDARDS 2—9

T he introduction to the Common Core State Standards stresses the importance of information reading:

> To be ready for college, workforce training, and life in a technological society, students need the ability to gather, comprehend, evaluate, synthesize, and report on information and ideas, to conduct original research in order to answer questions or solve problems, and to analyze and create a high volume and extensive range of print and nonprint texts in media forms old and new. (4)

You'll notice that this is not a "pore over the pictures and cool facts and say *wow* to your friend" kind of reading. This is reading to learn, reading to follow an author's reasoning, reading to analyze claims and support those claims with evidence. It is not a one-text sort of reading. Right from the first mention of nonfiction reading, the Common Core emphasizes synthesis, evaluation, and comparative textual analysis. The standards' focus is on the sort of nonfiction reading that we might associate with a college student who is majoring in journalism, economics, or political science.

As always, the standards present a pathway toward what they regard as college-ready work. As noted in Chapter Two, the standards for reading informational texts share the same grid as all the reading standards: There are ten standards, nine denoting skills and one related to text complexity. As you read across the grade level specifics of each standard, these skills are developed from simpler iterations to more complex. The grade level specifics for informational reading follow the same logic as those for literature. The difference lies in the kind of comprehension involved. When reading informational texts, the standards focus readers on the work of analyzing the claims texts make, the soundness and sufficiency of their evidence, and the way a text's language and craft may reveal points of view; the emphasis is investigating ideas, claims, reasoning, and evidence, rather than themes, characters, figurative language, and symbolism. The level of analysis called for by the information reading standards is no higher than that called for in literature—the Common Core standards for reading literature demand extremely sophisticated reading practices.

The specific standards for reading informational texts are located in two places in the CCSS. There are standards for reading informational texts that are part of the ELA standards for K–12. Then there are also standards for reading informational texts in science, social studies, and technical subjects, grades 6–12. We focus in this chapter on the standards for reading informational texts that are included in the ELA standards for K–12. These standards invite readers into a highly analytical mode, where the reader must read for much more than information, including delving into how a text conveys and persuades readers of claims and points of view. This is new reading work for most teachers as well as students. Therefore, in this chapter, we offer an overview of

- reading informational texts for key ideas and details
- reading informational texts for craft and structure
- reading informational texts to integrate knowledge and ideas

We end the chapter by offering pathways for implementing these levels of reading informational texts in your school and classroom.

Because this reading work is, we are convinced, new terrain for many adults, we want to invite you into an activity right away. The goal of this activity is to get you inside the Common Core standards for informational texts so that you grasp the reading work called for by these standards. This activity will illuminate the anchor standards and allow you to experience the reading practices that upper-elementary and secondary readers are expected to be able to do. After this activity, we'll move into implications for instruction, helping you think about ways to support your students in doing the information reading you will have experienced.

To get started, we suggest that you gather a few colleagues, and have at hand one text—choose something dense, short, and engaging. Perhaps one of Malcolm Gladwell's articles or a chapter from *Freakonomics*. We're going to read a short article by Guy Martin. It's from the June 22, 2009,

New Yorker, and it's about a water pistol role-playing assassination game played by high school students. Perhaps you'll want to work with this article as well. It's called "Shoot-Out" and you can access it online at *The New Yorker*'s website. As we read, let's try out the Common Core reading standards for informational texts, in order, from anchor standard 1 through anchor standard 9. If you use a different text, that's fine—notice the work we describe and try it out on your text.

READING FOR KEY IDEAS AND DETAILS (ANCHOR STANDARDS 1—3)

As you get ready to read, you'll want to keep in mind the first three anchor standards for reading informational texts. These standards are the foundation for the rest of the reading work the Common Core standards ask readers to do.

Reading Closely and Making Logical Inferences (Anchor Standard 1)

We want to alert you to your first job, which will be to say back what the text has taught you so far. This is the work of anchor standard 1, which asks readers to "read closely to determine what the text says explicitly" (10). The Common Core standards don't concern themselves with what you already know, or think you know, or how you feel about the topic. This is textual analysis, not personal response. If you read two or three lines and then get sidetracked into thinking about related personal experiences or your own opinions, refocus on what the text says explicitly. Unless you've chosen a long text, you can probably put anchor standard 1 to work after you have read just the first paragraph or two. Our article, for instance, begins by telling the reader that Killer has become a year-end ritual at many high schools in New York City, and that it is a game of water pistol ambush that leaves one last man, or team, standing:

> Killer, the last-man-standing game of water pistol ambush, has become a key-end-of-the-year-ritual in several New York City high schools. At St. Ann's, a private school in Brooklyn Heights, the game lasts two and a half weeks and is especially ferocious. Over the years, students there have developed a seventeen-point rule book, a map of the safe zones around the school, an entry fee (currently twenty dollars per team; it goes into the

winners' pot), and a nonplaying senior-class "judge," to arbitrate disputed kills and rule violations. The judge also makes a pie chart of death—the order of killing assignments, which he or she then distributes to squads shortly before opening day.

When you read this, you may find yourselves remembering other role-playing games, wondering if only private school kids play this, or worrying if virtual violence is becoming the new norm for young people. We thought those things too—but we reined ourselves in. This activity is meant to be an exercise in Common Core reading and for now, our job is to read in such a way that we "get" the text. We should be able to turn around and teach someone else everything we've learned so far. Try it. Pause, think what you'd say to teach someone what you have read. You might even cover the text, then try saying back everything you've learned so far.

You might start things off by saying that so far, this article teaches a role-playing assassination game called Killer that some high school kids in New York City play. If you are doing this retelling with colleagues, one of your colleagues might add that the game lasts over two weeks. Another might add that there is an entry fee, a rule book, and a student judge. It seems like kids massacre each other using water pistols. Someone might add that this article focuses on one school, St. Ann's, a private school in Brooklyn where kids play this game at the end of the year as a ritual.

Chances are, just to restate the contents of the first few paragraphs, you will find yourself peeking at the text again or reminding one another of details. It's surprisingly challenging to actually restate what the article said. That's because of two factors: One factor is that you haven't read enough yet to determine what the significant ideas are, so you're trying to hold onto a lot of details in case they turn out to be important. And the other factor is that this is a relatively complex text (we would probably level it at X/Y, a seventh-grade level). Like a lot of upper-level informational texts, it conveys a lot of information very quickly. This first standard does involve intellectual work, as we described in Chapter Three, on text complexity. Because there are so many details, your mind has to sort them into something coherent, and as you retell, you'll often find yourself restructuring the details, so that it sounds something like: "So far the article teaches about a game called Killer. The most important aspect of the game so far is that it is a role-playing game in which kids assassinate each other, using water pistols. This article focuses on one place where kids play this game, a private school in Brooklyn, New York. There are a few important rules we've learned so far, including. . . ."

Reading to Determine Central Ideas and Themes (Anchor Standard 2)

Now let's move to anchor standard 2 and read another chunk of the text, in the service of this second standard. The second anchor standard asks readers to determine central ideas and to summarize the text, linking key ideas and details. A hint: This is very hard to do if you didn't do standard 1 well, so if you're not satisfied that you've grasped the text, go back, reread, and try retelling what the text said in a more coherent, structured manner. Determining the central idea is also going to be hard if you're waiting for a bold subheading to steer you. There are no subheadings in this text—you have to read carefully for what the text suggests, for the ideas it forwards. We'll give you some help. Try asking the same question that you ask of literature. With stories, you ask yourself: "What is this story starting to be about?" Try it now: "What is this article starting to be about?" Then, as you notice ideas emerging in the text, gather up some of the information in the text as evidence for those ideas.

In "Shoot-Out," when we read just a few more paragraphs from where we stopped, we find out more:

"I'm looking for some good massacres early," this year's judge said as the competition began, the second week in May. (Summoning what his classmates referred to as his "inner lawyer," he asked that his name not be used.) "I've arranged at least one boyfriend–girlfriend kill that should be interesting."

Initially, each team of up to four students is given only the identities of its immediate prey. All the other players are anonymous, so that in the days leading up to the game the school becomes a souk of intelligence-gathering and disinformation. In 2007, Jake Protell, a freshman, distinguished himself by ferreting out the itinerary of a field trip that two targets were taking to Tel Aviv. Protell took a car to Newark Airport, found the victims before they passed through security, and dispatched them using two bathtub "squirt fish."

"I had to get special permission from the judge for the squirt fish, because I didn't want to take my gun anywhere near an El Al counter," Protell, now a junior, recalled, as he paced Pierrepont Street, three water guns shoved inside the pocket of a hoodie.

You may have a lot of personal responses when you read this, but you should cordon them off so that you and your colleagues don't detour into your lives and opinions, diverting your focus from this text. Ask yourself, "What is this text starting to be about?" In this article, for instance, you'll probably note that by now a central idea appears that kids can be remarkably ingenious. Another idea might be that role-playing games lead kids to extreme levels of engagement. Or a colleague might offer that Killer seems to lead kids to be independent in their actions. The Common Core leads us away from the mindset that texts are about one "main idea." Complex texts are often about more than one idea, so for the second anchor standard, you should launch a few main ideas that you can continue to investigate.

Remember that once you have stated some central ideas, you need to fill in some information from the text that supports those ideas. So go back and gather up the details that bolster your ideas. For example, the central idea that Killer leads kids to be ingenious might draw on supporting evidence in the way one boy, Protell, figured out his classmates' travel plans, thought through that he needed an alternate weapon and permission to use a squirt fish, and got himself to the airport. Notice how we pointed to specific details to support this idea? This is what anchor standard 1 describes as citing specific textual evidence, and standard 2 describes as determining central ideas and supporting details. You'll notice already how, to meet standard 2, you incorporate the work you did with standard 1 in support.

Listen to your conversation with your colleagues at this point, and remember that your work right now is to analyze the article's central idea, not your own. Hold yourself to what the article actually *says and suggests*. That is, the article does not *say* that the young people take this game extremely seriously or that they work with ingenuity, but the article absolutely suggests this. If you are reading a different article, what does your article say and suggest? When we've tried to read this article with colleagues, we have found the conversation often veering toward our feelings about these kids, our judgments of their game, and our own associations. All of this took us away from *close analysis of the text itself* and away from the standards. You may find the same, so stay within the corners of the text to do this Common Core type of close reading.

Now, at this point we need to warn you that in order to keep going, you need to keep doing all the work we have already mentioned as you read on, and as you try to practice the rest of the Common Core reading standards for informational texts. For instance, you must make sure you are clear on what the text actually says explicitly as you keep going. You'll also need to keep asking, "Is the idea that I thought was central to this text turning out to still be central? Is the article forwarding other ideas more strongly?"

Reading to Analyze How Individuals, Events, and Ideas Develop and Interact Over the Course of a Text (Anchor Standard 3)

Anchor standard 3 becomes increasingly important as you move along in the text and keep tracing central ideas. Standard 3 asks readers to analyze how "individuals, events, and ideas develop and interact over the course of the text" (10). Readers, therefore, need to notice the sequence of events, analyze relationships and connections, and discern cause and effect.

In our article, when we read another five or six paragraphs, for instance, we find ourselves following the stories of a variety of interrelated individuals. We learn about Willis Cohen, one of "a couple of tenacious ninth-grade holdouts," who has eluded a team of senior assassins. We find that in their pursuit of Cohen, these seniors stake out his house. They sleep on futons and in vans borrowed from their parents. They use a cell phone to call him, deploying the caller ID of Cohen's teammate. "The call had been engineered," we learn, "from a remote computer by a squad member with prodigious hacking skills." Cohen, who becomes accustomed to exiting his house secretly through the back, hopping fences, and grabbing cabs, finds one day that his cab driver refuses to put the windows up. Following Cohen's story, we infer that the seniors finally take him out through bribery and deceit. We also return to Jake Protell, now a junior, and find that his squad is co-led by Paulie Lowther. Paulie Lowther, it turns out, was a member of the winning team for the two prior years. The Protell–Lowther team racks up kills all over the city and its suburbs. On Memorial Day alone, Lowther, according to the article, "in five hours, shot a boy sitting on his stoop in Boerum Hill, a second as he ventured from his country house to Cobble Hill, and a third whom he duped into coming to a party in the Village."

As readers, you should analyze all these individuals and events, making sure you see how they are related. Cohen was an example of a tenacious ninth grader, who succumbed finally to seniors' knowledge of bribery and treachery. Protell, another ingenious ninth grader, has grown into an expert, efficient junior. Lowther moves with incredible speed across vast distances, sometimes acting as a sniper and sometimes as an undercover agent.

You're far enough along in the text now that you should be able to tackle anchor standards 1, 2, and 3. Try to restate, locate ideas, and support them with related details. If you are doing this work with our article, you might begin to notice that the details in the article lead you to begin to conclude that these kids not only show ingenuity, but also show incredible confidence—hacking computers, moving across the city, roaming from backyards to outer boroughs and beyond. Or you might spotlight the fact that the game leads kids to become strategic. You might claim that Protell's moving through protocols to attain his squirt fish, for example, shows not just ingenuity but also foresight and strategy. Either way, you'll need to go back over earlier parts of the text as well as the more recently read portions to produce examples that support the second or third central idea that you put forward.

READING FOR CRAFT AND STRUCTURE (ANCHOR STANDARDS 4–6)

Let's move on to anchor standards 4, 5, and 6. These are the standards that invite you to look at *how* a text is written—its craft and structure, and how the craft and structure affect your understanding.

Reading to Interpret the Language Used in the Text (Anchor Standard 4)

Anchor standard 4 asks readers to interpret the technical, connotative, and figurative meanings of words, and how the specific language shapes meaning. To do this analysis, you might look back, asking yourselves if some words seem more important or suggestive than others, or if some words seem surprising, or symbolic.

Looking back over our article, we might note that the words used to describe the game are often told in the language of war. Just list examples and say them out loud: *kills, targets, dispatches, massacres, intelligence gathering, pie chart of death*. This militaristic language turns a squirt gun chase game into something much more serious. The same language also works at multiple levels. On the one hand, it is a language of violence that intends to shock, to compel the reader to visualize kids practicing the art of assassination. The tone of the language also makes the article sound like a dispatch from the front—it has the rather analytical tone of an embedded reporter. Yet at the same time, the warlike language is set against the language of childhood—the squirt fish, the water guns tucked into a hoodie, the sudden reference to the mom who had been tipped off. The language of childhood colors the rest of the article, making the militaristic tone seem a bit tongue-in-cheek. That's what makes the article funny and interesting: it's how the text stirs up multiple emotions. When we keep looking closely at the language and how it affects meaning, we notice the adjectives used to describe the kids: their "prodigious" hacking skills, their "tenacious" intelligence gathering. The connotations of that language suggest admiration for the kids, which influences the meaning the article conveys. Instead of positioning readers to judge the students for their affinity for violent games, the text channels readers to notice the students' cleverness. Remember, *you* may have opinions that are different than the author's, but anchor standard 4 asks you to study how *this* text's craft conveys meaning.

Any text you're reading will reveal its stance through the language choices the author makes. Start by looking at the words in your text more closely, noticing if some words seem more important than others, and if there are categories or kinds of words used as there were in our text. If this work is new, you might try it out on a few texts, because it's often easier to *see* language choice when you compare the different kinds of language that authors choose. Notice if the words are biblical, or apocalyptic, or poetic: do they stir up dread, or sympathy, or distaste, or religious zeal? Think, for instance, of Abraham Lincoln's Gettysburg Address, which begins:

> Fourscore and seven years ago our fathers brought forth on this continent a new nation, conceived in liberty and dedicated to the proposition that all men are created equal. Now we are engaged in a great civil war, testing whether that nation or any nation so conceived and so dedicated can long endure. We are met on a great battlefield of that war. We have come to dedicate a portion of that field as a final resting-place for those who here gave their lives that that nation might live. It is altogether fitting and proper that we should do this. But in a larger sense, we cannot dedicate, we cannot consecrate, we cannot hallow this ground.

You can't help but be stirred up by the religiosity of the language in this excerpt. Lincoln's language conveys that this mission is a sacred one, even before he quotes God's will later in the text. It is also a language that conveys a sense of destiny—the nation that was conceived, dedicated, consecrated.

Think of the language of Dr. Martin Luther King's "I Have a Dream" speech, and how he makes the reference to this country having written a "bad check," in that it has not lived up to its democratic covenant of equal rights for all. So where Lincoln used religious language to stir up emotion, Dr. King evoked financial language to rationalize civil rights as "good business."

Now that you're alerted through this Common Core work to study the language as well as the ideas, you'll see how these language choices are so fascinating. These word *choices*, as they pile up, convey figurative meanings.

Reading to Analyze the Structure of a Text (Anchor Standard 5)

Anchor standard 5 moves the reader to also pay attention to how the text is structured. You might want to finish your text in order to really analyze how the structure leads the reader into meaning. In ours, there are only two more paragraphs, and we find that the Protell-Lowther team wins the game, and they celebrate with a spaghetti dinner. The closing paragraph states:

> In the late innings of Killer season, some kids occasionally sleep in the deeper recesses of St. Ann's itself. The game's valedictory message is built into its architecture: school is the safe ground. And, keen as the graduating seniors may be to leave, the game tells them that the world outside is not.

Take a moment to reconvene and reconsider the central ideas now that you've finished reading the article. We might adjust one of our ideas to the claim that Killer teaches kids that the world may be dangerous, but they are ready for it.

It is partly the structure of the text that leads us to adjust our thinking. Sometimes it feels as if the author is almost speaking to you directly, and, in the last part, the text is kind of a reflection. To analyze structure, do this: Look back over the text, and ask yourself if you could divide it into parts. Look at the text as if you were in a plane, flying above it. Instead of seeing fields divided by a ribbon of roads, you see paragraphs. Think about the meanings in those paragraphs, about the different sort of work that is being done in one part of the text, another, and another. Ask what work each part does.

Looking back over "Shoot-Out," for instance, we might notice that it begins with a kind of minilecture, or explanatory paragraph, and that paragraph gives us a lot of facts about the game in a sort of objective tone.

Then the text shifts and lays out some gripping anecdotes about a few key players, one alongside the next. Each one is interrupted, so that we don't find out who is winning the game. Instead, the anecdotes stir up sympathy for certain players and invest the reader in the game. The anecdotes also give more evidence of the extraordinary lengths kids go to in the game. The tone of these anecdotes is slightly admiring, full of precise adjectives that elevate the kids' ingenuity. Then suddenly the tone and structure change at the very end of the game, and the text ends with the author speaking to the reader. He states explicitly a new meaning—that this game teaches children that the world outside is not safe. This new idea is structured to intersect with the dominant earlier idea—that kids are ingenious, determined, and independent. The two ideas, therefore, converge, coming together to form the claim that while the world outside is not safe, kids are ready for it. The structure of the text leads the reader to this claim.

Reading to Assess the Author's Point of View and How It Shapes the Text (Anchor Standard 6)

Anchor standard 6 asks readers to assess how the author's point of view or purpose shapes the content and style of the text. This work, determining the author's point of view and how it influences the text, stands on the shoulders of anchor standards 4 and 5. To do this analysis, look back at the language choices in the text you are reading. Ask: How does the choice of words, the tone of the language, illuminate the author's point of view on the topic? As we saw in the Gettysburg passage, the decision to use a specific kind of language helps convey meaning. We are able to discern the author's point of view in our article, "Shoot-Out," not only from the author's explicit statement at the end of the text but also from the admiring language he uses to describe the students' game, with repeated references to the students' ingenuity, prowess, and determination. One can gather that the author is impressed by their intelligent use of strategy. Although he may end by stating that the world outside the boundaries of the school is not safe, it is clear based on the language used throughout the text that he believes that these children are learning to handle the world around them. This point of view—that children can prepare for an unstable environment—shapes the entire text. The author chooses to include examples that are consistent with this stance and to perhaps exclude examples that would make a different point. He also carefully chooses the language that will best convey the message he wants his readers to accept.

You'll notice that we are once again incorporating earlier anchor standards as we tackle the later anchor standards. When we discuss structure, for example, doing the work of anchor standard 5, we notice where the tone shifts, and to talk about the shift in tone, we review language, which is addressed in anchor standard 4. When we discuss structure and craft, we also analyze how those choices convey meaning, which brings us back to the work of anchor standards 2 and 3. And all along, we make sure we are sticking within the boundaries of the text, explicating what the text says and suggests, which is called for by anchor standard 1.

READING TO INTEGRATE KNOWLEDGE AND IDEAS AND THINK ACROSS INFORMATIONAL TEXTS (ANCHOR STANDARDS 7–9)

At this point, to tackle anchor standards 7–9, you need to read a text that is in some way related to the first text. Anchor standard 7 asks us to integrate and evaluate content in different media. You might, for instance, research variations of Killer. Over six million viewers recently watched "The Great Office War," a video of a Nerf gun assassination game (available for viewing at www.youtube.com/watch?v=pVKnF26qFFM). If you view it, you might note how this digital text begins with a calm office scene, introduces you to a few characters, and then slowly moves into what looks like a coffee break that becomes a full-on Nerf battle, with quick costuming, violent overthrows, and mayhem, spiraling into a battle that lurches toward its final end—the simulated and highly choreographed death of all involved. We might compare that message to that of "Shoot-Out." Or we might compare the tone. You can see the same arch tone, sudden violence, intense participation, and inner choreography—and perhaps we would talk about how the video makes the game seem more playful, whereas the article makes the game seem more serious, but how both seem to mock the death throes of the players. There are Protell-like characters, Cohen-like characters, and Lowther-like characters in the adult office war as well, which might lead us to rethink these characters as archetypes—the unlikely hero, the likable villain.

Or you could try playing *Call of Duty: Modern Warfare 2*, which sold 4.7 million copies on its release day alone, and you could compare what you learn from playing that game, to what you learned from reading about kids playing Killer, or watching adults play an office Nerf battle. The point is, you'll come to a more nuanced understanding of the article by comparing it with another text. You'll know more about the topic because you will have more information, but more importantly, you will see more because you will be comparing one text with another.

Let's move on to the next standard. Anchor standard 8 is also easier to do when you are comparing texts, especially primary documents, though it is possible to do through textual analysis within a text. It asks readers to evaluate the evidence that the text lays out, weighing the validity of the author's claims based on the sufficiency and soundness of the evidence and reasoning. Essentially, anchor standard 8 asks you to analyze the trustworthiness of the supports that the author provides for his or her claims, and the soundness of the logic that links the supports to the claims. If you want to do this by thinking about the one text alone, it helps to remember what you noticed about the craft and structure and to try to capture *how* the author persuaded you. In the article we read, you will remember, the author told us the stories of particular students and wrote about them with an admiring tone. The language of war was contrasted with the language of childhood and this made the argument somewhat lighthearted and therefore easier to digest. Thinking back over the structure, we can also add in some of the thinking we did as we worked on anchor standards 2 and 3. We might add that the author led us slowly toward a claim that this game teaches lessons about whether a person is safe in the dangerous outside world of life. Overall, we might say that his claim that the kids display ingenuity is well supported. But his claim that the game teaches important lessons about the dangers of the world is not supported by the same amount of evidence. Do you see how this time, we not only determined central ideas, but also analyzed the validity of the author's support for those ideas? Our goal was not to weigh whether we agreed with the ideas, but instead, to trace the argument the author made and to assess its validity.

If you read an article different than ours, try anchor standard 8. Try the within-text analysis (intratext) as well as cross-text (intertextual) analysis. This may seem like work that is new to you, but think to yourself that you are assessing texts just as you might pick up two peaches and assess their weight, ripeness, and freshness. As you compare two or more texts, you are also doing the work of anchor standard 9, which asks readers to compare two texts on the same subject, looking specifically at the ways those texts develop similar claims.

※　※　※

That's a lot of reading work—a lot of Common Core reading work. That's the work the standards outline for reading informational texts. You and your colleagues will probably want to pause at this point and talk about what you make of all this—what does this imply for developing your own reading practices, as well as for the teaching of nonfiction reading?

You will probably find yourself saying that the Common Core reading standards can deepen students' reading of nonfiction. But our hunch is that the more profound implication will be that the Common Core reading standards can deepen the reading skills of adults as well. For our students to read this way, we need to read this way. There is some work here that has the potential to take teachers as well as students to new places. That's an exciting thought, and one that can inspire you to want to give school-wide attention to informational reading.

We're going to assume now that you and your colleagues feel at home inside the standards for informational texts, and we're going to move forward, to recommendations for implementation. Within these recommendations, we unpack the grade level specifics a bit more closely so you can see some of the skill progressions articulated by the standards.

Pathways for Implementing the Informational Text Standards

In this section we offer pathways to help you and your school implement the CCSS for reading informational texts. However, before you can begin to think about how to successfully teach your students to do the work of the Common Core reading standards, it is important to acknowledge the obstacles that may be in place.

Current Challenges to Implementing the Reading Standards for Informational Texts

If you are going to take important steps to radically improve your students' experiences in information reading, you will probably need to start by owning the problems in your classroom and your school—and frankly, our hunch is the problems are serious.

Students are not reading enough nonfiction texts. First, consider the sheer volume of nonfiction reading your students are doing. For K–8 students, the CCSS advocate that 45% of students' entire academic reading diet (taking into account the reading they do all day long) be composed of informational texts—and this 45% figure includes everything the students read during social studies, science, and math, as well as all the reading they do within nonfiction units of study in ELA. So you might be thinking that your students are doing well over the requisite amount of information reading suggested by the Common Core.

Investigate before you come to this conclusion. In your school or classroom, look at how many pages of expository text an average student reads in a week, counting all that he or she actually reads across every subject. Compare the number of pages of expository text with the number of pages of fiction text. You will be astonished. A fourth-grade reader who regularly reads twenty-five pages of fiction during a single day's reading workshop in school—125 pages a week—*plus* an equal number at home often reads only two pages of expository text a day, or eight pages a week. (Of course there are exceptions, but look at the norm.) Readers who regularly read a handful of fiction books a week or month will read just a fraction of that many nonfiction books.

If this is what you find in your classroom and your school, know that you are not alone. Recent studies found that "students today are asked to read very little expository text—as little as 7 and 15 percent of elementary and middle school instructional reading, for example, is expository (Hoffman, Sabo, Bliss, and Hoy, 1994; Moss and Newton, 2002; Yopp and Yopp, 2006)" (CCSS 2010b, 3). If you see an absence of nonfiction reading in your school—maybe not an absence of time looking at the page, but an absence of volume of actual reading accomplished—you'll want to figure out what is going on. Chances are good that some of the factors we describe now, and perhaps others, are playing a role.

Students are not reading just-right informational texts. Above all, if your school is like most in the nation, many of the nonfiction texts your students are reading are almost surely too hard or too poorly written to engage students intellectually. Ask them to read aloud a small section, and listen to see if they are reading with the necessary fluency—with enough fluency that the oral text has the intonation and pace one would expect of normal conversation. Are they reading with at least 96% accuracy (a level that the vast majority of reading researchers believe would be a low level of accuracy, suggesting the text already contains more words that are hard for the reader than there would be in any text we picked up to read)? Jeanne Chall and her colleagues (1996) studied twenty-eight science textbooks that were listed as being at the fifth-grade level and found that none of the texts was actually written at a fifth-grade level; they were all harder, usually by two years and in four instances, by four years. And remember, even the phrase "written at the fifth-grade level" means that such a text is appropriate for the average fifth-grade reader, so almost half of fifth graders are likely reading below that level! What's so ominous about some of these textbooks is that they are difficult in part because they are also poorly written. They summarize, they organize, but they do not engage students in complex reasoning.

Students are not engaging with informational texts in the appropriate way. Then, too, students may accomplish only limited amounts of expository reading because they may be reading with pen in hand, taking notes about information they could look up with ease or that they don't even know yet will be significant once they read more. They are recording "the facts," as soon as they encounter them. We have a number of concerns with this activity, and we address some of these concerns later, but for now, let us simply point out that when nonfiction reading is a stop-and-go process, the expectation that a student pause every few lines to record facts almost guarantees that the student will progress very slowly, resulting in a limited volume of nonfiction reading.

Students have no choice in what to read. Finally, students may be reading without engagement—and engagement is the sine qua non for learning. Now, there is absolutely nothing about nonfiction that necessarily leads to a decrease in engagement. Think about the nonfiction texts you read—the books on your hobbies, the newspaper, the blogs on whatever passions are especially important to you, the vacation guides, the recipes, the reviews. We are quite sure that you read those texts with as much engagement as you read other texts. But it is worth noting that those nonfiction texts are embedded in your passions, the things you want to accomplish, and your daily comings and goings. The fact that you *choose* those texts is probably important. If your students are not devouring nonfiction texts with rapt engagement, it could be that they have no choice over what they will read. Remember, kids are reading nonfiction to figure out what to do with their lives. They need to read, and want to read, to discover the careers and hobbies they will pursue. Then, too, even if students are able to choose nonfiction texts, there isn't a school in the country that has nonfiction classroom libraries that match the density, accessibility, and availability of their libraries of fiction books. This endeavor has to be shared with a whole community.

Overcoming the Challenges to Implementation

Now that we have walked through the obstacles that may be blocking your pathway to student success with information reading, it is time to think about how to overcome those obstacles. We offer you four paths to improve your students' experiences in information reading.

Get more high-interest nonfiction books into your classrooms. The first challenge is to supply students with the high-interest, just-right informational texts that will be necessary if they are going to develop CCSS skills in information reading. In these times of bone-deep budget cuts, it will not be easy to marshal the necessary funds for you and everyone else in your school to develop the nonfiction section of your classroom library. Still, this needs to be a priority. Improving reading instruction is hard to do without lots and lots of well-chosen books. You and your colleagues will want to brainstorm ways to raise money to improve the nonfiction section of your classroom libraries, and you will want to become more adept at accessing digital sources.

How Can You Put More High-Interest, Just-Right Nonfiction Books into Kids' Hands?

+ For resourceful teachers, there are endless possible *grants* to be secured. In New York City, teachers who write a one-page-long donor choice grant application can easily secure five hundred dollars of funding to support a mission as important as that of improving students' nonfiction reading.

+ Actively seek the *high-interest nonfiction books* that make it possible for a student to read the whole text, whether they are the DK Readers (which are inexpensive, print-rich, and written at several levels on high-interest topics, like secrets of the Bermuda Triangle), or biographies, or sports reporting like *The Blind Side*. Any books that get kids to read nonfiction with the same volume and rate at which they read fiction should be treasured and replicated.

✦ Build *text sets* that offer multiple perspectives on a topic so that students can practice the high-level analysis and comparative work that the Common Core promotes. Try to build text sets that get at deeper issues within topics, and the various sides of those issues. For instance, if you build a text set on sports, include videos and print articles about the pros and cons of competitive sports for young people. Extend these text sets into academic subjects, such as human rights or green energy. If you need some help getting started, we worked on text sets with educators in 2010, and have many of these text sets posted on our website (http://readingandwritingproject.com/resources/classroom-libraries/archive.html).

✦ Get many, many *high-quality, print-rich journals* into the classroom. Not *Teen Vogue* or *Entertainment Weekly*, but *Upfront Magazine*, *Scope*, *Junior Scholastic*, *Sports Illustrated*, and *National Geographic*. These journals, written by award-winning investigative reporters, encompass some of the best nonfiction writing available. Get a teacher's subscription, which gives you multiple copies and online access. Ask students, parents, and friends to donate copies. Ask students to bring in special-interest magazines, on dance, cars, horses, ballet. Remember, kids are reading nonfiction to find hobbies and careers.

✦ Access *digital sources*. The journals we have mentioned all have online archives. There are also digital sources such as informational videos, which you can make available on laptops. PBS, Discovery, The History Channel, etc., all have science and history videos for children, teens, and adults. We make available a list of websites and journals on our website that thousands of teachers access (http://readingandwritingproject.com/resources/classroom-libraries.html). There are also *digital archives* online with the major libraries, including archives for teens.

✦ *Letter writing* pays off. Try writing to publishers and asking if they happen to have any seconds of books, or books that are now out of print, that they might be willing to give to your students. Write to anyone you know who is an expert on a topic, and ask for funds to support a shelf of great books on that topic. If the person works for an energy company, then the books can be about gas, oil, solar power, electricity. If the person is a chef, then develop a shelf of books on food and marketing.

✦ One textbook often costs about thirty thousand dollars for classroom sets. And often these texts can't begin to match the complexity of good primary and secondary sources. If you are aligning instruction to the Common Core, you will need students to read well-crafted texts that are written with particular (and different) perspectives. This suggests that your school will need to *channel whatever resources you do have away from textbooks and toward trade books.* Leaders in your school may not have yet realized that this is the writing on the wall and may still be investing in text books: history textbooks, biology textbooks. Help them consider using the budget they may have allocated toward textbooks to purchase nonfiction trade books.

✦ Do an *archeological dig* at your school. Look in any store rooms or closets, and dig through the layers of discarded kits and programs that probably line many classroom walls in the school. Most of those discarded programs are accompanied by texts, and some are nonfiction. You can separate the texts from the kits, level the texts, and put them into classroom libraries.

Infuse more information reading into content-area classes. You will also want to think about ways to infuse a lot more information reading into all of your content-area classes. We want to stress a few important steps you can take. First of all, one of the challenges is that usually all the classrooms in a grade level proceed in synchrony through a sequence of social studies and science units. So whatever accessible texts you have on a topic—say, civil rights—are all under demand at the same time and must be distributed among all the classes in that grade level. Some teachers have found it worthwhile to vary the sequence of units by just a bit so that they can rotate texts across classrooms. Or, you can consolidate and share the books by not keeping them only in one classroom. Consolidate all the nonfiction texts related to a unit onto a bookshelf-on-wheels, and move that collection of books between any remaining classes that are studying the same topic at the same time. This will mean only one class of students will be allowed to bring the books home to read on any given night, but chances are good that reading nonfiction won't be an every-night assignment anyhow.

We also want to suggest that when you and your colleagues plan your sequence of units in social studies, science, and perhaps math, you actually plan which of your units will be writing intensive, which will be media intensive, and which will be reading intensive. You won't have time for your students to do all aspects of content literacy in every unit, so you might as well decide that some units will emphasize one kind of work, others, another kind of work. Then you will want to get an excess of nonfiction books on the topics within which you will especially emphasize nonfiction reading. Some units of study are particularly easy to match to nonfiction text sets, as there are many children's and young adult nonfiction texts already existing.

Match your readers to nonfiction texts. Your effort to supply your students with lots of high-interest nonfiction books and to give them choice over what to read, when possible, will all add up to very little if you don't figure out how to match the books you bring to your classroom with the real readers in your room. You probably already have a system for leveling your fiction books and channeling readers toward books they can read with at least 96% accuracy, fluency, and comprehension. Increasingly, schools provide students with that sort of guidance and place a great priority on differentiating instruction so that all students are working within their zone of proximal development.

But if you are like the teachers we know best, chances are very good that you do not have an equally well-developed system for matching readers to nonfiction books. There are lots of reasons for this. First, many people have more mistrust for efforts to level nonfiction books. Time and again teachers have come to us with a handful of books that some expert has declared to be equally difficult, and the teacher have asked, "How is it possible that these books are of equivalent difficulty?" We often agree with their question, and of course this raises further questions. Is there a system for leveling nonfiction books that has inspired enough confidence that teachers should all adopt that system? Is it reasonable to level informational books as if there is some way to judge the challenges these books pose without knowing the reader's prior knowledge on the topic? Doesn't prior knowledge trump almost everything else when a reader is reading an informational book?

Definitive answers to these questions will probably not be available for a long time. You will therefore need to move forward in the face of uncertainty. There are, still, some commonsense guidelines that can help you match readers to carefully calibrated nonfiction texts.

Guidelines for Matching Readers to Nonfiction Texts

✦ When students are reading nonfiction texts, you can use the same tools and methods that you use to assess their abilities to handle fiction texts. That is, you can ask a student to read a text aloud, and note whether he or she reads with fluency (it sounds like talk), 96% accuracy, and comprehension (at the very least, the reader can teach you what he or she read). You needn't use a formal tool—assess a reader with any book for which you know the level of text difficulty. But if you want a tool, Fountas and Pinnell have one, and they bring a long track record to this work.

✦ Expect that on the whole, your students will usually be far less experienced as readers of expository texts than as readers of fiction. When in doubt, move students to expository books that are one notch easier than the fiction books they can read and ask them to read a lot of texts. The exception will be if the student is an avid reader of nonfiction or if the reader has deep knowledge of the topic.

✦ If a student wants to read an informational text that you believe might be a bit too difficult, the best way to support the reader is to teach that reader how to find more introductory texts on the same topic. This essential skill will be a lifesaver in college.

✦ If a student has never seen a vocabulary word before and mispronounces the word, see if the student can ascertain what the challenging word means. If he or she has the meaning right and can say a close approximation of the word, this suggests the student is making sense while he or she reads. If the reader can do this work with

95% of the otherwise "too hard" words, then the reader's miscues suggest the book may be within reach for him or her.

✦ Be aware that the colorful and dramatic pictures often make nonfiction texts look easier to read than they are. Don't be fooled by the pretty pictures.

Once you have matched readers to books and given readers more time to read nonfiction texts, you will be able to begin helping students do the work of the Common Core standards for information reading. That is, there is little sense in asking a reader to ascertain the central ideas in a text that he or she can barely plow through—but once you have matched readers to texts, and taught your readers to monitor their own comprehension, you are still a long way from having accomplished the work of the standards.

Move students up levels of text difficulty. Matching readers to texts is not enough. You then need to accelerate readers' progress up the gradient of text difficulty, especially for readers who come into your classroom not able to read grade level complex texts. The most important way to do this is to help readers accomplish vast amounts of minds-on, engaged reading of just-right expository texts. If a reader is reading level J books and it comes time to send some books home to be read that evening, send four books home, not one. You may worry. "Isn't that too much homework?" Remember, it's important for children and young adults to develop the habits that will sustain them through middle, high school, and college.

Then, too, you need to have a plan for when each of your readers needs to be reassessed and hopefully, moved to a higher level of texts. That process of assessing needs to be no big deal so that you do it regularly. Just ask the reader to try a text that is a notch harder, and see how the reader does with it. You will want to make sure that you are assessing every month if the reader has some catching up to do. It isn't okay to assess twice a year if a reader needs, ideally, to move up six text levels in one year. For older students, be sure they can self-assess, or assess with a reading partner.

There are lots of ways to give readers just a leg up of support so they can handle a text that otherwise might be just a bit too challenging. It helps if you read the first portion of the text aloud and engage the reader in a discussion of the text. During that discussion, you can embed domain-specific vocabulary that you see (at a glance) the reader will be asked to handle. It also helps if you set readers up to read a text together, stopping at regular intervals to retell what they have learned so far. You can even mark places in the text where you want the students to pause and recap.

Amassing a Collection of Challenging, Well-Crafted Texts of Varying Views and Perspectives to Meet the Standards

When you are working to provision readers with the texts they need in order to meet the Common Core expectations for information reading, there are a couple of other considerations for you to take into account. First, if you look at the text exemplars that are mentioned in Appendixes A and B of the CCSS, you'll note that the informational texts are all focused, short books, researched articles, or primary sources. The Common Core booklist doesn't tend to include long books on a topic, nor textbooks or other synopses or summaries on a topic. Instead the texts range from Donald Crews' *Trucks* to *National Geographic* articles or letters from John Adams, Winston Churchill, and Frederick Douglass. These texts are mostly special topic texts and articles. The CCSS comes right out and spotlights the importance of articles. They do this while arguing that students should be reading harder texts (a topic we take up later)—and they say that college students are encountering more challenging texts because, "as a 2005 College Board study (Milewski, Johnson, Glazer, and Kubota, 2005) found, college professors assign more readings from periodicals than do high school teachers" (CCSS 2010b, 2).

Also, in order for students to do the work the CCSS expect readers of informational texts to be able to do, it will be important that either you or your library include small collections of texts representing different perspectives on a topic, or you give students the support they need to seek out and find such text sets themselves. Starting in the primary grades, readers are asked to compare how more than one text deals with a subject. Young students compare ideas and information, while older students compare craft and structure, while still older students compare perspective and reasoning. But always, this work involves comparing texts that address the same topic differently, and so you will want to collect text sets on a topic. Ideally those text sets will contain some digital texts, and will contain texts that represent different perspectives. A text set on the pros and cons of bottled water may contain an article written by Danone Group, which makes Evian mineral water, for example, making it likely that even young students will be able to detect bias and to question the warrant behind an argument.

We've spent many hours making digital text sets available through our website on high interest and academic topics for teachers in our schools in 2011, These text sets include articles and informational videos, all available online, that offer a range of levels, and also different perspectives on topics from sports (good or bad for kids), to great white sharks (a danger to us or in danger from us), to green energy, child soldiers, and censorship. You might want to join this effort, so that more classrooms are better able to accomplish the critical reading across texts that the Common Core advocates.

Developing a Knowledge Base of Higher-Level Reading Skills for Nonfiction

If one of your major challenges will be providing the texts and the time for students to engage in the information reading that is emphasized in the Common Core reading standards, the other biggest challenge will be for you to develop the knowledge base to teach in ways that match these standards. Here again, your first step probably must involve realizing that you have a lot of work to do before your teaching is aligned to the CCSS. Chances are good that currently, most of the information reading that your students do is reading to accumulate information. The Common Core standards ask that we shift away from this type of reading and toward helping students learn to read to develop concepts, discover ideas, and to follow (and analyze) arguments.

To take stock of your current teaching and to understand the work that the standards ask you to do, imagine you'd asked your students to read the article that we discussed earlier, "Shoot-Out," and to do their very best reading work. What would be the mental operations going on in their minds?

Our hunch is that most American students believe that reading informational texts well means creating a duplicate copy of the article within the reader's mind, so the reader can reel off the facts: the name of the school that is featured in the article, the names of the three boys who are described, the place where one boy apprehended another, the nature of his weapon. Chances are good that a large percentage of the information reading your students currently do is reading to learn facts. Look, for example, at the notes students currently take when reading informational texts. Do those notes aim to help the reader retain just facts and information—the very stuff they could have at hand at any given moment on a classroom computer or their smartphones?

If a child is reading about polar bears, for example, notice if that child has jotted down how many polar bears there are in the North Pole, but has neglected to note the radical decline in their numbers or to muse about the relationship between the melting of the polar ice cap and the decline of the polar bear. Or note the high school student who writes down how many men died at Gettysburg but nothing about the significance of that battle as a turning point in the Civil War. Or imagine that some of your instruction in information reading involves the traditional emphasis on readers asking questions, then reading to answer those questions. What sort of questions have your students learned to ask? Do they ask questions about the author's perspective, about the way the author uses language and structure to advance his or her ideas? Or are the questions more factual; are they just short-answer questions? Consider the times you provide questions for readers to answer—say, after reading a chapter in social studies or science. Do you ask short-answer questions, or ask them to define a term, to cite a statistic? Or do you provide your students with invitations to compare two texts on a topic, to examine the warrant behind an argument, to question the if-then logic an author has presented?

If there is one overwhelming aspect of the Common Core standards for reading informational texts, it is that they move students away from reading to accumulate information, to reading to discern ideas and concepts and analyze texts critically for their reasoning and perspective. Think again about the article we read about the game of Killer. If we came away remembering that the name of the school was St. Ann's, or that there were seventy players in 2009, what good would that do us? According to the Common Core reading standards, the point is not those details. The point is that reading the article will make a reader think about what it means for kids to play this intense, far-ranging game. Whether the reader ended up changing his or her mind about how hard kids will work when they are motivated, or comparing the game to the Iroquois's lacrosse games, the point of the text is to teach ideas. The details are important for how they support larger concepts.

If your school decides to adapt its informational reading instruction, then, the first step will be to provision students with texts they can actually comprehend, and the next step will be to make sure students have long chunks of time to actually read, read, read these texts. Then you will want to think carefully about how teachers at every grade level across the school can help the school make the transition from seeing reading informational texts as a way to download facts toward seeing this as a way to wrestle with ideas and, ultimately, to form opinions.

Grade Level Specifics of the Reading Standards for Informational Texts

Teachers of six-year-olds can see that the Common Core asks even very young readers to read to determine ideas and supporting details. And even at this very early age, students are expected to understand how text features (illustrations, captions, glossaries, etc.) contribute to the reader's understanding. The point isn't for them to label the features correctly, but for them to use these features as helpers as they read. By second grade, students are not only asked to identify the main topic of a text and its details but also to identify the subtopics of paragraphs/parts within the text—so the standards assume these readers are beginning to sort out central ideas and subordinate ideas. In Gail Gibbons' *The Pumpkin Book*, a second-grade reader might figure out, for instance, that a main idea of the book is that pumpkins need resources to grow, and then she might also figure out that there are different kinds of resources—seeds, soil, light, and so on. Sorting and categorizing, which are important in information writing, are important in information reading as well. There is simply so much information that the reader has to analyze and sort it, even at a very young age.

By fifth grade, students are determining two or more central ideas and showing how they are supported by key details, and the standards assume that students will have to infer and make connections across the text in order to do this work. You can see that the CCSS has high expectations for the intellectual work students will do with informational texts. The standards explicitly move kids to thinking as they read, rather than trying to accumulate a slew of details.

As we have mentioned earlier, the standards want students at any age to become conversant with *how* texts are written, which means learning to pay attention to their craft and structure. This is part of introducing the idea early on that nonfiction is not *the* truth, but rather someone's *perspective or side of* the truth, a significant idea to learn. Again, this work actually begins even before fifth grade. Our youngest reader may begin to notice whether the images of snakes that are found in his snake book make snakes seem fascinating and beautiful or terrifying and deadly. A first or second grader's efforts to look closely at images, then, is the beginning of reading more analytically. By fourth and fifth grade, students are asked to compare different accounts and perspectives on the same topic, noting how authors use similar or different information, or how they structure their texts to organize and develop ideas. By seventh grade, they should be paying attention to all the craft and structure elements that younger students did, while also evaluating how the author's language suggests connotative meanings. They're also asked to weigh the author's evidence, to assess the soundness of the author's reasoning, and to determine whether the claims made in the text are sufficiently supported.

This move toward analyzing and comparing texts, looking closely at how they work as much as at what they say, is the most significant aspect of the Common Core standards for reading informational texts. The goal is, according to the CCSS, that students "work diligently to understand precisely what an author or speaker is saying, but . . . also question an author's or speaker's assumptions and premises and assess the veracity of claims and the soundness of reasoning" (7). This work is not about reading to be entertained. Nor is it about reading to memorize. It is about reading to think.

CHAPTER SIX

OVERVIEW of the WRITING STANDARDS

What Do They Say and What Does This Mean for Us?

If we were asked to describe the two or three most striking features of the Common Core State Standards, one of the things we'd say straight away is that the standards place a tremendous emphasis on writing. In effect, the standards refocus the nation on students' proficiency as writers. NCLB, the last large-scale reform movement in literacy, called for an emphasis on phonemic awareness, phonics, vocabulary, fluency, and comprehension. Writing was nowhere in the picture. In the Common Core State Standards, in contrast, writing is treated as an equal partner to reading, and more than this, writing is assumed to be the vehicle through which a great deal of the reading work and reading assessments will occur. The CCSS, then, return writing to its place as one of the basics of education. In order to help you grasp the Common Core's rallying cry around writing, in this chapter we discuss the standards' emphasis on

- three types of writing
- the writing process
- the quality of student writing
- writing as integral even for very young students
- writing across all disciplines and for real purposes

The Standards' Emphasis on Three Types of Writing

In the prelude to the Common Core standards, there is a section titled "Key Features of the Standards" (8). This synopsis emphasizes that although the writing process applies to all kinds of writing, different types of writing place different demands on students:

> The Standards acknowledge the fact that whereas some writing skills, such as the ability to plan, revise, edit, and publish, are applicable to many types of writing, other skills are more properly defined in terms of specific writing types: arguments, informative/explanatory texts, and narratives.

The standards themselves are organized in a way that highlights the demands these three broad categories of writing place on the writer. The first standard delineates expectations for opinion and argument writing, the second, for informational writing, the third, for narrative writing. Although these three "types of writing" standards represent just under a third of the ten standards, if one were to count the pages devoted to the writing standards and count the pages devoted to explicating the three types of writing, one would find that these first three standards occupy fully half of the CCSS for writing. The later standards illuminate how students should go about doing the work of the first three standards. For example, standard 5 is the writing process standard, and presumably, students will use the writing process that is detailed in this standard as they write the argument, informational, and narrative texts described in standards 1–3.

It is interesting to note that the standards refer to these as *types* of writing, not as *genres*. This makes sense because within any one type of writing, one can lodge many different genres of writing. In the New Standards Project, an earlier effort to create nationwide standards, the committee of twenty who wrote those standards (which included Lucy Calkins) wrestled with the issue of kinds versus structures versus types versus genres of writing and came to the decision that the whole world of writing could be divided into five (not three) kinds of writing: narrative, informational, persuasion and opinion, functional and procedural, and poetry. The Common Core's divisions are roughly in line with those earlier ones, although functional and procedural writing is now grouped with informational writing, and poetry is overlooked. In the New Standards effort, the committee created a chart that delineated the genres of writing that could be classified within any one of the types of writing. You might, with colleagues, try jotting down the genres you would put under these major categories, and then consider how often your students have opportunities to engage in the three main types of writing. You will probably come up with a list like this:

- **Narrative Writing:** personal narrative, fiction, historical fiction, fantasy, narrative memoir, biography, narrative nonfiction
- **Persuasive/Opinion/Argument Writing:** persuasive letter, review, personal essay, persuasive essay, literary essay, historical essay, petition, editorial, op-ed column
- **Informational and Functional/Procedural Writing:** fact sheet, news article, feature article, blog, website, report, analytic memo, research report, nonfiction book, how-to book, directions, recipe, lab report

For each of these kinds of writing, the Common Core State Standards delineate the way in which expectations grow each year, standing on the shoulders of the preceding year. And so, for example, first graders are expected to write opinion pieces in which they introduce the topic of the book they are writing about, state an opinion, supply a reason to support that opinion, and provide some sense of closure. By sixth grade, students are expected to write arguments (not opinions) to support claims with clear reasons and relevant evidence. In these arguments, students are expected to introduce the claim(s) and organize the reasons and evidence clearly; support claim(s) with clear reasons and relevant evidence, using credible sources and demonstrating an understanding of the topic or text; use words, phrases, and clauses to clarify the relationships among claims and reasons; establish a formal style; and provide a concluding statement or section that follows from the argument presented. You'll want to look yourself to see how these expectations escalate for twelfth grade!

The standards not only describe the progression of skill development that is expected to occur across grades in a spiral writing curriculum in which one grade builds upon the next, but also provide annotated exemplar texts to illustrate what these pieces of writing might look like and to answer the question, How good is good enough? When looking at the pieces that are provided as illustrations of one type of writing or another, it is important to note that even the pieces selected as exemplars do not adhere to all of the defining characteristics of a genre.

The standards not only define and describe the three kinds of writing and show how students' work with each of those kinds of writing should progress across the years, but also call for a distribution of writing experiences that gives students roughly equal amounts of time and instruction in argument, informative, and narrative writing. The balance tilts more in favor of narrative writing in the elementary grades and then tilts toward argument and informational writing in high school.

In the Common Core, the discussion of the distribution of writing between these types of texts is situated under the subheading of "Shared Responsibility" (4) as part of an emphasis on writing instruction belonging in the hands of all disciplines and every teacher. That is, if fifth-grade students are expected to write narratives 35% of the time, information and explanations 35% of the time, and opinions and arguments 30% of the time, and writing is expected to be woven into math, social studies, science, gym, and music, then presumably a good deal of the explanatory and informational writing will occur in science (lab reports), in math (math journals reflecting on the students' processes), in social studies (summaries of texts read, responses to questions asking students to synthesize information from several sources), and in reading (reading notebook entries, quick analytic jottings, preparations for partnership and book club conversations). This suggests that the CCSS recommend that a large portion of the writing done during ELA be narrative writing. Our next chapter, on the standards' expectations for narrative writing, illuminates this point further.

The Standards' Emphasis on the Writing Process

Writing standard 5 describes the writing process, and standard 10 describes the need to write routinely as part of that process. Both standards will be an integral part of students being able to work toward all the other writing standards as well. The grade level specifics of anchor standard 5 are almost the same across all the grades. Always, this standard says that students should be able to "develop and strengthen writing as needed by planning, revising, [and] editing" (18) with expectations for revision increasing with age and with expectations for independence increasing as well. Anchor standard 10 calls for students to "write routinely over extended time frames (time for research, reflection, and revision) and shorter time frames (a single sitting or a day or two)" (18). These are not low expectations!

Let's start by noting that the standards call for students to write often. "Write routinely" means to make writing a habit. Even noted writers describe how they have to push themselves to ensure that they write every day. Novelist Margaret Atwood, who has published dozens of fiction and nonfiction books, and has received almost every known award for her writing, claims: "The fact is the blank pages inspire me with terror. What will I put on them? Will it be good enough? Will I have to throw it out? The trick is to sit at the desk anyway, every day" (Murray 1990). It is not surprising that the standards emphasize writing often. Writing is just like any other practice—playing piano, running, knitting. The more opportunity you have for practice, the better you get.

The image of a routine for writing is not just about sitting down to write, however. A writing routine involves understanding what it means to work at your writing. Writing anchor 5 states that writers will "develop and strengthen writing as needed by planning, revising, editing, rewriting, or trying a new approach" (18). The CCSS are closely aligned, then, with the practices researched by Pulitzer Prize–winning journalist Don Murray, documented in *A Writer Teaches Writing* (2003). Murray described how journalists learn, even when writing to deadline, to revise on the run, to try out different leads and endings, to consider and reconsider each word, comma, sentence structure in order to convey precise meaning: they know that writing is a process.

Volume is also related to rate, and the standards are very specific about the expectations for production. Fourth graders are expected to produce a minimum of one typed page in a sitting, and fifth graders, a minimum of two typed pages in a sitting. That level of production requires practice. If you've ever practiced piano scales, you know that when you first sit down after a long stretch away from the piano, your fingers are slow. It's the same if you haven't exercised in a while, or if you haven't picked up knitting needles in five years. You know the skills, but your legs or fingers don't respond with the speed you expected. On the other hand, as you begin to knit, or run, or play piano, or write, you'll find that for every day you do it, the sheer discipline of moving your pen across the page, or your fingers across the keyboard, you will become faster and more fluent.

The Standards' Emphasis on the Quality of Student Writing

Although a reader of the writing standards will probably notice first that the standards emphasize three broadly defined types of writing and second that the standards call for frequent engagement in the writing process, the most important thing is that the standards issue a call for extremely high levels of proficiency. One has only to look at the descriptors of what students are expected to do at each grade level, or more importantly, to glance at the sample texts included in Appendix C, to realize that the Common Core State Standards are calling for higher expectations in writing than those that have been commonplace. One realizes this especially when seeing that the sample texts included in the appendix are meant to illustrate not the work that strong writers occasionally produce, but the work that *all* students should be expected to produce—and to produce regularly, with independence.

Let's look, for example, at even just the first portion of a piece of writing from Appendix C that represents what all eighth graders should be able to do as narrative writers:

> Miss Sadie no longer sits in her rocking chair on her porch on summer days. But I still can see her. The old chair squeaking with every sway of her big, brown body. Her summer dresses stained from cooking in her sweet smelling kitchen. I see her gray hair pulled back in that awful, yellow banana clip. Most of all, I hear that voice. So full of character and wisdom. (52)

The writer manages to convey a sense of love and intimacy, from the small details she includes about this long-ago scene. She creates a sense of a character. This is pretty good writing, and we'll be happy if our students can generate this kind of prose.

The emphasis on the quality of writing is also clear from the descriptors used to characterize students' writing at every grade level in the main CCSS document. By grades 9–10, for example, the lead paragraph to a narrative story should "engage and orient the reader by setting out a problem, situation, or observation, establishing one or multiple point(s) of view, and introducing a narrator and/or characters; create a smooth progression of experiences or events" (46). And all of that just describes the opening few lines to a story! One can't help but think, "Could *I* write like that, let alone teach a fifteen-year-old to write like that?"

The expectations for writing in the CCSS are also carried by anchor standard 4. At every grade level, starting in grade 3, standard 4 says that students are expected to "produce clear and coherent writing in which the development and organization are appropriate to task, purpose, and audience" (18). Note that a spotlight is placed on clarity and structure, as opposed to vividness or voice. This is interesting to us because we have often felt that one can look at various theories about writing instruction and ask, "Does this prioritize the sort of good writing one finds in picture books and poems, or does it prioritize the lucid, clear writing that one finds in William Strunk and E. B. White's *Elements of Style?*" The CCSS lean toward the latter.

The standards, you'll recall, focus on expectations and not methods. They detail what students should know and be able to do and do not specify practices that teachers should use to teach students the skills they need to meet those expectations. School districts and teachers are left to decide on an instructional program that will elevate the level of student writing so that all (or most) students reach these ambitious expectations. We discuss the implications of these standards in Chapters 7–9, but for now, it is enough to say that the standards are nothing to sneeze at. One can't help but think that they will require a planned, sequential, explicit writing program, with instruction that gives students repeated opportunities to practice each kind of writing and to receive explicit feedback at frequent intervals.

The Standards' Emphasis on Writing as Integral Even for Very Young Students

In thousands of schools across the nation, teachers start the kindergarten year off by saying to children, "In this classroom, each one of you will be an author. Each one of you will write stories and letters and songs and recipes and all-about books." Although this instruction has spread like wildfire, it is still far from the norm. In the majority of classrooms, kindergarten is a time for socialization, for learning the alphabet, for perhaps copying the whole-class text, with an emphasis on penmanship. The Common Core State Standards convey a crystal-clear message opposed to this practice. The message is this: Kindergartners can write. They can not only invent their own spellings and write with fluency and power, but also write long, well-developed, shapely texts.

One of the sample pieces (corrected for spelling) for kindergarten included in Appendix C goes like this:

Today before we had writing groups Mrs. John read us a story about frogs. We had to write about frogs. We have a tadpole in the science center. It has two back legs and when it has two front legs its tail disappears and it cannot eat when its mouth is changing. Then the skin gets too little and the frogs pull off their skin and they eat it. Some of the frogs blow bubbles. Frogs laid eggs that look like jelly and the fish eat some but some hatch to tadpoles. It grows bigger and bigger and bigger. (7)

This piece has created a stir among many kindergarten teachers. If the message of the standards is "All children should be able to accomplish this," many teachers question whether it is realistic to expect that within the one fleeting year of kindergarten, all children will be able to write like this. It is unlikely that a child who enters kindergarten with little knowledge of the concepts of print, little knowledge of sound–letter correspondence, and little experience with academic English will be able to produce a piece of writing like this. If, on the other hand, the message is that some children will have been reading and writing and using academic English long before they come to kindergarten and will be positioned to be able to write texts such as this, that's another message altogether.

The important thing about the primary writing standards, then, is not the specific expectations of each grade, but rather the fact that all of the skills that are considered to be essential for a high school student actually have their beginnings in the primary grades. The standards do not suggest that young kids write just stories and older students write just essays. Instead, kindergartners, like twelfth graders, are given repeated practice in writing their opinions and then supporting those opinions with reasons. Kindergartners, like twelfth graders, draft, revise, edit, and publish their writing. Implicit in the CCSS is the presence of a spiral curriculum. A child who has been learning narrative craft for thirteen years should, by the end of twelfth grade, be extraordinarily skilled, ready to spin an anecdote from his or her own story into an engaging college essay or scholarship application. A child who wrote opinions in the primary grades, then moved to carefully constructed arguments in middle school, is going to be ready to embark on learning the skills needed to contextualize an argument, acknowledge and refute the counterargument, and analyze the research base and bias of sources. The standards suggest it would be hard to achieve this high level of craft and knowledge if students weren't moving steadily along a spiral curriculum, practicing and extending skills in each type of writing each year. We discuss this in greater detail later in this chapter, under "Implementation Implications of the Writing Standards: Some Essentials."

THE STANDARDS' EMPHASIS ON WRITING ACROSS ALL DISCIPLINES AND FOR REAL PURPOSES

There is no question but that the Common Core State Standards emphasize writing (and reading) in the content areas, across every discipline. The message is clear that just as every teacher needs to be a teacher of reading, so too, every teacher needs to be a teacher of writing. For example, the Common Core State Standards do not expect that informational writing will be taught only within English language arts. Rather, people who call themselves authors of the CCSS often refer to the writing standards as a shared responsibility within the school that all subject areas support. In addition, the CCSS promote the value of writing often—routinely, they say— including writing for shorter time frames, and in response to specific tasks. The CCSS reiterate the emphasis on writing across the disciplines this way:

> To build a foundation for college and career readiness, students need to learn to use writing as a way of offering and supporting opinions, demonstrating understanding of the subjects they are studying, and conveying real and imagined experiences and events. They learn to appreciate that a key purpose of writing is to communicate clearly to an external, sometimes unfamiliar audience, and they begin to adapt the form and content of their writing to accomplish a particular task and purpose. (18)

Some speculate that one reason the CCSS place such an emphasis on the higher-level literacy skills that are important in a discipline is that when the country cannot agree on basic ideas about American history and science—on the existence of evolution, for example—it is unlikely that states will ever ratify shared standards in the disciplines. The CCSS may be the closest we come to content standards. If students can read and write well in science and social studies, this will hold up the level of discipline-based work.

Then, too, in this day and age, the ability to convey knowledge is becoming as important as the knowledge itself. Researchers share findings, clients expect clear communication, consumers give feedback, colleagues compose collaboratively—all through writing. As the Internet has provided global access to information and ideas, it has become even more important to write. Whether our students become scientists, engineers, activists, or analysts, they'll need to be able to write well to do well.

Implementation Implications of the Writing Standards: Some Essentials

The implications of the writing standards are clear. Writing must become part of the bill of rights for all students. Just as it would be unacceptable for a K–5 teacher to say, "Math's not really my thing," and to focus on other subjects, bypassing math, so too, in the world of the Common Core, it will be indefensible for a teacher to say, "Writing is not really my cup of tea," and then to teach writing only on Halloween, St. Patrick's Day, and Mother's Day. Instead, writing will need to be given its due, starting in kindergarten and continuing throughout the grades. Teachers will need to assess and teach writing, to track students' progress, and to plan interventions for those students who need extra help in writing. In short, writing will need to be treated just as reading and math have been treated in the past.

That part is clear. What is not clear is what, exactly, it means to teach writing. Although some educators have emphasized the teaching of writing and others have not, those who *have* taught writing have seemed almost uniformly to draw upon the tradition that was established by experts such as Pulitzer Prize–winning writer Don Murray, journalist Roy Peter Clark, writers Annie Dillard, Mary Oliver, Anne Lamott, and E. B. White, to name a few, and educators including Peter Elbow, Georgia Heard, Ralph Fletcher, and our own organization, the Teachers College Reading and Writing Project. Moreover, this writing process approach, emphasizing the importance of students rehearsing, drafting, revising, and editing their writing, has been as essential in colleges as in K–12 classrooms, creating a cohesion in the teaching of writing that has not existed in the teaching of reading. Across K–college, the writing workshop has been the accepted forum for teaching the skills and strategies of effective writing.

This is not to say that the arrival of the Common Core State Standards didn't ignite reforms in writing workshop instruction. When the Common Core State Standards were released, experts in the teaching of writing did, of course, take note that the standards call for a new emphasis on argument writing. Although most experts in the teaching of writing have always emphasized persuasive, opinion, and essay writing, there are new features to the standards' emphasis on argument, and this has led to a flurry of excitement and innovation. Then, too, the emphasis on writing across the curriculum has led experts in writing, including members of the TCRWP, to beef up that venue for writing instruction. Lastly, the quality of writing the Common Core demands is higher than what many educators may have aimed for in the past, as evidenced by the exemplar texts in Appendix C.

This last emphasis has led teachers to look closely at their schedules for writing, following a student across a week, seeing how much time is actually available for that student to write, and paying attention to how much writing that student actually produces during one sitting. In every school where kids become powerful writers, they have extended time to write, and they write daily. Don Graves, pioneer reformer in writing instruction for children, often said that if writers couldn't return to a piece of writing at least three times a week, it wasn't worth doing at all (2003). The kids would just be too far away from their writing to remain committed to it.

Mostly, then, the Common Core writing standards seem utterly aligned to the writing process tradition that is well established across the states, with a few new areas of focus and a raised bar for the quality of writing we should expect students to produce. This quality of writing can be achieved by mandating the explicit instruction, opportunities for practice, centrality of feedback, assessment-based instruction, and spiral curriculum that have all been hallmarks of rigorous writing workshop instruction.

CHAPTER SEVEN

THE CCSS and COMPOSING NARRATIVE TEXTS

The first three anchor standards for writing begin with argument, proceed to informational writing, and end with narrative writing, but learners grow into these genres in just the opposite direction. Human beings grow up on narratives, on stories. We come to know our parents by hearing their stories of growing up. We make friendships by sharing the stories of our lives. We get jobs and scholarships by telling the stories of our studies and careers. We stay in touch by regaling each other with the news of our comings and goings. We plan and daydream and work and worry in narrative; we recall and remember in narrative. We comprehend fiction and biography and narrative nonfiction by synthesizing what we read on one page, another, and another into narratives that we hope are coherent and satisfying.

Narratives are important not only because they are, as Barbara Hardy (1977) says, the primary mode of knowing, but also because they are an essential component in almost every other kind of writing. Listen to TED talks—models of persuasive and informative speaking—and you will find that mostly, those speeches are mosaics of stories. Read a terrific informational text, and you'll find that you are reading stories.

We begin unpacking the writing standards, then, by examining anchor standard 3, the narrative writing standard, and we suggest that when you study the writing standards, you do the same. Chances are good that you are more familiar with the craft of effective narrative writing than that of argument or informational writing, and therefore an analysis of standard 3 is a wonderful place to come to an understanding of how the writing standards, in general, are constructed, and of the considerable contribution they can make to your teaching. Our analysis of the narrative writing standard will undergird our analysis of the other types of writing outlined in the CCSS.

Writing anchor standard 3 states: "Write narratives to develop real or imagined experiences or events using effective technique, well-chosen details, and well-structured event sequences" (18 and 41). We focus on three particular aspects of this standard that we think can help you raise the quality of narrative writing, and writing in general, in your school:

- The CCSS' expectations for narrative writing are ambitious.
- The structure of the writing standards presents helpful learning progressions.
- The standards emphasize skills a writer will need to know to write any type of text.

We end the chapter by proposing pathways for implementing the narrative writing standards.

THE COMMON CORE'S EXPECTATIONS FOR NARRATIVE WRITING ARE AMBITIOUS

Listen to the start of this piece of writing, produced on demand by a fourth grader, and included in Appendix C of the CCSS as representative of the level of writing that fourth graders should be able to produce in a single sitting:

GLOWING SHOES

One quiet, Tuesday morning, I woke up to a pair of bright, dazzling shoes, lying right in front of my bedroom door. The shoes were a nice shade of violet and smelled like catnip. I found that out because my cats, Tigger and Max, were rubbing on my legs, which tickled.

When I started out the door, I noticed that Tigger and Max were following me to school. Other cats joined in as well. They didn't even stop when we reached Main Street!

"Don't you guys have somewhere to be?" I quizzed the cats.

"Meeeeeooooow!" the crowd of cats replied.

As I walked on, I observed many more cats joining the stalking crowd. I moved more swiftly. The crowd of cats' walk turned into a prance. I sped up. I felt like a rollercoaster zooming past the crowded line that was waiting for their turn as I darted down the sidewalk with dashing cats on my tail. (27)

For a nine-year-old, this is some pretty skilled writing. The writer knows something about building tension, about the art of specific detail, about using dialogue to develop characters and action. Our point is that whether you look at exemplars from younger or older students, the conclusion is the same: students are expected to write well-crafted, tightly structured stories. These are not mere accounts; they are children's versions of literature. The expected levels of achievement are well within reach of students who have grown up within a rigorous course of study in narrative craft, but the expectations are beyond reach for most students who have not had the advantage of instruction in the skills and strategies of narrative writing—much more so than in other types of writing, such as informational writing, where the Common Core exemplars do not set the bar as high.

Contrast, for example, the start of this third-grade report on horses, also from Appendix C, with the start of the story about the shoes.

HORSES
Why I Chose This Animal
I chose horses because I like to ride them. I also like to pet them. At the camp I go to everybody gets to have horses back [*sic*] riding lessons. Horses are so beautiful and fun to ride.

Horse Families
A mother or female horse is called a mare. A father or male horse is called a stallion. A foal is a baby horse. (18)

As an exemplar of informational writing for third grade, this text does not intimidate. There is no unusual level of skill displayed, either in the detail, the structure, or the logic of the writing. The narrative exemplars, on the other hand, set a higher bar.

The Structure of the Writing Standards Presents Helpful Learning Progressions

If you try to understand the narrative writing standards by turning immediately to the grade you teach, and reading the descriptors for that grade, you'll probably find the expectations to be overwhelming. Before you dismiss the standards as unrealistically high, you need to read them in an entirely different fashion. Start with kindergarten, and read those grade level skills. Imagine a very simple story that meets those descriptors. Then reread just the first part of the kindergarten description, and now read to the right, noting what added work first graders are expected to do. By proceeding in this way, reading in a horizontal fashion, setting the descriptors for each skill from one grade alongside the descriptors of the preceding grade and noting the new work that is added at each subsequent grade, you'll come to understand the trajectory along which writers can travel. This trajectory will, in fact, make the writing standards something that students will be able to achieve, especially if they have the opportunity to grow up within a strong writing curriculum.

We have found that it is actually helpful to not only read the standards this way, but also imagine what a piece of writing might look like if it matched the kindergarten standards, the first-grade standards, and so on up the ladder of narrative writing. Let's do this together, skipping some grades (and some descriptors) for the sake of expediency.

The kindergarten standards for narrative writing ask writers to do the following:

- narrate a single event
- provide a reaction to what happened (19)

So perhaps our story, which we may tell with pictures and words, goes:

The grade 2 standards include all the skills from kindergarten and first grade, plus the following:

- elaborate the event(s)
- include details for actions, thoughts, and feelings
- provide closure (19)

First of all, we know that now we need to add some elaboration, and specifically, the standards call for details that describe "actions, thoughts, and feelings." Also, we know we're being asked to provide some closure. We can't just write, "I got on the roller coaster. It went up the hill. I was scared. The End." We can't stop a roller coaster while we're at the top. Let's try:

> I got on the roller coaster. I was scared. My stomach felt sick. It went up the hill. I was more scared. I thought about accidents. I wanted to cry. We got closer to the top . . . then we raced down and up and around. I was afraid I would be sick. I was sick. But I was alive and it was over.

By grade 4, the standards include the following additional skills:

- establish a situation
- orient the reader
- introduce a narrator and/or characters
- organize a sequence of events that unfolds naturally
- describe actions, thoughts, and feelings to develop experiences or events
- use dialogue to show the response of characters
- use concrete and sensory language to convey experiences precisely
- use words and phrases that show the movement of time
- create a conclusion that follows from the events (20)

Now is when we start to sweat. Already, by grade 4, students are supposed to write like Nabokov. Remember, though, that this is a list of skills that fourth graders should be able to demonstrate, but this doesn't mean that every narrative must contain all of these characteristics. A study of the exemplars in Appendix C shows that no one piece does everything listed in the standards for that grade. For our story, let's start with "orient the reader by establishing a situation" (2010a, 20). We could interpret this to mean that we shouldn't just launch into the middle of our story, the roller coaster ride, which is pretty much what we've done so far. We should instead set up a situation, introduce our narrator and characters to the reader, and probably provide some details about setting to orient the reader. So maybe we start like this:

> I stood in front of the roller coaster with Lisa and Patty. Lisa loved roller coasters. Patty loved roller coasters. I did not. I was scared because I hate

roller coasters. I was also scared because I had just eaten cotton candy, fried dough, and a huge root beer. And now we were about to get on a roller coaster. Lisa and Patty were two very popular girls. I knew I had to pretend I wasn't afraid of roller coasters.

Now we think, "What next?" Let's look back at our fourth-grade list of skills. Okay, we're working on thoughts and feelings; those are coming along. We haven't gotten to any action yet, so maybe we want to move to that. Oh, and it says we're supposed to include sensory details, concrete language, and dialogue to show how characters respond to events. Let's give those a try:

"Let's get on it," I said.
"You sit in the middle," Patty said, and she grabbed my arm for a minute, pulling me close to her.
"We're friends," I thought, and I looked at Patty, with her shiny long hair and her perfect outfit. My stomach did flip-flops. I tried not to think of the fried dough, cotton candy, and soda I had just eaten and drank.

The grade 8 standards ask writers to do everything we've already described and, in addition:

- establish a context and point of view
- consider pacing
- signal shifts in time and place
- reflect on events in the conclusion (43)

The question of context is interesting. It pushes us to ask, "What am I doing here, at this roller coaster?" Perhaps, among other additions, we might add:

There I was at the roller coaster again. It felt as if every summer, the day came when I stood in front of the roller coaster, and had to decide whether to stand by the side or get on it. If I stood by the side, I felt like a baby. If I got on it, I would be miserable. I would be immobilized by fear. I wouldn't even be able to open my eyes. My body would be so clenched with terror that my muscles would ache for days.

> This time, I wouldn't chicken out. This time, I was almost in high school. This time, I was determined to not be a baby.

Perhaps we'll work in some of that shifting of time or place as well:

> Later that night, I stood at the laundry room sink in the basement, trying to clean the mess off my shirt. As I scrubbed at the stains, I realized how little had actually gotten on me. Most of it had landed on Patty.

The grades 11–12 standards ask for all the skills that came before, plus these:

- set out a problem and establish its significance
- sequence events so that they build on one another
- create a particular tone
- convey vivid pictures
- provide a conclusion that reflects on what is resolved (46)

To do all of that, we probably need to write a longer narrative. For now, perhaps we might try the notion of a reflective conclusion. Do we learn anything from the roller coaster experience?

> That year was a hard one. The summer had begun with me standing in front of the roller coaster again. Lisa had looked at me and said: "Don't be a baby. Come on, let's go."
> I should have said no. Then I wouldn't have thrown up on Patty, the most popular girl in the school. But then I wouldn't have learned that sometimes, being brave means being able to admit you're afraid.

Corcoran, Mosher, and Rogat, who have researched the qualities of effective learning progressions, wrote that one of the most essential components of learning progressions is that they denote "levels of achievement or stages of progress that define significant intermediate steps in conceptual/skill development that most children might be expected to pass through on the path to attaining the desired proficiency" (2009, 17). We've found that these CCSS progressions are a rather elegant series of steps, and that if we can help our writers achieve these stages of development, they'll be more proficient narrative writers—and they'll learn skills that apply to any genre.

THE STANDARDS EMPHASIZE SKILLS A WRITER WILL NEED TO KNOW TO WRITE ANY TYPE OF TEXT

We were so enamored with the process of reading the grade level standards horizontally, noting the relatively small, incremental advances that occur at each grade, that it took us a long time to see another source of coherence in the anchor standards. If you look across all three types of writing in the standards (anchor standards 1–3), you'll see that always, the first descriptor of each type of writing (or for K–2, the first part of the description) details the way in which writers will begin their texts. Then, for each type of writing, the next descriptor describes ways writers will develop the text, elaborating and using specific details to do so. The nature of the specifics change, with narrative writers supplying actions, thoughts, and feelings and information writers providing concrete details, quotations, and examples, but either way, writers learn to develop, to elaborate. Of course, hand in hand with elaboration, writers must supply linking words or, if they are older, linking phrases and transitions, which create cohesion and clarify the relationships among parts of the text. And whatever the type of writing they're producing, writers need to create closure, preferably by linking backward to earlier portions of the text.

This cohesion of the standards across the three writing types is important because it means that as a teacher moves from teaching one type of writing to teaching another, it will be economical to remind writers of the strategies they have already learned, helping them to do similar work in the new type of writing. This way, when starting an argument or informational piece, for example, writers will expect that they need to orient the reader and one way to do this in an informational text is to introduce the organizational structure. Whether the writer is establishing a situation, orienting the reader, creating an organizational structure, or establishing a focus, these are all variations on the same kind of work—namely, beginning a text—and they all require many of the same proficiencies. Likewise, when a writer learns that a roller coaster story can't leave people hanging midway through the roller coaster ride, she'll learn something about endings that will help her with argument and informational writing as well.

Pathways for Implementing the Narrative Writing Standards

As we've researched the effect of the Common Core State Standards in classrooms, we've seen two ways in which you can harness the writing standards to raise the level of student writing. The first is to lean on teachers' familiarity with narrative writing as a starting point for studying the Common Core writing standards and becoming expert with the grade level expectations and skill progressions. The second is to launch writing habits and structures—the writing process and writing workshop—that will sustain students across all types of writing. In this section, therefore, we look at these two pathways to implementing the writing standards in your school.

Accessing Teachers' Familiarity with Narrative as a Starting Point

We, in education, are good at adding and multiplying the things we are to teach. We are good at jumping from one priority to another, then another. Although surely there is no harm in the Common Core leading a school to add this or that to the curriculum, the most important work that teachers, or a school, can do in order to adopt the Common Core State Standards is to become accountable to teaching whatever they are already teaching in ways that accelerate achievement. The real work lies not in telling students about this cool new thing they could try, but in moving students along whatever progression is already in place.

Schools that have studied the writing process approach to teaching writing are apt to already teach narrative writing, and they are, therefore, poised to be able to use the standards to lift the level of narrative writing in ways that can take both students and teachers to new heights. The narrative writing progression in the standards can, above all, help teachers tap into the power of learning progressions, seeing ways in which a clear trajectory of progress can inform their plans for units of study, their minilessons, their choice of mentor texts, their feedback on student writing, their conferences, and their small-group work; that is, it can help them with all of their teaching.

Adopt or create a learning progression. In "The Lowdown on Learning Progressions," James Popham, professor emeritus at UCLA and an expert on assessment and testing research, explains that "a learning progression is a carefully sequenced set of building blocks that students must master en route to mastering a more distant curricular aim. . . . This sort of backward analysis can isolate the key tasks a student must accomplish on the way to mastery" (2007, 83). How helpful it is for teachers to be able to specify what constitutes a simple, clear narrative, and then to specify also the moves a writer can take to make that simple narrative into a more sophisticated one. Once writers are producing this new level of narrative writing, they'll want to know: "What's next?"

We encourage you, therefore, to put together teams of teachers at each grade level and across grade levels to study the descriptors of grade level skills in narrative writing, and to use these skill progressions to provide the necessary scaffolding to lead more students toward these skills. Some of this work will entail teachers writing their own demonstration texts, as we illustrated earlier in this chapter with our roller coaster text. Some will entail teachers agreeing that each grade level will teach these skills and give students repeated opportunities to practice them. That is, teachers will need to agree on some specific units of study in narrative writing that each grade will teach collaboratively, so that the grade levels above can count on all students entering the year with some level of expertise and fluency in these skills. Students simply won't achieve these high levels of writing unless they get consistent instruction and practice, across the grades.

Use a continuum of narrative writing to assess your students' progress. Another collaborative process you'll want to do with your colleagues is to collect student work as exemplars, and study those within and across grades, so that you can monitor your students' progress and scaffold them into writing higher-level texts. We and our colleagues at the Teachers College Reading and Writing Project developed our own continuum of narrative writing. We established a step-by-step progression of benchmarked narrative pieces, and showed how traits such as *show don't tell* unfolded in progressively more complex ways across that continuum of work. This continuum revolutionized teaching and assessment in many schools, and we expect the Common Core State Standards for narrative writing can do likewise. Teachers who are interested in accessing the *K–8 Continuum for Assessing Narrative Writing* (which is fully aligned to the CCSS) will find the tool available at no cost on the TCRWP website, at www.readingandwritingproject.com.

Here are our suggestions for how to use the continuum for narrative writing in ways that will help lift the level of instruction in your school and classroom:

1. *Start the year by asking students to write their best on-demand narrative pieces.* We say to students, "Write a personal narrative, a small moment, a true story of one experience. Make this your best narrative writing." We offer no additional coaching, no reminders; we want to see what students can do without assistance.

2. *Afterward, collect student writing and lay it alongside the continuum of narrative pieces, representing twelve levels of development.* We ask, "Where in this continuum do most of my students fall?" and then we look at the pieces of writing and the descriptors of those pieces to see the next steps students need to take, tailoring our planned unit of study to support that next level of development.

3. *After teaching a unit of study on narrative writing and publishing the pieces to great fanfare, again set aside a day for on-demand writing, and provide the exact same instructions.* We look to see whether students' narratives have moved up a notch (or two) in the continuum, and regard their progress (or lack thereof) as our progress. That is, if we teach writers well, it is not just their published pieces—the pieces that we've reviewed, coached into, and supported—that get better. It is, ideally, the writers who improve, and this is revealed to us in the progress we see in students' on-demand writing.

   Now that the Common Core standards have provided all teachers with a continuum of sorts, we hope that teachers across the nation will begin, in a similar way, to preface writing instruction with an assessment that helps them tailor instruction to students' current level on the learning progression laid out by the standards. We also hope that teachers everywhere hold themselves accountable to teaching in ways that affect not just the writing, but the writers. This will be evidenced when students are given a postassessment in which they have the opportunity to show what they can do.

4. *It will also be important for teachers across a grade level to be transparent about the progress their students do and do not make.* If one teacher in the grade level has taught in ways that have especially accelerated student progress, then by all means, other teachers need to

visit that room and ask, "What did you do that we could try?" It will be this spirit of accountability, this laserlike focus on results, this willingness to engage in an ongoing cycle of improvement that will make our classrooms truly standards based. One note of caution when using the CCSS as a way to tailor instruction: The language of the CCSS is academic—it's not intended for kids. If seventh graders, for example, knew what "establishing a context and point of view and introducing a narrator" (43) meant, they would be doing it. You'll have some work to do, translating the CCSS language into language that not only students, but teachers, can employ effectively.

Provide students with clear goals and effective feedback. John Hattie, of the University of Auckland, talks about the importance of clear goals and feedback in his seminal work *Visible Learning: A Synthesis of Over 800 Meta-Analyses Relating to Achievement* (2009). In his summary, he draws six major conclusions that he casts as "signposts towards excellence in education" (238). In one key conclusion, he writes, "Teachers need to know the learning intentions and success criteria of their lessons, know how well they are attaining these criteria for all students, and know where to go next in light of the gap between students' current knowledge and understanding and the success criteria of: 'Where are you going?,' 'How are you going?,' and 'Where to next?'" (239). These three feedback questions are intended for both teachers and students. What is critical, Hattie posits, is that students are participants in their own learning process. Both teaching and learning should be visible. That is, teachers need to monitor student learning, provide feedback, and let students know when learning is successful (37).

We agree that if you want to accelerate kids' prowess as writers so that they quickly learn to write coherently and independently, it's helpful to provide a clear path for kids to follow, rather than to show them all the alternatives they could wander among. What matters is that students understand that writing is a learnable craft, as Murray explained (2003). We have found, though, that it moves a school forward when teachers agree on predictable pathways, so that kids share common understandings and build on their writing skills across grade levels. Popham reiterates this, sharing research suggesting that "almost any carefully conceived learning progression is more likely to benefit students than teachers' off-the-cuff decision making" (2007, 84). Creating continua helps teachers and students share a vision of what the writing they are trying to achieve looks like, including steps along the way.

Launching Writing Workshop and Using the Writing Process to Sustain Students Across All Types of Writing

Having crystal-clear goals will not make one whit of difference if students don't have protected time in school to work on achieving those goals, and if teachers don't have time to convey feedback and coach their writers in the act of writing. Writers need time to write, which means they need time to take their writing through the steps of the writing process. When we've seen students *not* develop as they should as writers, it's often because the time for writing has been "outsourced." That is, students have been assigned writing in class, perhaps even given some instruction, but then they've been expected to produce their writing elsewhere. Aside from the fact that this structure privileges students who receive coaching and support outside of school and assumes that kids all have clear time and space to write once they leave school, when you outsource writing time, you lose all opportunity to coach and give feedback to writers while they are in the process of writing.

In the work Doug Reeves (2010) has done with schools to demonstrate the power of feedback, he reiterates one aspect of feedback again and again—and that is that feedback needs to be immediate and in the midst of kids' work. In the summer of 2011, when Doug was working with hundreds of school leaders in Boston, he described how, in his visits to schools with the mission to see what affected student achievement, he saw the best feedback happening in the music rooms and on the playing fields. Music teachers and chorus directors launched their kids into some work, watched and listened carefully, gave their students attentive feedback, and then had the kids do it again. Repeated practice combined with carefully calibrated feedback makes a tremendous difference. What was shocking and initially disheartening to those who headed English departments was Reeves' finding that feedback that came later or was subsumed under grading had very little, if any, effect on student achievement. Doug gave the analogy of a diving coach asking a student to dive, then coming back a week or two later and saying, "Remember that dive you did? Well, I'd give it a seven out of ten."

The writing process and writing workshop give students and teachers the time, structure, and place to produce first drafts of writing (which are the teacher's research data), to give and get feedback (from teachers to students in the form of conferences, and from students to teachers in the form of their subsequent writing), and to enter into a system of continuous improvement. We urge you to launch a writing workshop model in your school and classroom, beginning with narrative writing. We suggest launching with narrative writing because most teachers already believe that for students to produce powerful narrative writing, they should take their writing through more than one draft. Most teachers already incorporate some study of mentor texts in their narrative writing units, which means some of the writing process is done in class. Many teachers are also skilled at giving feedback in narrative writing, as they have worked in this type of writing as readers and writers for years. If you can get solid structures in place with narrative writing, you should be able to carry these structures, and the habits they instill, across other types of writing and across the curricula. Once students are inculcated with the habits of drafting, revising, and seeking and responding to feedback, they'll carry these habits to their other writing.

We encourage you, when you have classrooms in your building that model this system of continuous improvement in writing, to open these classrooms to other teachers, including content-area teachers. We can't tell you how illuminating it has been to science teachers, for example, to realize that students could learn to revise their lab reports in response to feedback. So get the writing process and writing workshop going in your school, beginning with narrative writing. Or, improve your workshop model so that it is really successful. Then take this success to other types of writing across the school.*

---

* If you feel that your teachers need support with the writing process and the writing workshop model, or with using these structures to raise the level of narrative writing quickly, consult the many professional resources listed on the TCRWP website, www.readingandwritingproject.com. We particularly like Ralph Fletcher's *Writing Workshop* (2001) for helping new teachers begin workshop. Many teachers have found the *Units of Study for Teaching Writing*, by Calkins et al. (2006), to be useful for the collections of minilessons and predictable conferences. Carl Anderson's *How's It Going?* (2000) continues to be the watershed text on conferring—though we also find his *Assessing Writers* (2005) extremely helpful. There are many, many more professional texts, by authors such as Katie Wood Ray, Randy and Katherine Bomer, Roy Peter Clark, and others, listed on the website that we recommend heartily.

CHAPTER EIGHT

THE CCSS and COMPOSING ARGUMENT TEXTS

A rgument writing is a *big deal* in the Common Core State Standards. If you had a hunch that this was so from its place as number one on the list of writing types or the odd sense of déjà vu you got as argument-related expectations seemed to pop up across all areas of the standards, you were on to something. In fact, the writers include an entire section in Appendix A titled "The Special Place of Argument in the Standards" (24) to emphasize their strong belief in argumentation. The sections begins, "While all three text types are important, the Standards put particular emphasis on students' ability to write sound arguments on substantive topics and issues, as this ability is critical to college and career readiness." To support their argument, the authors refer to statements by college professors who each make additional claims for the centrality of argument in universities. Gerald Graff, for example, claims that the university is largely "an argument culture" (2003, 24). It is with this particular vision of university life, which your own experiences may or may not confirm, that the standards writers mapped their expectations for argument writing from high school graduation backward.

It seems important to note that this belief in the essential nature of argumentation, at least on the part of the writers of the standards, colors many areas of the document. There is a push for logical reasoning, analysis of claims, and reliance on clear evidence and evaluation of sources throughout the grades.

The pace at which the opinion and argument standards develop is breathtaking when you study them longitudinally. Kindergarten and first grade begin simply enough, expecting a student to introduce a topic and supply some opinion for it, perhaps with a reason. But then in second grade, the student is already expected to structure his or her writing in support of his or her claim. In fact, in some respects the complexity of second-grade argument writing, at least in terms of the text of the standards, seems to outpace that of the other two writing types. In second-grade informational writing, the main emphasis seems to be only that the texts include a variety of details, whereas the expectations for argument writing are more extensive.

You will want to study this standard with the expectation that you, and your students, probably have a lot of new work ahead. This is certainly work that can be accomplished; it will just take some careful focus and attention.

We think three important ideas will help you study the Common Core standards for argument writing:

- The continuum of expectations for opinion and argument writing is steep.
- Writing arguments eventually includes refuting counterarguments.
- Writing arguments eventually includes using sources, evaluating them, and using this analysis to engine convincing arguments.

We conclude this chapter by discussing the implications for instruction in argument writing.

The Continuum of Expectations for Opinion and Argument Writing Is Steep

It is worth noting that if you ask a group of first-grade teachers to list the kinds of writing they teach their five- and six-year-olds, chances are good that none of those teachers will include "opinion writing" in his or her list. This is *not* because young children aren't engaged in this kind of writing—children who are lucky enough to participate in writing workshops typically work on units of study in writing persuasive letters and writing persuasive reviews, for example. Instead, the issue is that the term *opinion writing* is not a term most primary teachers use. The label *opinion writing* is a generalization, and teachers are more accustomed to teaching and talking about specific genres, including persuasive letters, persuasive reviews, book reviews, and petitions. Essays, of course, qualify as opinion writing, but even the Common Core authors don't see essay writing as belonging in K–2 classrooms.

The expectations for this type of writing are well within reach for kindergarten teachers who have received help in teaching writing: students are asked to "use a combination of drawing, dictating, and writing to compose opinion pieces in which they tell a reader the topic or the name of the book they are writing about and state an opinion or preference about the topic or book" (19). This standard will seem especially age appropriate if one emphasizes that children can be writing their opinions about *topics* as well as about texts, and they can use dictation and drawing as well as writing to share those opinions. That is, a kindergartner can use drawing and writing to write a piece that essentially says, "I love, love, *love* my mom," and that child will have met this standard. A caveat to this is a strange misalignment between the text of the standard and the sample pieces in Appendix C. The sample piece for kindergarten opinion writing raises the bar in dramatic ways, and one is left unsure which is the actual expectation for kindergarten work: the descriptor in the standards, or the exemplar piece? The piece, written in five-year-old font and spelling, does a great deal more than tell the name of the topic or book and state an opinion. Here it is, corrected for spelling and grammar:

> My favorite book is *Do You Want to Be My Friend?* The mouse asked the horse if you will be my friend. The horse said no. The mouse found a friend. The mouse asked the little mouse if you will be my friend. The little mouse said yes. They dug a hole in the ground. My favorite part is the horse. (6)

The second-grade sample for opinion writing is a book review that was produced in class. So again, although the standards acknowledge that opinion writing can address a host of topics, the opinion writing samples in the appendix feel less rooted in children's own interests and passions than the rest of the K–5 writing samples. We challenge the assumption that opinion writing should only be book reviews or responses to teacher-selected prompts, but for now it is enough to note that it is not until fourth grade that the sample opinion pieces veer from being book reviews. Even when a piece that is not a book review is finally included, the topic, which relates to a whole-class field trip, seems teacher sponsored. That is, although writing persuasive letters comes naturally to kids ("Dear Mom, I want, I *need*, more allowance. I've got to have more allowance. The other kids all get like a dollar a week. How come I only . . ."), as does writing reviews of television shows, restaurants, ice-cream flavors, and toys, the samples included don't capture the authenticity of this kind of writing in the lives of young children.

The descriptors of opinion writing suggest that a third grader can essentially write, "I love horses," and then write and support one reason for loving horses. After supporting that one reason, the third grader can think, "Hmm. Why else do I love horses?" and can then produce a second reason. Having stated the second reason, the third grader can generate some support material for it. This allows the writer to approach a piece of writing, whether it is about loving horses or about a character in a book demonstrating a particular trait, without having pre-thought the essay as a whole. The writer can think and write in a piecemeal fashion, entertaining one reason for his or her idea and recording that before thinking, "Hmm. What other reason can I write?" This means that the third-grade writer's thesis statement needs only a claim and need not also forecast all the paragraphs (and reasons) that will follow.

The descriptors for the fifth-grade argument writing standards (20), on the other hand, suggest that by this time, a writer is expected to write something like, "Fifth grade is different from fourth grade," and then produce *a logical structure* for the reasons he or she will provide to support this claim. The logical structure might rely on the logic of chronology, for example, in which case the writer's entire thesis statement might be: "Fifth grade is different from fourth grade from the start to the finish of the day." Such a logical structure would suggest that the first support paragraph might start with a topic sentence that reflects the chronological structure of the essay. The first body paragraph, then, might read: "There are many ways the start of the day in fifth grade is different from the start of the day in fourth grade."

Although the descriptors for fifth-grade writing suggest that a logical structure is critical at this stage, in fact the sample pieces in Appendix C do not bear this out. There is no fifth-grade argument writing in Appendix C. There are, however, two sixth-grade argument pieces. Neither the persuasive letter to Mr. Sandler (36) nor the personal essay about the author's cat, Gus, being "a cuddle bug" (38) include an organizational structure in which ideas are logically grouped unless you regard "The first reason . . . ," "Another reason . . . ," and "The last reason . . ." a logical grouping. The descriptors for these pieces suggest that transitions like "One reason" and "Another reason" suffice for the Common Core authors as evidence of a clear organization.

WRITING ARGUMENTS EVENTUALLY INCLUDES REFUTING COUNTERARGUMENTS

In explaining why argumentation skill matters, the CCSS note that learning to compose convincing arguments not only develops *writing* skills, but also propels thinking and learning and researching skills. That is, the CCSS value the skills that precede the actual writing of argument. They value the ability to assess whether a source of information is trustworthy and to weigh the warrant behind evidence. They value looking for sides of an issue, and weeding out bias, and tracking the development of ideas. We can't help but think about the advertisements that promise a Barbie or Ken body in just thirty days, the websites that promise instant cures for every woe, and the platforms of politicians that promise to support every program without raising a dollar of taxes. In a world when even young children are flooded by language trying to get them to buy, vote, choose, hate, or promote one product, cause, or candidate over another, the Common Core prioritizes critical judgment. Although it is not new news that secondary school students need to be able to write academic essays in which they state and defend a claim, the Common Core's expectations show that the authors of this document believe that the study of argument writing can teach students of all ages to be critical consumers as well as composers of logic.

But the argument writing standards require not only skills of weighing and judging, but also skills of reasoning. The standards ask that secondary school writers study patterns across data to develop ideas, and then, through a process of logical thinking, bring others along a persuasive, compelling chain of thought that might go like this: "If we assume that this is true, then doesn't it suggest that . . . And if we agree on that, then can't we also say that. . . ." High school students, especially, are expected to be able to forge as well as to follow links in thinking—their own and other people's—and to do this in ways that allow them to question assumptions, to disentangle complex ideas, and to sort through evidence supporting or refuting an idea.

In the middle school standards, "opinion writing" shifts to being called "argument writing." You won't be surprised, then, to see that the biggest new element in the middle school standards is that now, for the first time, students are expected to not only argue for their claims, but also be able to argue against opposing sides. It is no longer that I just have an opinion about my cat being a better pet than your dog; now I am actually going to argue against any point you could possibly make advocating your dog as the better pet. The CCSS expect that students at this level can entertain the possibility that someone else may hold a conflicting opinion, can take it in, can perhaps agree with parts, and can then refute the counterargument.

Between grades 7 and 12, the standards lay out a skill progression for dealing with counterclaims in argument writing. This progression begins with "acknowledge alternate or opposing claims" in grade 7 (42) and then builds to "acknowledge *and distinguish* the claim(s) from alternate or opposing claims" (italics added to distinguish new expectations) in grade 8 (42). In grades 9–10, students then should not just distinguish claims but also "develop claim(s) and counterclaims fairly, supplying evidence for each while pointing out the strengths and limitations of both in a manner that anticipates the audience's knowledge level and concerns" (45).

This is high-level work. Once counterargument plays an important role in the work students are doing, then the topics, themselves, need to become generalizable. It is hard to counter an essay that claims, "This is my favorite book," or "I love my mother." Those claims are so personal that they are tough to contradict. This means that in secondary schools, writing instruction in argument must help writers think more universally so that they consider points that really are debatable. The writer who originally wanted to write, "I love my mother," will be supporting a debatable claim when she takes a step back to instead say: "Most young girls idolize their mothers." The necessity of counterclaims channels writers to take on universal and provocative issues, pushing them toward compelling, controversial ideas.

This means, then, that in the essays written in middle school, it is not enough for the writer to say, "Most young girls idolize their mothers in that they want to dress like them, act like them, and be able to make their own decisions like them." Now the writer also needs to say, "I know some will argue that girls actually want to be very different from their mothers." This writer will even need to take on that point of view and imagine what that person's argument might possibly be. Perhaps she'll end up writing,

"They might argue that girls often wear very different clothes and many tend to like things that their mothers do not." To do the work of the CCSS, especially at the highest levels, writers need to be able to mull over the counterclaim, and even show that mulling over in their writing in order to help readers logically follow their chain of thinking. For example, they might pick up the claim, consider it, and then reclaim their original point: "It's true that some girls do appear to act very differently from their mothers; some may even purposefully like music and hobbies and sports that their mothers disapprove of. However, this does not mean they do not still idolize them. Paying so much attention to their mothers that they act completely differently still shows how carefully they study that parent." When a writer considers, weighs, and refutes counterarguments, this strengthens and clarifies the writer's position.

One final note: Although the standards call for a formal style, this does not mean that writers need to avoid personal pronouns, nor does it mean that writers must always use formal language. Many of the student exemplars in Appendix C adopt the first-person pronoun and write in an informal, warm tone that one might find in one of Malcolm Gladwell's best-selling books or Carl Sagan's elegant and accessible texts on the solar system. The CCSS are clear that all standards are "end-of-year expectations" (4), and so student writers should learn to emulate different voices and note the different effect of each, being sure to master switching into a formal style but not being bound to make all assignments sound this way.

Writing Arguments Eventually Includes Using Sources, Evaluating Them, and Using This Analysis to Engine Convincing Arguments

The Common Core encourages teachers to shift instruction so that students do not just spout information they have learned from sources (whether print, digital, or experiential), but instead analyze that information and those sources. The argument writing anchor standard asks that students are able to support their claims "in an analysis of substantive topics or texts" and that those claims are strengthened by "valid reasoning and relevant and sufficient evidence" (18). Whenever the standards mention evidence, it is then important to also look carefully at writing standards 8 and 9, in the "Research to Build and Present Knowledge" grouping of standards. Standard 8 describes expectations for types of sources and a level of citation across grades and standard 9 asks students to "draw evidence from literary or informational texts to support analysis, reflection, and research" (18).

Standard 8 is easy to follow. In the younger grades students should learn to draw information from "experiences or gather relevant information from print and digital sources" and simply "provide a list of sources" (21). In middle school and high school, this shifts to collecting "relevant information from multiple print and digital sources," being certain to "assess the credibility and accuracy of each source" (44). These older students should also know how to use a "standard format for citation" (44). All clear expectations that, though not always easy to help students in using, one could imagine students attaining.

Now move to standard 9. This standard expects not only that information is derived from literature and informational texts, but that a high level of analysis takes place before bringing that work to writing. We have often jokingly said to one another that this is the standard with twenty standards hidden within it. Literally, this standard asks students to apply all of their grade level reading standards when using source information for writing. Look at writing standard 9 for fourth grade, for example:

a. Apply *grade 4 Reading standards* to literature (e.g., "Describe in depth a character, setting, or event in a story or drama, drawing on specific details in the text [e.g., a character's thoughts, words, or actions].").

b. Apply *grade 4 Reading standards* to informational texts (e.g., "Explain how an author uses reasons and evidence to support particular points in a text"). (21)

In essence it says that to pull evidence from sources and to cite them, you have to first read them well. The writing standards are asking all teachers of writing to draw on good reading teaching, and vice versa (this is a particularly important point for those districts in which there is one reading teacher and one writing teacher and never the two shall meet).

You could think of standard 9 in another way: it is the standard that suggests sophistication for content. When looking at what can sometimes appear as unclear or repetitive descriptors from grade to grade, this standard presses on the content that students are writing about, really upping the bar of what is expected in writing. Compare how fourth graders might include an author's "reasons and evidence" within their opinion writing with how an eighth grader is expected to think about his or her sources (italics added to emphasize new expectations):

a. Apply *grade 8 Reading standards* to literature (e.g., "Analyze how a modern work of fiction draws on themes, patterns of events, or character types from myths, traditional stories, or religious works such as the Bible, including describing how the material is rendered new").

b. Apply *grade 8 Reading standards* to literary nonfiction (e.g., "*Delineate and evaluate the argument and specific claims in a text, assessing whether the* reasoning *is sound* and the evidence *is relevant and sufficient; recognize when irrelevant* evidence is *introduced*"). (44)

Go back, now, and look at the first subskill that writers should be able to draw from literature. These standards may take your breath away, even within one grade. Take fourth grade, for example. It is true that many upper-elementary students will be accustomed to drawing information from literature and nonfiction texts and maybe even synthesizing information from all those texts into amalgamated reports (written in the students' "own words"). These writers, though, might not tend to "describe in depth" a character's thoughts, words, and actions when arguing a point about a book or movie in a review. They are even less likely to be well versed in noticing that informational texts represent varied, distinct points of view so they can be ready to "explain how an author uses reasons and evidence to support particular points" when writing why that author's opinion is true and important in their own opinion essays.

Until you teach otherwise, fourth graders (and even eighth, ninth, or tenth graders, for that matter) will probably not do much more than mention specific authors or sources in in-text references for direct quotes or in bibliographies. The Common Core suggests that students should not just lift quotes from texts and plop them into their opinion and argument writing, but instead analyze their sources of information with more and more nuance, and then use that analysis within their writing. Now, you might ask, "What does this look like?" Unfortunately, again, the exemplar pieces provided in Appendix C do not reveal the level of complexity described here. Below ninth grade, most pieces labeled "argument" or "opinion" are samples of students drawing on experience.

The ninth-grade example, a piece arguing that the book version of *The Boy in the Striped Pajamas* is better than the movie version, is the first instance of more careful reading work leading to writing. In one overtly reading-connected paragraph, the sample reads:

> Characterization is very important to a story and influences how a person interprets the novel or movie, and one important way that the book differs from the movie is how Bruno's mother is characterized. In the movie, she is unrealistically portrayed as an honest woman with good moral values, and is almost as naive as Bruno is about what is going on at Auschwitz. When she discovers what her husband is doing to people at the camp she is deeply disturbed. Mortified by her husband's cruelty, their relationship declines. In contrast, she is a far more sinister character in the book. Though Bruno is too young to understand what his mother is doing, one of the reasons he dislikes Lieutenant Kotler is that, ". . . he was always in the living room with Mother and making jokes with her, and Mother laughed at his jokes more than she laughed at Father's" (162). (57)

The writer goes on to use this analysis of character in both the book and the movie to argue that the book version is more compelling, that in the book, Bruno, the young protagonist, is just as unaware of what is taking place in Auschwitz as he is about his mother's temper and apparent alcoholism. It's a sophisticated move, and a compelling one for teachers to study.

PATHWAYS FOR IMPLEMENTING THE ARGUMENT WRITING STANDARDS ·

The argument writing section of the Common Core has tremendous implications for instruction, the most important of which is just that argument matters. Providing that federal and state budgets for education do not get scrapped entirely in the next few years, the next generation of high-stakes tests will probably emphasize students' abilities to write arguments. But that is not the only reason to take this call for reform seriously. Think of any cause that matters to you. Is it global warming? The growing gap between the rich and the poor? Or violence in video games? Whatever the cause, you probably believe that the world would be a better place if people who care about that cause had the courage and the literacy skills to make their views heard. If young people grow up learning to participate in logical, reasoned, evidenced-based arguments, this will mean that they are given a voice. Our democracy is dependent on an educated, concerned citizenry, exercising the right to be heard.

The Common Core State Standards in argument writing *are* worthy of special attention. We say this knowing full well that the Common Core spotlights more priorities than one could possibly adopt. So why are we emphasizing this priority?

Something dramatic needs to be done to ratchet up the level of students' literacy skills. Consider first the essential but difficult to implement straightaway push toward informational reading. We are all for that. But that reform will not be easy. The work that the Common Core State Standards call for in informational reading is important, but given budgets that have been cut to the bone, such reform will be challenging to implement in a large-scale fashion, starting tomorrow. There are few schools in which classroom libraries brim with informational books that are leveled and that are truly accessible to the real students in those classrooms. As we discussed in Chapter Five, the system of leveling informational books and of matching readers to books is not yet up to speed in most schools.

Reforms in writing instruction, in contrast, take no additional resources; schools *can* right now begin to emphasize writing in general and opinion writing in specific, and we believe this work will empower writers, make learning more active, help vitalize reading, and elicit more civic involvement and engagement.

This being said, although the standards' emphasis on argument writing is highlighted by the writers, the standards will not provide you with clear pathways for proceeding. One option is for schools to retreat to methods of teaching argument that were in fashion hundreds of years ago, when argument was very much a part of classic writing instruction. Sometimes, even, the policy makers who have written the CCSS and others who claim their connections to them seem to suggest as they travel the country that this would be a way to go. We do not think so.

Teachers who want to accelerate instruction in argument writing can draw upon a robust field of knowledge in the teaching of writing. Reinstating the classic emphasis on argument writing need not mean retreating to methods of teaching writing that have long since been discarded. The last thing we need is a return to daily assigned topics or an overemphasis on the content of debates instead of on the skills of argument, the methods of teaching writing that were once commonplace in traditional high school literature classrooms—the ones that produced the opposite of growth and achievement *for all* over the last several decades.

Here are a few ideas, then, that will probably undergird a successful effort to implement the Common Core State Standards in argument writing.

First, consider that when you teach a new and challenging kind of writing, the demands of the new type are complicated enough that it is especially helpful to make other aspects of the writing less challenging. That is, if a teacher's end goal is to teach students to write argument essays, it makes sense that instead of also making the content of that writing challenging—like tackling elements of literature when writing to argue for a particular interpretation of a book—the teacher first teaches students to write argument essays around subjects that are especially accessible to the writers. Give writers a supported arena in which to develop the skills, strategies, and genre knowledge necessary to write the new and demanding kind of text well. Then, once the writers have mastered the writing type, guide them in applying their skills to more remote subject matter. This does not mean there is no place for channeling students to tackle new or unfamiliar ideas, or to dive into work such as that suggested in standard 9; all of this should be included as you plan long term across a unit and a year. Imagine if you were asked to write an essay arguing why one of two texts that address the same theme differently is a more correct point of view—that would be a challenge enough to learn to do. Now consider if you could draw on books or films that you know and love—the project would be altogether different than if you were required to center this work on books you found so tedious you could hardly read them, and so impenetrable you could hardly understand them.

Second, when you teach argument writing, it is helpful to make sure that writers have a variety of opportunities to write in this genre, with some of those opportunities allowing writers to work over both long and short periods of time on a piece of writing, receiving coaching and instruction along the way. That is, a skier learns to ski by the instructor saying, "Watch me," and then demonstrating a move. The skier then skis just to the next rise while the teacher watches. Then the teacher and the student confer, with the skier getting feedback and new instructions before tackling the next portion of the hill. In the same way, it is important that when students learn to write argument essays, they do much of this work in school, with the teacher showing a technique, then inviting students to try it while the teacher watches, and then leading individual or small-group conferences to give feedback and channel writers toward the next step in their writing. In this way, the writing teacher might show essayists how to angle an anecdote to make a point, how to unpack that anecdote in ways that link it with the idea being advanced, how to cite passages from a text and then turn around and mine the passages for their noteworthy features, and so forth. Opportunities to work on this kind of writing should be repeated across even one unit of study, and even other times outside the ELA classroom. In the writing workshop, students should probably vary the time they take to write a draft, with perhaps some draft writing and revision taking a few weeks and some happening in just a day or two. That is, early in a unit of study on essay writing, the essays written by, say, seventh graders might look like the essays written by third graders as they focus more on good structure. Then with instruction and practice, students will begin writing essays that look more like a fifth grader's and so forth as each cycle through the writing process includes more and more sophisticated teaching points. First allow students to practice the skills and strategies of argument writing within a writing workshop, then teach students to draw on the writing skills they develop in that context in order to write outside the ELA classroom. With repeated instruction, practice, and feedback, students will advance along a trajectory of progress.

Finally, as always, instruction in opinion and argument writing should be informed by assessing student writing. In the previous chapter, we mentioned an assessment that the Teachers College Reading and Writing Project has developed in order to help teachers evaluate student progress along a continuum of narrative writing development. The TCRWP has also developed an assessment for opinion and argument writing. For opinion and argument writing, teachers ask students to write an essay about an issue they care about; the same prompt is given to five-year-olds and to fifteen-year-olds. Students have an hour to write the piece; often the youngest do not work that long. In many instances, teachers were skeptical about even asking students to do this writing. "I don't think they'll have a clue what to do," teachers said. Many students did surprisingly well. In an hour, they were able to take subjects that were dear to their hearts—why every family should have a dog, the significance of fathers, the injustice of certain school or family decisions—and write fairly well structured pieces. Some students turned out to be secret experts, who wrote convincingly of the need to recycle, or to use green energy, or to adopt animals from shelters rather than buy them from breeders.

Once students have each produced a piece of writing, we then take the work and assess it against pieces that have been benchmarked, levels 1–12, on our continuum. To do this, we mostly match the piece of student writing against the benchmarked pieces, taken as wholes, but there also are descriptors for many aspects of those pieces, and we keep in mind those descriptors. You'll find, when you do this work, that no one piece meets all the benchmarks, as they are not meant to be met in a single piece, but instead are a set of competencies for a writer to achieve across a year.

The writing continua are enormously helpful for teachers, in much the same way as the Common Core State Standards, themselves. The biggest difference is that the continua we at the TCRWP have developed are based on a progression of student work, so the predictable problems are delineated, providing teachers with guidance with some of the hard spots of teaching argument writing.

When you do this work together in a community, you'll find colleagues sharing insights and expertise. In Seattle, for instance, middle school coaches and teachers gathered hundreds of pieces, selected ones they thought clearly demonstrated CCSS benchmarks, and published these as a set, with annotations such as those the Common Core presents in Appendix C. In the end, it was the work they did together that was more valuable than the collection—the thought collaborative of teachers studying student work raised the level of student achievement.

The Reading and Writing Project has also developed performance assessments for every grade level, K–8, that were vetted by several members of Achieve, the organization that manages PARCC, that could assess research-based essays. In these assessments, students are asked to read a small collection of short texts with varied complexity levels (one text is a documentary video) on a topic. The texts advance conflicting ideas on the same topic, and the warrants behind the texts vary. After summarizing the texts, each student is asked to decide on his or her own view about the question at hand and to write an argument supporting that view, using the texts as part of the argument. For tenth graders, students not only read the texts given to them but also must (in short order) search for and use an additional text on the topic.

This assessment was given to thousands of K–8 students in New York City schools and was being given before and then after a unit of study on argument writing that was being taught alongside a parallel unit on reading across informational texts. When we piloted this assessment, we were not surprised to find that very few students were writing, reading, and thinking at the CCSS levels. Few incorporated more than the most perfunctory amount of textual evidence, and when they did, they didn't even seem aware that the texts they had just read presented contradictory views on the topic. They simply saw those texts as rather like storehouses of facts, any one of which could be loosened from the larger text and plopped into the students' essays.

When the teachers who used the assessment then taught the unit on argument writing (which followed the suggestions in this chapter) and a parallel one in reading workshop on informational reading, lo and behold, in a matter of weeks, students began to think of the texts they were reading as coherent arguments and to notice the claims and supports in those texts. They began to note, too, the authors of those texts, and when evidence was readily available suggesting the validity or bias of the authors, they began taking this into account. Human beings want to learn, and this was clear open ground for new learning.

A Final Thought About the Opinion and Argument Writing Standards

The standards writers laud argument as hugely important, essential—the heart of college and career readiness. Our suggestion is to take the call for rigorous, thoughtful opinion and argument writing instruction seriously. But also, don't panic. Now is not the time to grab at anything stamped with "Achieve CCSS Argument Standards!" nor is it the time for a return to classroom methods of the past that yielded little results for all learners. Build upon strengths, take research on best practices seriously, and continue to revise your curriculum with your students' work in front of you, not a textbook or mandate. The opinion and argument writing standards will be achieved by teachers making smart, student-based choices in their classrooms.

CHAPTER NINE

THE CCSS and COMPOSING INFORMATIONAL TEXTS

In order to understand the Common Core State Standards for informational writing, it is helpful to pause for a moment and think of all the informational writing that students do in school. Although research reports and nonfiction books spring to mind right away as examples of informational writing, this category of writing is far broader than that. Informational writing could include entries, Post-it notes, and summaries written in response to reading, as well as lab reports, math records, and descriptions of and reflections on movies, films, field trips, books, interviews, and experiments. Under the umbrella of the broad category *informational writing*, one finds the answers students write in response to questions teachers ask—whether those are oral questions, questions found at the end of textbook chapters, or questions discussed in class. The CCSS authors highlight how broad this type of writing is in Appendix A:

> Informational/explanatory writing includes a wide array of genres, including academic genres such as literary analyses, scientific and historical reports, summaries, and précis writing as well as forms of workplace and functional writing such as instructions, manuals, memos, reports, applications, and résumés. (23)

In essence, the skills required to write informational texts are not just part of a writing type; they are tools for thinking about subject areas, books, and life.

Let's clarify something before diving much further into this topic: Although the Common Core seems to call for a larger percentage of the writing that students do across a day to be informational writing, the truth is that for teachers in grades K–5, the Common Core asks only that one-third of that writing be informational writing. That is, writing in science and social studies and art and computers all adds up to that chunk of informational writing time. And then, for grades 6 and above, the informational writing standards are presented both as ELA standards and within separate standards tailored more to science and social studies teachers. Therefore, English language arts teachers need not throw out their entire curriculum and replace it with all informational writing all the time. For most teachers, this is no referendum.

We start this chapter, then, by noting that while spokespeople for the CCSS interpret the standards as placing new demands on schools in the area of informational writing, for many schools the new aspect won't be the expectation of students devoting a greater percentage of their writing to texts that fall under the broad umbrella of informational writing (it is already commonplace for one-third of the writing that students do to be informational writing). Rather, the new element will be that the Common Core expects students to apply the same standard of craftsmanship to informational writing as they would to short stories, memoirs, essays, and poems. That is, traditionally, when students wrote about reading (whether literature or history or science), the goal has been for them to show that they have done the reading, gleaned the necessary knowledge, and developed some thoughts. Prior to the arrival of the CCSS, it wasn't usual for their informational writing to be held up to the same standards as essays and short stories. Now, a reader of the CCSS can quickly see that across all three kinds of writing, there is a parallel emphasis on elaborating with specific information, details, examples, and citations or quotes, and on synthesizing those details and specifics so they are linked to and controlled by key ideas or themes.

The standards require that writers of informational writing, like writers of fiction and essays, be given opportunities to rehearse, draft, revise, and edit. Although an emphasis on writing process instruction is not explicit in the Common Core informational writing standards, in order to create well-structured, coherent, carefully crafted informational texts, young writers will need to be taught how to make and revise plans for a text, to study mentor texts, to draft and revise and embellish and rethink a text, and to seek and use feedback from teachers and peers. And not only will they need to do all this within a writing workshop, where the focus is on developing skills as writers, but they'll also have to transfer these skills to the content areas, doing this work on the run, quickly, in the service of discipline-based learning.

We believe there are several aspects of the informational writing standards that merit further attention:

- The parallel structure of the standards for all three writing types presents a helpful learning progression.
- It is especially important that information writers learn to sort, categorize, and elaborate on information.
- Writing about a topic extends learning about it—and therefore, informational writing belongs in and also beyond the ELA classroom.

We end by looking at some pathways for implementing these standards.

THE STANDARDS' PARALLEL STRUCTURE FOR ALL THREE WRITING TYPES PRESENTS A HELPFUL LEARNING PROGRESSION

Once you have studied anchor standards 1 and 3—the argument and narrative writing standards—it is not hard to understand anchor standard 2. Standard 2 parallels the standards for the other two types of writing. For example, just as standard 1a describes what an *argument* writer should do at the beginning of a text and standard 3a, what a *narrative* writer should do at the beginning of a text, standard 2a describes what an *information* writer should do at the beginning of a text. Similarly, standards 2b, 2c, 2d, and so on describe what an information writer should do in the middle and end of a text. The expectations are further aligned because, for example, in all three types of writing, writers are asked to elaborate. The method for elaboration differs a bit between the different kinds of writing—writers are asked to use details and dialogue when writing stories, reasons and examples when writing arguments, and facts and citations when writing informational texts. Still, in all three types of writing, writers are asked to elaborate, and in all three types of writing, writers are expected to write an ending that refers back to earlier sections of the text, creating closure.

Then, too, whether you are studying the narrative, argument, or informational writing standards, the standards need to be read horizontally, across the grade levels. The standards do not ask teachers at any one grade level to work miracles. Instead, they ask that all the teachers across a student's schooling work together to support a progression of skill development. That is, if a fourth-grade teacher looks only at the expectations for fourth grade, that teacher is bound to panic. But if that teacher looks at what students are expected to be able to do in kindergarten, first, second, and third grades, the incremental developments asked of fourth graders will seem entirely reasonable.

To understand this, start by reading what is expected of kindergartners. You'll think, "That's no big deal." Next, read the first-grade standards, pen in hand, underlining *just the new words* that describe the *added* work that a first grader should be expected to do. Again, you'll probably say, "Well if kindergartners could do that, then this is totally doable." Continue this process with the second-grade standards. We've demonstrated this work here with italics:

- **Kindergarten**: "Use a combination of drawing, dictating, and writing to compose informative/explanatory texts in which they name what they are writing about and supply some information about the topic." (19)
- **First Grade**: "Write informative/explanatory texts in which they name a *topic*, supply some *facts* about the topic, *and provide some sense of closure.*" (19)
- **Second Grade**: "Write informative/explanatory texts in which they *introduce* a topic, *use* facts *and definitions to develop points*, and provide *a concluding statement or section.*" (19)

As you move up to third grade, you'll notice that this is the grade when skill sets begin to appear in list form (this is true for argument and narrative as well). But these substandards, or subskills, do in fact build upon the earlier grade levels. Now, we've italicized the new words in third grade.

- **Third Grade**: "Write informative/explanatory texts *to examine* a topic *and convey ideas and information clearly.*
  a. Introduce a topic *and group related information together; include illustrations when useful to aiding comprehension.*
  b. Develop the topic with facts, definitions, *and details.*
  c. *Use linking words and phrases* (e.g., also, another, and, more, but) *to connect ideas within categories of information.*
  d. Provide a concluding statement or section." (20)

Reading horizontally in this way, highlighting just the new words that appear at a grade level, you can climb the staircase of Common Core expectations for informational writing. Note that the specifics of the prior grades can help you adjust your teaching so that you are able to assess a student's entry point in this trajectory and to bring that student along a progression of work. Note also that if you look *above* your grade level, you can see what's coming next—realizing that you don't, in fact, have to tackle all those skills yet, but that you have a horizon to reach toward.

Implicit in the standards is the expectation that students will need time, strategies, and explicit instruction that will enable them to plan, develop, draft, and revise their work, no matter what type of text they are writing. Across all three types of writing, students are asked to plan the structure of their writing; to work on introductions that, as students get older, preview what is to come; to work on elaboration, and to do so in ways that become more deliberate and bound to conscious purposes as students move up the grades; and to work on endings, which, as students progress, are expected to hold whole texts together by harkening back to what has already been said. The point is that writers will be working on these skills not only in informational writing, but in all the writing they do.

It Is Especially Important That Information Writers Learn to Sort, Categorize, and Elaborate on Information

If you ask teachers or students to read a published nonfiction text and to notice aspects of the text that are especially admirable, both teachers and students are apt to point to a passage containing vivid language or evocative detail or lush, descriptive language. It is highly unlikely that either a teacher or a student will say, "What I really admire about this text is its structure." For many people, the structure that undergirds a text is invisible just as the foundation and the bearing beams in a house are invisible. The Common Core standards for informational writing remind us that although these structural features are often invisible, they are nevertheless as crucial to an informational text as the foundation and bearing beams are to a house. The Common Core standards expect that as children grow up, they learn to use structures to construct their texts, and they emphasize the link between structures and ideas—hence the emphasis on "logical structures." The CCSS also expect that writers of informational texts will read informational texts differently, noticing the infrastructure to those texts, thinking about the structural decisions that other authors have made.

The Common Core asks teachers and students to turn informational texts—their own and those written by others—inside out so as to study the designs that undergird the texts, noting the parts and the ways that the different parts have been brought together.

Let's look more specifically at the staircase of expectations for organizing informational writing. In the primary grades, students are simply expected to name a topic and "supply some facts" (19). The grade 1 sample from Appendix C, "My Big Book About Spain," illustrates this, and can be contrasted with the grade 3 exemplar "Horses" to understand the progression students are asked to go through between first and third grades.

The first-grade piece (which has created quite a stir among first-grade teachers because it is surprisingly long) shows a writer who has a topic, the country of Spain, and who lays out facts like a tossed deck of cards. Here is an excerpt of this piece, with the original spelling:

Spain has bull fights and I would want to see one. I think Spain looks like a upside down hat. In some of the fiestas the people are loud. Some of the fiestas are even beautiful and colorful. Spain has alot of diffrent people. (11)

Now look at an excerpt of the third-grade piece, "Horses." Remember that in third grade, children are now expected to "group related information together" (CCSS 2010a, 20).

Horse Families
A mother or female horse is called a mare. A father or male horse is called a stallion. A foal is a baby horse.

Markings
A star is a little white diamond on the forelock. The forelock is a horses forehead. A race is a white line down the middle of the horses face. A blaze is kind of like a race but wider. . . . (CCSS 2010d, 18)

You can see that the simple skill of organizing—categorizing, sorting, and then presenting in a deliberate order—is important. The expectations for organization progress just a bit between third grade and fourth grade:

- **Grade 3**: "Introduce a topic and group related information together." (CCSS 2010a, 20)
- **Grade 4**: "Introduce a topic *clearly* and group related information *in paragraphs and sections*." (20)

Starting in fifth grade, the standards ask that the writing contain a "general observation and focus" and that the information be grouped *logically*. This new expectation is extended in middle school when writers must organize not only facts and information but also ideas and concepts—which is no small expectation!

- **Grade 5**: "Introduce a topic clearly, *provide a general observation and focus*, and group related information *logically*." (20)
- **Grades 6, 7, 8**: "Introduce a topic; organize *ideas, concepts, and information*." (42)

In high school, writers are expected to do even more organizational work, putting all concepts under one larger and cohesive umbrella:

- **Grades 11–12**: "Introduce a topic; organize *complex* ideas, concepts, and information *so that each new element builds on that which precedes it to create a unified whole*." (45)

In the Common Core, structure takes precedence over other qualities of informational writing. These standards are brief, so the decision to highlight the way writers progress along a continuum in their abilities to organize information and, eventually, ideas, is deliberate and represents a decision to deemphasize other aspects of informational writing. We agree with the emphasis on structure, especially when writing informational texts, because this type of writing requires that the structure be created—planned, drafted, revised—based on an understanding of the content and an attention to readers who become students of the topic.

Indeed, structure is foundational to writing informational texts. It is as if the writer of an informational text has an enormous armload of information, and that information, like a pile of laundry that has just been taken from the dryer, needs to be sorted. Just as laundry can be sorted according to different principles—his, theirs, and mine, or "needs to be ironed" and "doesn't need to be ironed"—so too, a topic can be sorted in multiple ways. The same basic information about soccer could be categorized by roles on a team, or by famous players and what they do, or by the eras in the history of the sport, or by what one journalist learned when beginning to understand the game and then after becoming embedded in a team. To complicate matters, a book on soccer will probably combine several different organizational structures. For example, in the grade 7 piece that is included in Appendix C, "A Geographical Report" (42), all the specific information within each subsection of the text is organized to support a larger concept about vernal pools. Take, for instance, the section explaining the importance of vernal pools:

- First, there is a paragraph that forwards the idea that vernal pools are easily disturbed (and it is implied that we then need to be careful around them: "Even grazing or off road vehicle use in the summer, when pool species are dormant and people could think they are just a dry hole, can damage them" [43]).
- Then the next paragraph advances the idea that surrounding mounds are equally fragile.
- Then the author makes the point that there is a need for more study of these ecosystems.
- Finally, the emphasis shifts to the fact that a large assortment of species lives in these pools (implying that these animals, too, are fragile and worth protecting).

A structure such as this emerges from the knowledge itself, so knowing about and thinking about information is a big part of writing informational texts well.

It is important to note that skilled information writers carefully select and craft the details they choose to include—and they often elaborate on them by explaining domain or technical language, providing multiple types of evidence, making comparisons, and using text features to link connected details to ideas. The CCSS expect that our students can independently include a variety of types of evidence, such as facts, definitions, and quotations, and use language that connects that evidence within sections and across an entire piece.

Essential here, though, is that students do not simply learn *what* to include, but *how* to craft their writing so these details become a cohesive part of it. We have all read dry pieces packed with facts, in which the writers seem to border on plagiarism. A student meeting college and career readiness standards will not write like this:

> The sun is a sphere consisting of plasma. It is 1,392,000 kilometers in diameter. Its mass takes up 99.86% of the solar system. Its surface temperature is 5,505 degrees Celsius.

That student will, instead, know how to gather essential details, elaborate on them when needed, and embed them within his or her writing so that the writer can accurately and clearly express ideas to readers:

> The sun is the largest object within our solar system, so large, in fact, that its mass accounts for 99.86% of it. Everything else—our earth, our moon, enormous Jupiter and Saturn and the other major planets, all of the planets' moons, asteroids, and other materials—makes up less than 0.2%. Imagine a glass full almost to the rim with water. The sun's mass is the water and everything else in our solar system makes up just the small line of molecules forming the surface tension on that glass.

While the informational writing standards detail the development of structure with a fine-tooth comb across grade levels, the document is less clear on how elaboration of ideas grows across grades. In kindergarten, students are asked to "supply some information" (19). In first grade this becomes "facts about the topic." And in second grade it becomes "facts and definitions." This incremental listing of elaboration strategies explodes in fourth grade, when students are expected to be able to use "facts, definitions, concrete details, quotations, or other information and examples" (20).

In "A Geographical Report" and other pieces in Appendix C of the CCSS, information writers use a variety of details, crafting them in such a way that they flow together. For example, in "A Geographical Report," there are lots of details, but a reader is not apt to feel as if all these details have been added just for details' sake. Reading these exemplar texts, you won't find yourself thinking, "Oh, there is a direct quote, and there is a definition, and there's another direct quote." Instead, the effect is similar to that of watching a PBS special or a documentary on National Geographic. The voice of the writer is that of an informed and passionate researcher:

> It does not take much to disturb a vernal pool. Even grazing or off road vehicle use in the summer, when pool species are dormant and people could think they are just a dry hole, can damage them. Most are disturbed by grading and flattening of their habitat, or by breakup of the impervious layer. With just flat land there would be no depressions for vernal pools to form; what would form would be "vernal mud." With no impervious layer the water would just sink into the ground, and would be there only for a short period of time, not enough for wetland plants.
>
> The mima mounds have to be protected too. If the watershed for the pools is changed, the condition of the pools changes. If there isn't enough water from runoff, then all plant or animal life in them disappears, because they need enough moisture at the right time, to live. If there is too much water, then the pool may turn into another kind of wetland, such as a bog.
>
> Although people have begun to study them, there is still a lot to learn. One thing scientists know is that they are a part of a larger environment. Many animals travel from other areas to feed on plants or animals, or drink from the vernal pools. For example, water fowl from many other places will stop at the pools to eat the fairy shrimp and snack on the plants. (43)

This piece shows not only a careful, coherent structure but also an attention to elaboration. As students progress in their development of informational and explanatory writing, the CCSS expect that we teach them not only to develop more purposeful structures, but also to use more and more varied details. In the end, it is the combination of elaboration, structure, and meaning that creates well-crafted informational texts.

Writing About a Topic Extends Learning About It—and Therefore, Informational Writing Belongs in and Beyond the ELA Classroom

There is a considerable body of research that suggests that when teachers pay attention to informational writing, teaching its processes and craft and then creating multiple opportunities for students to transfer those skills to the informational writing they do in every subject, the result is not just better writing, but also better learning. Doug Reeves, for instance, has shared research that shows students' outcomes in science, even on multiple-choice tests, improve when they have opportunities to write in social studies and science. "[W]hen students write more frequently and when they score higher on writing performance assessments, their scores on multiple-choice tests improve" (2000, 6). And interestingly enough, the payoff—better learning—seems to take place not only when a student writes about a particular topic, but also when the student studies *any other* topic. That is, a student who has learned to write about lots of topics ends up developing habits of mind (such as the habit to sort and organize information and to grow big ideas that link the specifics) and using them to grasp new material on a subject, whether or not the learner is actually *writing about* that subject.

This is not all that surprising. Return to the grade 7 informational text from Appendix C that we have been looking at—but think, as you read, about the learning (not the writing) that is reflected in this piece:

Vernal pools have a large assortment of rare and exotic flora and fauna (plants and animals). Five of them are on the federal list of endangered species, and one more is a candidate for listing. The plants and animals in vernal pools are unusual because they have only developed recently compared to other changes in evolution. As scientists study the pools more intently they are finding more and more unknown species. There are temporary pools in other places around the world, but California's vernal pools are different because of their long drought phase, which causes the plants and animals to adapt to the climate. They go into a dormant phase. For example, fairy shrimp lay eggs before the drought which hatch when it gets moist enough to be active. Some plants, in a short period of time, develop seeds; others appear to die out, but quickly spout again from the rain. Many of these species cannot survive outside vernal pools, and some are "endemic" (species found only in a very restricted geographical area). (43)

Teachers who have looked at this piece have often said, "Our students' informational writing—in social studies, in science—is *nothing* like that. Our students are more likely to just plop facts onto the page." The problem may be, then, not a writing problem, but that the students don't know enough about what they are writing about. You can teach students to use writing to extend their learning. Here the student has clearly digested information and incorporated it into his or her own ideas, through the act of informational writing.

In Appendix A, the CCSS authors claim that "with practice, students become better able to develop a controlling idea and a coherent focus on a topic and more skilled at selecting and incorporating relevant examples, facts, and details into their writing" (23). And they also become better at "differentiating different types or parts; comparing or contrasting ideas or concepts; and citing an anecdote or a scenario to illustrate a point" (23). We agree, although we would probably restate that claim like this: With direct, explicit instruction and with extensive opportunities to practice and to receive and use feedback, students become better able to do this work.

The important thing to realize is that teaching students to do the intellectual work involved in writing about a subject—any subject—means teaching them to organize and elaborate on facts and ideas, to decide on priorities, to look at information through different lenses, and to entertain questions and see the answer to one question as leading to yet more questions. This is vastly different work than the work that many students do when writing informational texts, which sometimes involves little more than moving information from one place to another. What is interesting is that when learning to write *from a place of expertise*, students are at the same time *becoming* more expert on the topic they are writing about. This, of course, teaches students that experts in any field are not just born "smart"; instead, they do the work to collect known facts, they think through those facts enough to organize them into bigger concepts, and they apply that system of organization to new scenarios (Bransford, Brown, and Cocking 1999). As the NAEP writing framework, which the CCSS explicitly draw on, says, "informative writing *helps both the writer and the reader to learn new ideas* and to reexamine old conclusions" (italics added; National Assessment Governing Board 2007, 13).

This, of course, has happened to us over the course of writing this book. Although we approached the task of writing about the CCSS confident that we had studied and thought about and taught these standards until we had developed expertise, the act of writing about them has amplified our command of the topic exponentially. Each time we returned to revise a draft, it forced us to reexamine the document, and our current ideas, and develop a more nuanced and more organized understanding.

The fact that writing well involves the same intellectual work that constitutes learning well means, then, that the act of writing informational texts actually supports strong learning habits. Numerous studies have linked the processes students learn while writing informational texts to the way they learn information through reading, lecture, and media, and ultimately to their success in school. The Center for Performance Assessment (2003) conducted research on 130,000 students in 228 schools in which more than 90% of students were eligible for free or reduced lunch and were ethnic minority students. The researchers looked at schools in which 90% of these students met or exceeded high academic standards. The study found that these extremely successful schools were characterized by an emphasis on informational writing across the school day. The Carnegie Corporation's report *Writing Next* (Graham and Perin 2007) also cites a high correlation between student achievement and many skills found in informational writing.

PATHWAYS FOR IMPLEMENTING THE INFORMATIONAL WRITING STANDARDS

Throughout this book, we have emphasized that adopting and understanding the Common Core Standards are not easy, but that the real challenge lies in accelerating students' achievement so that their work matches the ambitious levels set forth by the standards. Although the informational texts that have been included in Appendix C of the Common Core are nowhere close to as well written as the narrative and even the argument pieces, it is clear from the descriptors that the informational standards are still high, especially when one considers that students will be expected to produce writing that meets these standards even in discipline-based classes where, presumably, they will be given few of the support structures that are commonly found in writing workshops.

So the question stands: How do we recommend schools proceed if the goal is to be sure that all (or most) students are able to write informational texts such as those described in the CCSS?

The first answer must be to acknowledge that the jury is out on this question. If anyone announces that there is a clear pathway by which students across whole schools, districts, cities, and states can be assured of reaching the Common Core's levels of achievement in informational writing, he or she is wrong. If the pathway were clear, we'd see whole cities, whole states, where it was commonplace for seventh graders to produce essays such as the one on vernal pools quoted earlier, and that is not the case.

On this issue, as on most issues related to implementation, knowledgeable people in positions of authority will suggest different pathways, leaving educators in a position to make their own decisions. The curriculum writers associated with PARCC, for example, have created rough-draft templates of curriculum that suggests students be assigned to write answers to teacher-generated questions on texts the whole class is studying. This suggested curriculum for informational writing does not appear to allow for explicit instruction in writing, but instead assumes that informational writing skills will develop as a natural by-product when the emphasis is on learning about a content area.

Our experience suggests otherwise. If assigning writing on the questions the teacher or the textbook has raised were a method that produced high levels of writing, then it seems to us that schools everywhere—and especially secondary schools—would all be filled with students who *independently* could produce high-level informational essays. This is just not the case. Then too, if assigning writing, alone, led to high levels of achievement in writing, the profession of teaching would be filled with teachers who were confident as writers of informational texts. After all, many of us remember participating in this sort of instruction when we were students in traditional high schools of long ago. Our teachers would assign a question—What does the imagery in Hamlet suggest? or What sequence of events and underlying tensions led to the start of World War II?—and we'd write compositions in which we attempted to answer that question. Afterward, we'd receive a grade—one for content and one for mechanics in English classes—and move on to another day, another assignment. Of course, many schools continue to teach writing in this fashion, but the schools (and colleges, too) that produce stellar writers are far more apt to embrace a writing process approach to teaching writing.

Like most educators who are regarded as leaders in the field of teaching writing, members of our organization, the Teachers College Reading and Writing Project, have been profoundly affected by the revolution that occurred in the field of teaching writing. The approach that we use is built on the premise that just as there is a scientific method that is fundamental to scientists, so too, there is a writing process that is fundamental to writers, and this process is flexible enough to be applicable whether one is writing a poem or an editorial or an informational book. People who join us in advocating for the writing process approach to teaching writing have worked for decades to develop a tool kit of methods for teaching students effective writing techniques and strategies. These methods for teaching writing are all based on beliefs that counter the approach that asks teachers to assign students text-dependent questions to answer through writing. The writing process approach, in contrast, suggests that writers benefit when they can make some choices about their topics so that they can select angles, ideas, audiences, and forms. This approach to teaching writing is also based on the belief that students will invest themselves most in their writing if they can write on topics they know and care about, for real audiences of readers who do not know the same information as the writers know and who therefore stand a chance of wanting to learn from the writers. Above all, this method suggests that writers need demonstrations, guided practice, assessment-based instruction, and feedback—the same sort of teaching that readers receive—and need, even more than this, opportunities to practice by engaging in lots of writing and receiving feedback on that writing.

Educators who care about developing informational writing skills are left to decide whether to use the Common Core as an incentive to rally teachers into the work-intensive, time-intensive, and rewarding work of teaching writing, including informational writing, within writing workshops. This choice means that educators will rely upon all the tools, strategies, knowledge, and accumulated experience of an entire field of writing practitioners and researchers—and presumably will use these shoulders to reach for yet higher horizons.

We obviously advocate this approach. That is, we believe that educators need to bring all they know about teaching writing to the challenge of helping students write informational texts well and to do so in ways that help students grasp the many commonalities of effective writing across every genre. But we believe this with the following five qualifications.

First, alongside a focus on informational writing within the writing workshop, it is also important to promote and use informational writing across the entire curriculum. Although we absolutely believe that students need opportunities to write informational texts of many types—nonfiction books, feature articles, investigative research reports, journalism, and the like—within the writing workshop, once students have practiced some informational writing skills and strategies in the supportive context of a writing workshop, they need to apply those skills and strategies to their discipline-based studies, engaging in the same sorts of informational writing within their science and social studies curricula.

Second, we encourage educators to select an approach to teaching the writing process that draws on research to accelerate achievement. All writing instruction is not equally designed to promote accelerated progress. Some advocates of a writing process approach emphasize, above all, student ownership, suggesting that it is best if students within a workshop are each writing a different kind of text, a kind that matches that particular student's intention. This interpretation of a writing workshop probably promotes engagement, but we are not convinced that it is the most efficient means for promoting achievement. Hattie's research (2009), based on findings from 300,000 studies of achievement across a wide range of fields, suggests that learners achieve when they are working toward crystal clear and ambitious goals that they can envision, and when they receive feedback in the form of medals and mission—feedback that acknowledges the progress a learner has made and explicates next steps toward the goal. When teachers of writing draw on this research, this means that instead of inviting students to explore the whole wide world of informational writing, emulating whatever aspects of published texts appeal to them, teachers help learners work toward more of a crystallized shared goal. In a unit on informational writing, this means the teacher would decide on the specific sort of informational writing that he or she would rally students to produce, and then help writers work toward that specific goal. This is not, then, the sort of writing workshop where students collect a giant pile of informational writing of all shapes and sizes, and the teacher encourages each student to select a mentor text from all those choices and then study that mentor for qualities the student appreciates. Instead, the teacher settles upon an image of informational writing that he or she believes is within reach for the class, and the class as a whole talks about and annotates and analyzes the text, coming to understand how it is made. We furthermore suggest teachers prioritize texts in which there is a logical and visible infrastructure, perhaps shown through a table of contents that supports logically structured chapters, perhaps shown through headings and subheadings and topic sentences.

Third, we are convinced that teachers need to study student work, taking cues from instances when student writing improves and instances when it does not. The teacher needs to note what it is that seems to help students improve not only that day's text, but their capacities to write well another day on another topic. In Chapters Seven and Eight, we described a continuum of narrative writing and of argument writing that schools linked to the TCRWP have used to track students' progress as writers; not surprisingly, we have developed a similar continuum for tracking students' progress as information writers. These continua allow teachers to examine ladders of exemplar pieces—in this case, in informational writing. Of course, the Common Core includes some student writing in Appendix C, and that writing has been enormously helpful, but the samples of informational writing in the Common Core represent a scattering of grade levels, and do not in any way suggest the sorts of progress a student might make within a grade (which is, after all, what any given teacher cares about most). The pieces we assembled in our continuum for informational writing show a progression of development, with level 6 being a bit stronger than level 5 and a bit weaker than level 7. As you and your colleagues sit together to study the pieces in our continuum or in a similar one that you can make yourselves, you might find it helpful to consider the following:

- what you notice about how students progress in their use of structure and their knowledge of the genre
- what you notice about how students progress in their use of elaboration and development of ideas
- what you notice about how students progress in their decisions about meaning and purpose, and the ways these decisions link with the above skills

The texts in our continuum build directly from those of the CCSS but provide a more detailed progression. Our point is not so much that teachers across a school should all track student progress along levels 1–15 of our continuum for informational writing, but more that a school will benefit from collecting informational writing that is regarded as exemplary for a particular age of child, lining these pieces up, and then creating opportunities for students to produce on-demand drafts of completely independent informational writing so that teachers and students can then say, "This writer produced, today, a piece of informational writing that more or less seems equivalent to our level 6 benchmark." The teacher and the writer can then both work to help that writer be able to, another time, produce a piece of writing that more closely matches the level 7 benchmark pieces. Meanwhile, if one teacher at the grade level is regularly moving students up several levels, then other teachers across the grade will want to talk with and observe that teacher, asking, "What are you doing that is supporting such progress?"

Fourth, the informational writing standards, like all the writing standards, support the notion that teachers need to align instruction across the grades, making sure that at every grade, students are given strong instruction. We suggest that teachers take the broad term of *informational writing* and divide it into more specific genres, teaching different genres at different grades. Perhaps in first grade, students will write lab reports about their science investigations, in second grade, all-about books, in third grade, informational nonfiction chapter books, in fourth grade, investigative feature articles, in fifth grade, research reports, and so on. The powerful thing about such a progression is that if all those teachers recognize that ultimately, they are all teaching informational writing, and that the differences between the work at one grade level and another are nowhere near as important as the similarities, then the teachers can deliberately stand on the shoulders of the previous grade's instruction.

Finally, when working with informational writing, it is important to plan not only up and down the grades, but also across all the disciplines within a grade. Study the expectations of the informational writing standards, both the standards themselves and, when appropriate, the exemplar pieces in Appendix C (keeping in mind, as we have discussed in several chapters, that some pieces more accurately display what seems to be the intended rigor of the standards than others). Then, sit down as a grade level team, bringing your yearlong scope and sequence as well as the curricular maps for any unit that could contain informational writing. Almost certainly that is *every* unit in the content areas and specific ones in English language arts. There is a bit of art to not just repeating the work of others, but building upon that work. You might look at your curriculum as a matrix rather than a time line, including the content-area subjects, and sit down together with a simple, empty grid: the columns are months of the year (September, October, November), the rows are each subject area (ELA, science, social studies). Together talk out which point in the school year each subject area could take on an informational writing project. Next are two examples, the second a bit more rigorous than the first, though both are examples of how successful schools plan for the child, not just the subject area.

Option 1
- English language arts decide to do an "expert project" informational book unit in November, in which students write on subjects of their own choice.
- Social studies, though students will have been doing bits of informational writing all year, will focus instruction more purposefully on the skills of informational writing in December, writing about the Civil War, both traditionally and perhaps digitally.
- Science will use informational writing to develop and showcase students' knowledge of climate change in January or February.

And so on.

You and your colleagues could stop there, as even that sort of planning is already making huge strides toward the writing-across-the-curriculum approach the CCSS expect. You could, however, go a bit further, considering not just *what* to teach, but *which skills* of informational writing to address. In your early planning, before students arrive, it is helpful to talk this work out. As the year goes on, these plans should be revisited to be certain they match the needs of your students.

Here's option 2, with more skill-focused planning:

Option 2
- The English language arts "expert projects" in November will emphasize structure and elaboration.
- The social studies Civil War projects in December will emphasize research and citation.
- The science climate-change essays in January or February will emphasize the incorporation of visual information.

And so on.

These are just examples, of course—you could angle the units differently. The point is that here the teachers are thinking through how they can extend prior teaching, and they are divvying up some of the finer skills, so that no individual teacher has to teach everything in one unit of study.

What a gift to be able to say in March, "I know that in science you learned to diagram, chart, and graph information in compelling ways. As we embark on this new writing in social studies, let's think about how we can use that knowledge here as well, as we bring our focus over to structures for longer, more developed informational writing."

A Final Thought About the Informational Writing Standards

Adoption of the informational writing standards, like the entire CCSS document, could either become a point of stress and contention or a point of profound growth of the school community. Every subject area has traditionally involved some level of informational writing, and a study of this topic, including standards expectations, student work, curricular plans, and teaching methods, has the great potential to bring an entire school community together. In the Teachers College Reading and Writing Project schools, both elementary and secondary, that have made a mission of bringing all subject area teachers into the literacy fold, students do not bounce from one kind of expectation to a different kind throughout the day; they are less likely to hear that essays go like *this* in the morning but go like *that* in the afternoon. Instead, students experience repetition and a common culture, and for the staff, the tough work of teaching becomes even more shared. Teachers share plans, pass classroom anchor charts from room to room, and look at student work as a community, not in isolation. Schools can transform into open-door, collaborative communities, and the study of the informational writing standards is one powerful road to that end.

CHAPTER TEN

OVERVIEW of the SPEAKING and LISTENING and of the LANGUAGE STANDARDS

WHAT DO THEY SAY AND WHAT DOES THIS MEAN FOR US?

Rounding out the Common Core State Standards are the final two strands, the speaking and listening standards and the language standards. In the same elegant way the standards can, at times, make connections across the reading and writing strands, so too do these final sets of expectations mirror and support development of the other standards. So, while these additional sets of standards could feel like *more* work to do, when thought of as a piece of the larger whole, the expectations begin to feel more like a part of, not an add-on to, your instruction. This is not to say the standards are wholly perfect and completely easy to manage, as we discuss later in this chapter, but they do make clear attempts to help teachers connect all of the various dots.

In this chapter, we give an overview of the last two strands of the Common Core ELA standards: speaking and listening, and language. For both strands of standards, we provide

- a broad overview of the standards
- emphases we find within the anchor and grade-specific standards
- implications for instruction

SPEAKING AND LISTENING STANDARDS

Speaking and listening will be a strand in any set of English language arts standards. Glance at any state standards, though, and it will probably seem as though the speaking and listening standards weren't written for the occasion. Instead, it will look as if just before all the standards were released, someone found *another* state's speaking and listening standards and then did a fast job rewriting them so they could be plopped into your state's standards. Or perhaps the speaking and listening standards were just retrieved from the prior generation of standards and dusted off.

The Common Core State Standards in speaking and listening aren't as marginalized as is typical in state standards. The authors of the CCSS came to the work with some notable energy, ideas, and beliefs. These standards make a statement—one you may agree with or may not, but at the least, you should not overlook them. After all, talk (and the reciprocal work of listening) matters.

Overview of the Anchor and Grade Level Standards

Let's take a look at the structure and organization of the standards. First, there are only six anchor standards, instead of the ten found in the reading and writing strands. Here, the anchor standards are divided into two groupings: "Comprehension and Collaboration" and "Presentation of Knowledge and Ideas." The first grouping focuses on students talking together in order to understand texts; the second grouping focuses on students making oral presentations:

Comprehension and Collaboration

1. Prepare for and participate effectively in a range of conversations and collaborations with diverse partners, building on others' ideas and expressing their own clearly and persuasively.
2. Integrate and evaluate information presented in diverse media and formats, including visually, quantitatively, and orally.
3. Evaluate a speaker's point of view, reasoning, and use of evidence and rhetoric.

Presentation of Knowledge and Ideas

4. Present information, findings, and supporting evidence such that listeners can follow the line of reasoning and the organization, development, and style are appropriate to task, purpose, and audience.
5. Make strategic use of digital media and visual displays of data to express information and enhance understanding of presentations.
6. Adapt speech to a variety of contexts and communicative tasks, demonstrating command of formal English when indicated or appropriate. (CCSS 2010a, 22)

A glance at the high school grade level standards of the "Comprehension and Collaboration" grouping will tell you that the expectations for using language to collaborate around texts and topics are high. The goal seems to be that the intellectual conversations that sometimes take place in seminars at our most academic colleges become commonplace in K–12 classrooms. By high school, for example, the CCSS want all students to be able to listen to an editorial or watch a news report, noting places where the author's reasoning isn't persuasive or where the logic seems faulty. Implicit in this is a belief that academic literacy requires students not just to take in facts but also to position themselves as critics and reviewers in relation to the texts they read and hear. They are expected to borrow, learn from, reshuffle, clarify, qualify, and evaluate the work of others.

As students progress from one grade to the next, the standards expect incremental progress toward these ambitious goals. By the end of elementary school, the grade level standards suggest that students can keep a small-group book conversation going without needing nudging from the teacher. They can hear lulls in the conversation and jump in to say, "What we are mostly saying, so far, is . . . ," and "Could it be that there is another way of looking at this? Maybe it is. . . ." In the world of the CCSS, fifth-grade students can talk with a partner or a small group about a book, coming prepared to the conversation with notes, perhaps jotted on Post-it notes. A fifth grader can read over a classmate's writing, too, and make notes to talk through some key points with the writer: "Does the lead start too far from the action?" or "I can't picture this setting. Read the draft aloud?"

The "Comprehension and Collaboration" anchor standards call for students to become skilled collaborators; the "Presentation and Knowledge of Ideas" anchor standards call for students to become skilled presenters and critics of other people's presentations. Students are expected to be able to make oral reports that are organized to support main ideas and themes and that include audio and visual supports.

This emphasis on visual supports brings us to another point. The CCSS open up the definition of speaking and listening to include nonverbal forms of communication and viewing and interacting with multimedia. Anchor standard 2, which states that students should be able to comprehend and analyze various forms of media, partners with anchor standard 5, which asserts that students should be able to use media in presentations. For the CCSS, then, *speaking* is broadly defined to include nonverbal communication and *listening* to include interacting with multimedia. This makes sense, as the skills one might use to thoughtfully listen or carefully speak are replicated when interacting with these other forms of communication.

The Speaking and Listening Standards Hint at Questionable Curricular Methods

Anchor standards become especially important in the speaking and listening standards because, for some reason, it is in the speaking and listening grade level standards that the authors of the CCSS seem to shift between detailing expectations (as standards should) and suggesting instructional methods and structures. Not surprisingly, the primary authors of the standards, who are businesspeople, attorneys, assessment experts, and policy leaders, are less versed in classroom instruction than in expectations, and therefore sometimes their suggestions for classroom instruction will seem a bit unusual. Following are some of the most prominent curricular suggestions the CCSS promote in the speaking and listening standards. Our point is not that we disagree with these ideas for how a teacher might teach, but only that these are instructional decisions. These are not performance expectations but curricular suggestions.

The CCSS suggest that teachers assign students roles in discussions. Many teachers have learned that students do not need official roles in order to be successful in conversation. Harvey Daniels, famous for suggesting students in literature circles assume roles such as the illustrator or the encourager, revised that suggestion in his later books. He did this because he saw that the roles reduced student interactions instead of increasing them. Giving students specific roles within a small or large group is not necessarily a problem, but that decision should be left in the hands of teachers.

The CCSS require that students evaluate every speaker's point of view, use of evidence, and rhetoric. The standards emphasize that listeners should learn to take the stance of evaluator toward the speakers they encounter in school, examining points of view, reasoning, and rhetoric. The authors of the standards seem to have something in mind when they suggest that from fourth grade on, "speakers" will make arguments that students will evaluate: they seem to be channeling classrooms toward formal debate. While we agree with the merits of debate, we question if this is necessarily the only or even best way for a teacher to enrich a student's speaking and listening skills.

The CCSS prioritize the argument genre in formal presentations. The grade level standards ask students to present information orally in a style that supports clear comprehension, using various forms of media fluently to enhance presentations. What we find remarkable is that starting in fifth grade the only type of oral presentation the standards expect is argument, despite the fact that students will be expected to write in at least three genres. While it is easy to see the advantages of oral arguments, it is also easy to see advantages for oral presentations in other genres. Oral presentations have strong connections to student writing, so it would make sense that if students are asked to *write* stories, that they also be asked to *present* their stories.

The Speaking and Listening Standards Expect Students to Engage with Various Forms of Media

In previous iterations of state standards, some states have made minor nods to technology and media in the classroom, usually suggesting students learn to word process or that they view and discuss movie adaptations of books. The CCSS take a bold stance, making an expectation across grades that students become savvy consumers and creators of media. Anchor standards 2 and 5 address the importance of developing students who are adept in both understanding and creating multimedia. The CCSS authors state:

> New technologies have broadened and expanded the role that speaking and listening play in acquiring and sharing knowledge and have tightened their link to other forms of communication. Digital texts confront students with the potential for continually updated content and dynamically changing combinations of words, graphics, images, hyperlinks, and embedded video and audio. (CCSS 2010a, 22)

This is a major shift for many classrooms, especially those where the one computer in the back of the room is used only to type and print final drafts.

Your heart may be pounding a bit if you feel the learning curve for new technology is daunting. Before you throw your hands up, we would like to point out that the CCSS leave fairly wide open what technology you will use and when. The CCSS, while pushing very firmly and clearly for students to develop strength and fluency with multimedia elements, provide less definition of just which elements in particular.

Anchor standard 5, which requires students to "[m]ake strategic use of digital media and visual displays of data to express information and enhance understanding of presentations" (2010a, 22), may feel like it calls for the largest shift in instruction. The expectations for using multimedia ramp up more quickly from grade to grade than the expectations for viewing it. Second graders are expected to "create audio recordings of stories or poems" and "add drawings or other visual displays" to their presentations (2.SL.5; 23). By high school, students are expected to "make strategic use of digital media (e.g., textual, graphical, audio, visual, and interactive elements) in presentations" (9–12.SL.5).

The standards are clear that all of this is not technology for technology's sake. Instead, the authors were mindful to connect every use of technology to a purpose. Here are those second-grade and high school standards again, now with their entire text. Notice in the portions we've italicized that the adding of technological elements is connected to the students' purpose for writing or creating:

> Create audio recordings of stories or poems; add drawings or other visual displays to stories or recounts of experiences *when appropriate to clarify ideas, thoughts, and feelings.* (2.SL.5)

> Make strategic use of digital media (e.g., textual, graphical, audio, visual, and interactive elements) in presentations *to enhance understanding of findings, reasoning, and evidence and to add interest.* (9–12.SL.5)

The standards do not expect that you merely bring students into the computer room and let them play around with YouTube or let them have fun cutting and pasting images from Google. Instead, the CCSS suggest you embed the use of media in your instruction just as you might embed a novel.

Anchor standard 2 describes expectations for how students listen, view, and interpret various kinds of media (including pieces read aloud). Listening to media, in the elementary school grades, appears no different than listening to a person. That is to say, teaching students to be active listeners is similar whether they are listening in conversations or listening to a television newscast or a video clip. In second grade, students should be able to listen to or view media clearly enough that they can "recount or describe key ideas or details from a text read aloud or information presented orally or through other media"; third graders should be able to retell the "main ideas and support details"; fourth graders should be able to "paraphrase portions"; and fifth graders should be able to "summarize" what they heard or viewed (23, 24). The teaching you do around active listening can apply to both conversations and viewing media.

In middle and high school, the standards shift the role of listening or viewing media to one that seems to match the active analytic work students are asked to do in the "Craft and Structure" grouping of the reading standards. In the reading standards, students are asked to analyze how word choice affects meaning, how claims are developed with evidence, and how an author crafts a text to reveal a point of view. The second speaking and listening anchor standard expects students to do much of the same work with media. In early high school, for example, this standard reads:

> Integrate multiple sources of information presented in diverse media or formats (e.g., visually, quantitatively, orally) *evaluating the credibility and accuracy of each source.* (9–10.SL.2, emphasis added; 2010a, 50)

What seems clear from these standard 2 expectations and the ones from standard 5 is that the CCSS call for infusing a study of media into students' school year as part of an effort to develop more thoughtful communicators and consumers of information.

Implications for Instruction

Here is our suggestion: Pay attention to these standards. The good news is that you will probably be able to implement the speaking and listening standards, unencumbered by other people's expectations or the pressure of high-stakes tests. If you implement the CCSS in speaking and listening, this will motor major reforms in both reading and writing.

Regard these standards as an invitation to explore, invent, and pilot some new ideas. Do not think of these standards as a form of micro-control, as a mandate for how you must organize a curriculum of speaking and listening, but as a call to action. If you invest yourself in developing a powerful curriculum of speaking and listening, your work will have far-reaching implications for many areas of the curriculum.

Plan for rigorous, curricular-aligned conversations between students. Of course our students talk—they talk all the time—but development in this standard set, as well as getting the most you can out of it to support the other standards, requires purposeful interactions. In classrooms that work with the Reading and Writing Project, teachers make strategic decisions about conversations between students and see these as developing across the year. In a Common Core–aligned reading curriculum, for example, you might begin the first part of the year with students in reading partnerships, teaching these same-book pairs to do the work described in the "Comprehension and Collaboration" grouping of standards. With only one other peer to interact with, students can quickly build muscles for coming prepared to conversations, engaging with a listener, posing and answering questions, and so on. Students can also talk with partners in order to reach the reading standards. Think of the power behind one peer asking another, "What in the book made you think that?" The work partners do in conversation spills over into each individual's independent work. At the same time that these partnerships are developing, teachers tend to begin whole-class conversations from shared read-aloud texts, in which they teach students to develop ideas together in pairs, groups, and ultimately whole-class discussions. The whole class can practice digging into larger themes or studying authors' decisions while also learning the habits of positive interactions. Then later in the school year, students often move from book partnerships to book clubs, groups of three to five students reading the same text, taking what they have learned in pairs and in class conversations and working more independently, refining the skills they have been practicing all year. While this is an example of how the speaking and listening standards overlap with students' reading work, similar overlap takes place in the development of writing, as students have conversations with one another about their writing development.

See your role as facilitator, not leader, releasing ever greater responsibility so students can meet the CCSS goal of independence. Once you have made instructional decisions about speaking and listening, about where you will plan to develop this work within your curriculum, the next place to look is at your role. The standards are in no way suggesting that you be the arbiter of all conversations in your room; in fact, they are saying quite the opposite. They suggest that your role is to help students develop the skills of collaboration and presentation so that ultimately they can enact these skills independently, without your help. So your plan should be, just as it is with reading or writing, to demonstrate strategies, teach conversational moves explicitly, and then allow students to experiment, flub up, and fix up. Your teaching is then strategic, responding to greater patterns of need that bubble up across your classroom.

Think across students' entire day and year when considering how to handle some of the more overreaching suggestions of the standards. When it comes to the curricular suggestions the standards seem to be making, remind yourself that literacy does not develop only during reading and writing instruction and also that the standards are intended to be end-of-grade expectations, not descriptions of how every task must be devised for students. In other words, allow yourself and your colleagues to enjoy the invitation to experiment with oral presentations that involve "diverse media," as this is an intriguing suggestion, but do not be fooled by anyone into believing that now *every* time students wish to present ideas they must do so in a formal speech complete with poster boards or video clips. The same holds true for the implied suggestion that students should be involved in debate-style conversations. Again, teaching students to listen thoughtfully to other speakers, while also piecing apart the evidence for their claims, is a useful skill, though you may want to think about where in their day and year a little or a lot of this work may be most fun to study. Is it in social studies during the study of America's founders? Or perhaps in science, taking time to teach students to support the reasons why their hypothesis is correct? Making just a few of these debate opportunities available during the year will probably pay off.

For more about developing strong speaking and listening skills, you could use the series Units of Study for Teaching Reading (Calkins et al. 2010) as a resource.

Now that we have taken a closer look at the speaking and listening standards, and how this work will impact the high levels of reading and writing work also required of your students, let's turn to the language standards.

LANGUAGE STANDARDS

The language standards are written to suggest that language work should not be taught in isolation. Rather, language work should be interwoven across the day, so that conventions, vocabulary, and craft moves become a seamless part of the reading, writing, speaking, and listening already under way in your classroom.

Often, schools adopt exceedingly detailed and massive scope and sequence plans that lay out every precise bit that students must master at each grade level. Commas need to be controlled by third grade, semicolons, by fourth, and so on. The list goes on and on and on, and always, mastery is required. The expectations are often so excessive that it almost seems they have been written to be ignored. And indeed, just as most schools have these scope and sequence documents, many teachers ignore them. In this regard, the Common Core language standards help matters.

Overview of the Anchor and Grade Level Standards

There are six anchor standards for language, divided into three categories:

- "Conventions of Standard English," which outlines expectations for grammar
- "Knowledge of Language," which outlines how students should apply their knowledge of language as craft choices in their writing and speaking
- "Vocabulary Acquisition and Use," which outlines expectations for vocabulary

The language standards streamline what teachers need to focus on at different grade levels. One way in which the CCSS authors keep the standards lean enough to be achievable is by not unrolling a particular skill across time, thereby avoiding a situation in which the later grades have longer and longer lists to attend to. Instead, each grade mostly has its own particular set of skill expectations. There are several messages these language standards clearly convey.

First, by separating conventions into their own set of standards, the CCSS convey the sense that some students will be strong at other areas of writing—the structure, organization, and focus of their pieces, for example—while still needing work on grammar and punctuation. The need for development in one area does not necessarily connect to a need for development in the other.

Second, the language standards emphasize the applied use of skills in context—the *use* rather than the knowledge of rules.

Third, the authors also state that decisions about what is and is not acceptable vary over time and are amenable to change (11–12.L.1a). For instance, while someone might say that one can never begin a sentence with the word *and* or that paragraphs always have three to seven sentences, the authors of the standards are aware that conventions are determined by society, and they change over time.

And fourth, the emphasis across all the anchor standards is quite clear: the focus should not be as much on correctness as on increasing complexity of writing as students develop their skills in crafting language.

These points are revolutionary to many, and so we unpack them more in this chapter, the following two in particular:

- The CCSS break from traditional practice by recommending that language work be embedded in use of skills.
- The CCSS writers place an emphasis on using language skills as craft choices, not as separate from them.

The Language Standards Emphasizes Context-Embedded Language Work over Memorization of Grammar Rules

If you skim quickly through the words that begin each of the grade level language standards, you will quickly notice a pattern emerging. The CCSS use verbs such as *use*, *form*, and *produce* rather than *explain* or *define* when describing what students should know and be able to do with language. These standards describe students who can work with conventions and extend their vocabulary while writing and speaking, but do not first require students to define what they are doing or the words they are using. This is a marked departure from instruction that demands memorization of terminology and rules.

To be more specific, look at anchor standard 5, describing students' understanding of nuances in word choice, including the use of figurative language. There is no emphasis on students needing to define the differences between simile and metaphor; instead, when those terms first appear in grade 4 and grade 5, the focus is on interpreting the meaning of simple metaphors. This doesn't mean that a teacher won't give youngsters the labels that can help them talk and think about the sophisticated work they might be trying to do with language, but the CCSS stress *using* rather than *defining*.

This same emphasis is true in anchor standard 1, which describes the conventions students should master. The grade 4 standard reads:

Use modal auxiliaries (e.g., *can*, *may*, *must*) to convey various conditions.
(4.L.1c; CCSS 2010a, 28)

In an instance such as this, the CCSS do not channel fourth-grade teachers to tell their students, "Today we are going to learn modal auxiliaries," and then give them worksheets for practicing this and ask them to copy the definition from the board. The important thing is to teach students to think conditionally, rather than to define the term *modal auxiliaries*.

This emphasis on skills over memorization is also clear through the CCSS authors' direction toward "flexible use" of strategies within many of the standards in this set. For instance, the grade level specifics for anchor standard 4 explicitly state that students should be able to determine the meaning of unknown or multiple-meaning words and phrases by "choosing flexibly from a range of strategies" (CCSS 2010a, 29). The larger goal here is not memorization of vocabulary words; it is instead that students be able to independently choose from a range of skills to figure out meanings on their own. This is another fundamental shift in practice for many schools. Here, for example, is the third-grade list of strategies for anchor standard 4:

Determine or clarify the meaning of unknown and multiple-meaning word [*sic*] and phrases based on *grade 3 reading and content*, choosing flexibly from a range of strategies.

a. Use sentence-level context as a clue to the meaning of a word or phrase.

b. Determine the meaning of the new word formed when a known affix is added to a known word (e.g., *agreeable/disagreeable, comfortable/uncomfortable, care/careless, heat/preheat*).

c. Use a known root word as a clue to the meaning of an unknown word with the same root (e.g., *company, companion*).

d. Use glossaries or beginning dictionaries, both print and digital, to determine or clarify the precise meaning of key words and phrases. (29)

For students to meet this standard, they must be aware of these different strategies and, more importantly, be able to apply them when appropriate. The CCSS authors imagine a student, when confronted with a challenging word or phrase, who does not just make one attempt and move on but instead tries several attempts to arrive at a viable approximation.

The fact that the standards' expectations are for students to use grammar conventions with flexibility is in line with current research. For example, the Carnegie Corporation's *Writing Next* (Graham and Perin

2007), one of the largest recent meta-analysis reports of writing pro-grams and approaches, reviewed numerous quantitative research stud-ies on practices in writing and student achievement. In summarizing their research, the authors devote a section to what they title "A Note About Grammar Instruction." They write:

> Grammar instruction in the studies reviewed involved the explicit and sys-tematic teaching of the parts of speech and structure of sentences. The meta-analysis found an effect for this type of instruction for students across the full range of ability, but surprisingly, this effect was negative. This negative effect was small, but it was statistically significant, indicating that traditional grammar instruction is unlikely to help improve the quality of students' writing. Studies specifically examining the impact of grammar in-struction with low-achieving writers also yielded negative results (Anderson 1997; Saddler and Graham 2005). Such findings raise serious questions about some educators' enthusiasm for traditional grammar instruction as a focus of writing instruction for adolescents. (21)

While this meta-analysis concluded that systematic teaching of parts of speech and sentence structure does not yield effective results, the re-searchers did find that alternative procedures, such as sentence com-bining, are more effective than traditional approaches for improving the quality of students' writing. It seems fitting, then, that the CCSS assert that the study of language should be woven into students' authentic work, our next topic of discussion.

The Language Standards Promote Language as a Tool to Make Powerful Craft Moves

Bring to your mind a great speech, perhaps of a president or leader, or think of a writer you admire, maybe a novelist or a columnist. The topics the writer handles pull you in, and then it is the craft choices that writer makes that grab you and hold you. You are pulled to the works of Martin Luther King Jr. because of their impact on our nation's thinking, and you admire and study those works because they are artfully written. You don't admire him because he properly conjugated verbs or because he used conjunctions appropriately; instead it is the choices he made as he crafted the language that appeal the most.

Anchor standard 3 states: "Apply knowledge of language to understand how language functions in different contexts, to make effective choices for meaning or style, and to comprehend more fully when reading or listening" (CCSS 2010a, 25). This standard makes up the entire "Knowledge of Language" grouping. This standard suggests that writers choose the right figurative language, or best complexity of sentences, or even just the right words, to have the greatest impact on an audience. Specifically, the standard suggests that writers draw from all the other language standards when crafting their writing. What feels so important about this is that yet again the CCSS are elevating the teaching of literacy well beyond that of NCLB's belief that writing and reading were more or less equated only with phonics. The standards recognize that great writers and speakers use conventions and word choice as tools to reach their audiences. Perfectly formed sentence structure is not the only ingredient, but an equally important one to polished prose, strong arguments, and clear presentations.

As you read the grade level specifics of this anchor standard, several things will quickly become clear. One is that the asterisks that were present in anchor standards 1 and 2 are also present here. When reading, then, do not look only at your grade level; be sure to look at the previous grades for topics that you are expected to carry forward. Second, you will notice that in most instances the expectations laid out in the "Knowledge of Language" grade level standards complement those found in the "Conventions of Standard English" standards. For example, the grade 8 standard for anchor standard 1 in the "Conventions of Standard English" grouping states that students are expected to "[f]orm and use verbs in the active and passive voice" (1b) and "[f]orm and use verbs in the indicative, imperative, interrogative, conditional, and subjunctive mood"(1c) (52). Similarly, the "Knowledge of Language" standard for grade 8 also focuses on verbs: "Use verbs in the active and passive voice and in the conditional and subjunctive mood to achieve particular effects (e.g., emphasizing the actor or the action; expressing uncertainty or describing a state contrary to fact)" (3a; 52).

In third grade, a focus on nouns, verbs, and adverbs in the convention standards leads to the expectation that students should "choose words and phrases for effect" (3a; 29) in the "Knowledge of Language" standard. In fifth grade, expectations for the use of conjunctions is reiterated in the "Knowledge of Language" standards by a writer's ability to "expand, combine, and reduce sentences for meaning, reader/listener interest, and style" (3a; 29). The same is true for overlaps in other grades, with each stating that the mastery gained should not just be memorization of terms or rules, but the ability to apply that knowledge "for effect," "for interest and style," or "to achieve particular effects." Choosing words for effect and sentence combining for meaning, interest, and style are examples of powerful craft moves and ways in which writers use grammar flexibly to engage readers.

This is an essential piece of the Common Core State Standards' progressive move to promote the active use of skills, not just rote memorization. Students are expected to see conventions and vocabulary not as solitary points, but as a part of their larger literacy toolbox.

Implications for Instruction

We suppose a key aspect of implementing the language standards is to first step back and breathe. In our experience with schools around the country, we've found that sometimes well-meaning professionals, be they classroom teachers or principals or even district leaders, hear the term *grammar* or *vocabulary* and jump straight for methods they experienced as students themselves, even though those methods have historically led to only a percentage of the class reaching a level of proficiency while far more others fell behind. Equally, it is important to breathe when the workbook publishing representative comes knocking at your door and wants to show you the newest "Common Core–aligned" series of ditto sheets.

Hold, instead, to what is clearly the intent of these standards: to teach students the skills and strategies that will make them independent word solvers and writers and speakers who are able to apply meaning, structure, elaboration, and conventions as craft moves to their writing and speaking. The ultimate teacher is you, responding to the needs of your students as they progress along this continuum of expectations, not a series of prepackaged words or disconnected activities.

Here are a few ideas to support your implementation of the language standards.

Begin with assessment. By this chapter we sound like a song stuck on Repeat. One easy place to look is at your students' on-demand writing assessments (see Chapter Eleven for more on this) and/or writing pieces from their most recent standardized test if you have those available and they are not more than a month or so old. You could attempt to read on the level of detail across each student's piece, holding your grade level's CCSS as a list of criteria next to each sample, to check which standards the writer appears to have control over and which he or she does not. You could, however, just as easily skim, looking for broader patterns for students and for your entire class or classes. It is especially helpful to think within three categories, identifying what level the majority of your class is at for different skill sets: (1) general mastery of a skill with only occasional typos, (2) awareness of a skill but with misuse and perhaps confusion regarding its use, or (3) no apparent awareness of a skill. These categories can help you devise which areas you need to spend more whole-class instruction on, which areas are more appropriate for small-group or one-on-one instruction, and equally which areas you might spend more days on than others.

Teach the language standards in connection with the writing, reading, speaking, and listening work you are already asking students to do. The CCSS are clearly saying a resounding *no* to some practices that teachers describe thus: "I start by teaching sentence structure and students work only on sentences, then paragraphs, and then later in the year they are ready to write long compositions." Instead, the CCSS see all areas of literacy as developing in tandem. Consider the point that the language standards are separate from reading, speaking and listening, and writing. This is key in that they are intended to cross over all areas (a clear command of academic English makes you better at all of these areas) and also clearly indicates that one area is not more important than the others. Equally significant is how each area develops across grades. Even in kindergarten the writing standards are not suggesting you wait until students know how to use periods before starting to write. Instead all things are developing at the same time.

Know that when students take on new, more challenging work, sometimes the strategies they knew before fall back a bit. Carl Anderson has talked about the fact that in all aspects of writing, strategies students have mastered may slip when they learn new skills. He uses this analogy: If I asked you to ride a bike around the room right now, probably most of you could; you might wobble at first but you would get the hang of it again. Now, if I asked you to ride a bike around the room while juggling, your formerly proficient bike riding would completely fall apart as you focused more of your attention on not dropping the beanbags. This is important to have in mind as you work with your students on these skills. Do not lose complete faith when their paragraphs dissolve under the weight of a new type of comma usage. Remember, too, to build from strength. If you jump right to what looks like the most challenging work, your students will find little success and your efforts will take longer than you intended. Often, backing up a bit to get a good start helps all learners have enough steam to overcome the tougher bits.

Plan ahead for repetition of skills. As with everything, one time is not enough. All skills take repeated practice, repeated failures, repeated fix-ups, and repeated tries even past the point of proficiency to make the skill automatic. Mary's book *The Power of Grammar*, written with Vicki Vinton (2005), describes one possible way of laying out grammar instruction across the year, so that during each unit of study skills are repeated at less and less scaffolded points. For instance, a concept first taught during the editing phase of the writing process can be repeated in the next unit of study when students first begin drafting, and then again in the unit after that during collecting within student notebooks.

Be current on research on best practices and be prepared to both teach others and defend your practices to those who are trying to sell you something. We cited research on grammar instruction earlier in the chapter that is striking in the way it aligns with the expectations of the CCSS on more integrated teaching of language within the literacy areas. The body of research on learning vocabulary seems to agree on three instructional areas, equally progressive and in line with the standards:

1. Students need immersion in rich oral and written language, meaning they need to read a lot and be involved in literate conversations in literacy-rich classrooms.
2. Students do need some words to be specifically taught, but teachers should select words that cross many content areas and will be current and visible in students' experience. This is because for these explicitly taught words to stick, a student must experience them across contexts at least twelve to fifteen times on average. This means words of the week will not have lasting power unless they are attended to

in reading, writing, speaking, and listening across the day as well as across the year.

3. Students need to learn how words work and gain the sense that words can be formed from other words and that words with similar spellings often—though not always—can have meanings derived from one another. This means that vocabulary practices should not just be centered on word lists but should teach students to be active word solvers.

CHAPTER ELEVEN

CCSS–ALIGNED ASSESSMENTS FUEL WHOLE-SCHOOL REFORM

Education is at an important crossroads. The development and adoption of the Common Core State Standards have created forward momentum, but the future is still to be determined. Seymour Sarason, author of *Revisiting "the Culture of the School and the Problem of Change"* (1996), has noted that all too often educators plunge into the work of school reform as if zeal and passion alone can guarantee success. The mission of improving schooling is not a new one, and it is important to bear in mind that over the past forty years, there have been countless attempts at school reform that have aimed to improve teaching and learning—and mostly, those attempts have failed, leading to stagnant or declining levels of student achievement (Tyack and Cuban 1997; Elmore 1995; Goodman 1995; National Commission on Excellence in Education 1983). Recent reforms spurred on by No Child Left Behind legislation were no exception. Despite hundreds of millions of dollars of new funding for reading instruction, reading scores in the United States flatlined. There is a new spin to the current reform: the rallying cry is now for *all* children to become college and career ready. There is no doubt that the mission is a worthy one, but if things are to be different this time—if the promise of the Common Core is to be actualized—educators need to learn from our history of reform efforts and break new trails toward the horizon before us. How many years of failed efforts at school reform will we endure before we pause long enough to study the research on school reform and use the past to inform the present?

To emphasize the complexity of this school reform work, Michael Fullan points out, "If people were given a literal choice of 'change or die,' do you think most people would choose change? If you said yes, think again" (2007, 2). Fullan goes on to cite an article written by Alan Deutschman in which he writes, "'What if a well-informed, trusted authority figure said you had to make difficult and enduring changes in the way you think and act, and if you didn't you would die soon?' The scientifically studied odds that you would change, he writes, are nine to one against you" (2). This is why 80% of the health care budget is consumed by treating illnesses related to smoking, eating, drinking, stress, and insufficient exercise. Dr. Ed Miller from Johns Hopkins says, "If you look at people after coronary-artery bypass grafting two years later, ninety percent of them have not changed their lifestyle" (Deutschman 2007, 4). Deutschman points out that the only situation under which heart patients improved was when the call for them to change their habits was accompanied by weekly support groups. "If the threat of death does not motivate people who are ill [to change], what on earth is going to motivate teachers to change?" Fullan asks. He answers, "deep engagement with other colleagues and with mentors in exploring, refining, and improving their practice as well as setting up an environment in which this not only can happen but is encouraged, rewarded, and pressed to happen" (65).

Rufus Jones, the great American Quaker, once said, "I pin my hopes on the small circles and quiet processes in which genuine and reforming change takes place." This principle needs to guide any effort to align instruction in a school to the Common Core.

At the same time that we know we must focus intense attention and support on small teams of collaborators within and around our schools in order to make true reform happen, we also know that we cannot turn away from the high-stakes tests and culture of assessment that is a reality in today's schools. Even while we focus on building a culture that supports change, we know that to date, tests are the tail that wags the dog. They matter. And, although tests have always mattered, because people are increasingly attaching rewards and sanctions to scores and regarding them as a barometer for measuring the success or failure of a teacher, a principal, a superintendent, and a state, they matter more now than ever. Furthermore, when assessments are sound, we want them to matter; assessments need to inform and fuel not only our teaching but our school reforms. Assessments, at best, will give us crucial information, information we need about what exactly is working—and not working—for our students' education.

That is to say, any school reform effort must be deeply connected to the learning culture of the school, the collaboration of its teachers and school leaders, and also assessment—the true understanding of where our children are in their learning process and of what they need in order to progress.

Any one focus alone will not bring about the reforms we need most. In this chapter, then, we discuss first steps toward creating a culture and context for making meaningful school reform; then, we consider past, future, and current assessments and their relationships to the Common Core.

FIRST STEPS TOWARD CREATING A CULTURE AND CONTEXT FOR MAKING MEANINGFUL SCHOOL REFORM

Setting the stage for whole-school reform involves taking a few principles to heart:

- Don't interpret the CCSS as a mandate to shoehorn more stuff into an already overcrowded curriculum.
- Choose priorities, drawing on the school's strengths.
- Implement the selected reforms fully and seriously, then learn from that process and extend it to new areas.

Don't Interpret the CCSS as a Mandate to Shoehorn More Stuff into an Already Overcrowded Curriculum

The first thing to learn from research is that shoehorning more and more and more new programs and new initiatives into the crowded day is not apt to be an action that will take a school to Common Core levels of achievement. We say this because most school leaders' first instinct when they think about aligning their school to the Common Core is to add this or that new component to the curriculum: perhaps this time, the new work will involve a new emphasis on nonfiction text sets, perhaps on research projects, perhaps on high-tech publishing, argument writing, writing across the curriculum. . . . Yes, the standards justify work on all of those topics and a score of others, but the real work of the Common Core is not about curricular compliance; it is about accelerating student achievement. And for this to happen, schools need to build the ongoing systems of continuous improvement that make learning—on the part of students and teachers alike—part of the culture and infrastructure of the school.

Research, experience, and common sense all combine to tell us that the best way to lift the level of teaching and learning in a school is not by adding yet more "first-draft" teaching into the school day. Fullan draws on decades of school reform study when he says, "The main problem in public education is not resistance to change, but the presence of too many innovations mandated or adopted uncritically and superficially on an *ad hoc*, fragmented basis" (1993, 23). He adds, in *Change Forces: The Sequel* (1999), "The biggest problem facing schools is fragmentation and over-load. It is worse for schools than business firms. Both are facing turbulent and uncertain environments, but only schools are suffering the additional burden of having a torrent of unwanted, uncoordinated policies and inno-vations raining down on them from external hierarchical bureaucracies" (40). Right now, the Common Core looms above most schools, like a giant rain cloud, ready to release just that torrent of unwanted, uncoordinated policies and innovations that Fullan describes.

Our first suggestion to school leaders, then, is to guard against re-sponding to the Common Core with a knee-jerk reaction to add a host of new programs, each of which bears the label of Common Core. It is easy to add new programs—for decades, American schools have been character-ized by a constant stream of new, new, new, but the results haven't been all that impressive.

Choose One or Two Priorities, Drawing on the School's Strengths

The far more important and more challenging work is that of engaging teachers in the effort to accelerate student achievement. The best way for a community of teachers to do this is to study what teachers across the school are already doing that matches the priorities of the Common Core, and then to consider ways to invest far more deeply in a few of those al-ready ongoing initiatives, bringing more teachers into that work and help-ing everyone work with greater levels of fidelity. Then together, teachers across the school can reap the gains in achievement that are associated with doing something really well.

Currently, we know from a careful study by Nye, Konstantopoulos, and Hedges that "the variance due to differences among teachers [within a school] is substantial in comparison to the variance between schools" (2004, 247). This study goes on to articulate something that most of us al-ready know: encouraging teachers within a school to observe each other, to plan together, and to adopt shared teaching methods can dramatically improve teaching and learning in a school. Good practices in one classroom can become schoolwide shared practices. This work can ratchet up the levels of teaching and learning in a school while establishing schoolwide systems for diffusion of good ideas. Meanwhile, it can also build a culture of high expectations and professional study.

Imagine a school deciding that one of the defining characteristics of the education it offers all students will be that every K–6 teacher will assess the level of text difficulty that each reader can handle with 96% accuracy, fluency, and comprehension, and will help readers read a huge volume of within-grasp books. In such a school, teachers can all rally children to work with deliberateness and resolve so as to be able to access an ever wider span of books. By tracking students' progress up the ladder of text difficulty, and communicating with parents and the principal and next year's teachers about that progress, that school can create a system that scaffolds reading anchor standard 10. The good news is that research shows that the capacity to handle grade level complex texts, more than progress along any particular skill trajectory, provides students with successful school experiences.

Of course, the school could embrace entirely different goals. For example, perhaps one of the defining characteristics of the school is that every teacher up and down the grades embraces writing to learn, using writing to engage students in categorizing, ranking, comparing, predicting, questioning, connecting—in short, in thinking—in response to the information, ideas, and texts that they encounter throughout their days. Or perhaps the school embraces a spiral writing curriculum in which each teacher teaches two units of study on opinion, informational, and narrative writing, with those units designed to build on each other. The school might go further and use a shared continuum of touchstone pieces as a measuring scale for noting the level of work that each student can produce with independence in each of those types of writing, allowing teachers to track student progress and to develop interventions to intercede when a student is not progressing as hoped.

A school could embrace any one of those defining principles or a host of others, and of course, it could also embrace a combination of such principles. Either way, there is evidence to show that achievement accelerates when schools offer a coherent instructional approach, one that brings teachers in a school together and allows one year's teaching and learning to build upon the next.

But in order for all (or most of) the teachers in a school to go beyond giving mere lip service to the shared practice, a school leader will need to alter the mind-set some participating teachers may have that professionalism means autonomy. Dick Elmore, one of the nation's foremost researchers of school change, has often warned against this viewpoint. He lamented, "Educators equate professionalism with autonomy—getting to use their own judgment, to exercise discretion, to determine the conditions of their own work in classrooms and schools. In fact, professionalism outside of school is exactly the opposite of this definition. Professionals gain their social authority, not by exercising autonomy, but by subscribing to an externally-validated body of knowledge" (2004, 3). In a truly professional school, people visit each other's classrooms in order to identify and adapt best practices. Planning is collaborative, and every teacher draws on—and eventually, contributes to—a knowledge base that is bigger than any one individual. This does not mean that teachers do not need to think critically or make sound judgments based on their classrooms and their students—they do. It means that this thinking and reasoning does not occur in a vacuum. It is the result of excellent teachers opening the doors of their classrooms, creating an environment where not just one classroom, but an entire school, benefits from shared best practice.

To implement the Common Core, then, identify the strong teaching practices and innovations that are already present in your school, looking especially for the practices that could lift the level of learning not only in one discipline but across many (as is almost invariably the case for work on reading and writing). Keep in mind that researchers have suggested that 20% of what a school is doing makes 80% of the impact; one of the reasons schools rarely improve is that schools are rarely willing to give up anything so as to extend those high-impact practices. Think: What might those high-impact, CCSS–aligned practices be in your school? Of course, it takes capacity to develop capacity, and the good news is that you will be able to leverage those who are already doing this work to mentor those who need more support.

Think also: What resources do you need to take effective methods wide, deep, and high? You don't want to rally the school around a shared endeavor that isn't apt to pay off for all involved, because your larger goal is not just that the practice becomes shared but also that teachers across the school have a positive experience as they work together to go from good to great. That is, the real goal is for people at the school to learn how to learn together and, in doing so, to learn how to become a school where professionalism involves recognizing, implementing, and improving upon high-impact teaching practices rather than about individual teachers going their own way, oblivious to everyone else.

Implement the Selected Reforms Fully and Seriously

Doug Reeves (2010) of the Leadership and Learning Center recently illuminated the relationship between innovations and achievement in a study of innovations in two thousand schools. Reeves found, first, that many schools are flooded with a constant stream of new initiatives, few of which are implemented with any degree of rigor or with sustained attention over time. He furthermore found that innovations that are implemented with low and medium degrees of fidelity have no effect on achievement. In contrast, those that are implemented with 90% fidelity can have an extremely high effect on achievement. Reeves' findings are logical—after all, an innovation, a reform initiative, can affect achievement only when it has the power to alter behaviors, to change something, to constrain. And, if an innovation is disregarded or bypassed every time it chafes a bit, the result is a bit like being on a diet until one sees an eclair.

Of course, once a school has enjoyed working as a learning community to implement some innovations with high degrees of fidelity, then that school will be in a position to take on other innovations as well. As we mentioned in Chapter One and have discussed throughout the book, the Common Core State Standards absolutely spotlight the importance of higher-level comprehension skills; informational reading; writing argument, informational, and narrative texts; writing across the curriculum; content literacy; vocabulary development; progress up the ladder of text complexity; reading like a writer; and debate—among other skills—and schools will need to tackle some of these new territories, and do so with due speed. But hurrying to implement a host of innovations without full commitment and depth, implementing them in ways that actually do not affect student work or lead to improvements in teaching and learning, will mean that the forty years of failed efforts at school reform will set the stage for our future—and we cannot let that happen.

Once you and your school community have made the commitment to make the CCSS a lever that powers school reform, and once you have set priorities and goals you plan to work toward with intensity and fidelity, then you are ready to use assessments to help you actually lift the level of teaching and learning in those areas. In the rest of this chapter we explain ways that

- past assessments have led curriculum far afield of CCSS goals
- future assessments may (or may not) support whole-school reform
- present assessments can be created, revised, and critiqued to fuel school reform and lead to CCSS goals and beyond

PAST ASSESSMENTS HAVE LED CURRICULUM FAR AFIELD OF CCSS GOALS

It's only common sense that in a test-driven educational system, if high-stakes tests ask students to do little more than read a barrage of short passages and then answer multiple-choice questions that require low levels of skills, then the literacy curriculum will match those skill-and-drill tests. That is the situation in America today. That is, one important factor that helps to explain why America's students are not faring well on international benchmarks and why they are not graduating from high school with the skills needed to excel in college is that teachers across the country are teaching to tests that do not assess complex abilities. The tests do not measure students' abilities to write essays, compose compelling narratives, develop theories about characters and themes, read critically, synthesize across large swathes of texts, recognize assumptions and biases in texts, compare and contrast across texts, or engage in research. Today's tests do not measure students' mastery of high-level, complex skills.

When high-stakes tests ask little of students, schools that teach only low-level literacy skills can appear to be doing an acceptable job. In addition, published basal or textbook programs that merely ask students to fill in little blanks as a substitute for writing can appear to be satisfactory. Teachers who follow scripted "teacher-proof" programs, not thinking in response to what students do, can appear to be effective. They can all appear that way because the tests ask for only low-level work. The expectation of low-level tests functions as deadweight, dragging down what happens not only in classrooms but also in the educational system as a whole. That, essentially, is the situation in America's schools today.

This problem is made all the more intense by the fact that our country inadvertently created a system that rewards states for lowering the level of rigor in their high-stakes tests. That is, No Child Left Behind legislation pressured schools into producing a steady increase in scores on standardized tests. In order to produce that required result, many (if not all) states lowered the cognitive demand of their tests, or adjusted their scoring scales, so that a reasonable percentage of students would show the required Adequate Yearly Progress (AYP). The trend to lower the demands of the states' tests was accelerated by the fact that NCLB requires standardized tests to be given each year. In this time of declining budgets, the expense of that decision has channeled states to rely increasingly on cheaper, multiple-choice assessments, and multiple-choice questions tend not to assess higher-level comprehension and composition skills.

When one thinks about it, it is not surprising that when our country has a system in which each state is left on its own to design and adapt its own measuring stick—creating and calibrating its own high-stakes tests—and when the federal government gives advantages to states that achieve expected levels of progress on whatever scale those states adopt and punishes those that do not, states end up altering measuring sticks and scales so that it appears that students are making progress. The fact that this trend exists is especially obvious when one contrasts the scores students achieve on their states' tests with the scores they receive on the National Assessment of Educational Progress, the one and only measuring stick that has remained constant from state to state, from year to year. Given this, it is useful to keep Campbell's law in mind when considering the role—and impact—of high-stakes testing in this country: "The more any quantitative social indicator is used for social decision making, the more subject it will be to corruption pressures and the more apt it will be to distort and corrupt the social processes it is intended to monitor" (Campbell 1976).

This perfect storm of conditions has played a large role in explaining why millions of children today are given a skill-and-drill reading textbook curriculum that asks little of teachers and little of students. This is part of the explanation for why only nineteen out of every one hundred ninth graders are graduating from college within six years of graduating from high school. If we are going to educate students to handle the world's problems—the ever widening gap between rich and poor, the skyrocketing rates of obesity and autism, the decaying infrastructure across our country—then tests, the tail that wags the dog, need to assess skills that we value.

Given the context of American education today, in which the world of schools is driven by a laserlike focus on "results" (interpreted to mean scores), it is probably good news that the Department of Education has channeled 350 million dollars to two consortia—PARCC (Partnership for Assessment of Readiness for College and Careers) and SMARTER Balanced—that have been charged with developing standardized tests that can be given across participating states, tests that will not be controlled by any one state, and that supposedly will be aligned to the new standards, to each other, and to international benchmarks. In fact, there is probably no other initiative that has a greater potential to affect education across America than the development of those tests.

FUTURE ASSESSMENTS FROM PARCC AND SMARTER BALANCED MAY SUPPORT WHOLE-SCHOOL REFORM

A lot is known about the two groups charged with developing the assessments, and less is known about the assessments themselves. PARCC is led by a group of seventeen states, each playing a role in the decision-making process for the consortium. One representative from each of these states is on the leadership team, and this group is responsible for coordinating the development of assessments.

SMARTER Balanced is composed of twenty-eight states and supports approximately twenty-two million K–12 students. It is led by Judy Park (Utah) and Carissa Miller (Idaho), who are governing coleaders, and by Linda Darling-Hammond, the senior research analyst.

Although these consortia are working in competition with each other, the expectation is that the two groups will contribute to a shared body of knowledge, although they will be making two different tests. The new assessment has been predicted to be released by 2014, at the end of a four-year grant period.

You are sure to have lots of questions about the assessments. Will there be one national test? Will it be internationally benchmarked? Will it lead to a national curriculum? Will it be scored centrally? Will state results be announced against a comparison group composed of students in that state or students in all states within PARCC's or SMARTER Balanced's reach?

Many of the answers to your questions (and ours) are not available yet—and the answers that are available keep changing.

To date, the plan is for both sets of assessments to be taken on computers so that results can be returned more quickly and can therefore be more apt to influence instruction. The computer assistance will be especially integral to the design of SMARTER Balanced's assessment; currently the group is planning for an adaptive assessment. This means that if a student answers one particular question correctly, she will be channeled to a more complex portion of the test; if the student answers the question incorrectly, she will be channeled to a less demanding portion of the test. The diverging paths can continue throughout the test. At this point, both consortia plan to rely upon a combination of computer scoring and teacher scoring.

All in all, these new assessments may prove to be innovative and able to assess higher-level thinking, reading, and writing skills. That is certainly a clearly stated goal. On the other hand, the entire enterprise may amount to something far less radical or new than the drumroll suggests. You may be surprised to hear this, recalling that 350 million dollars have been invested in the effort. The important thing to realize is that 350 million does not come close to covering the cost of actually giving and scoring the new assessments.

For example, whereas existing high-stakes tests can be scored for eight dollars per student, the word is that the tests that are being designed may cost thirty dollars per student to deliver and score. If that is the case, will states adopt the new assessments? Then, too, consider the technological infrastructure that will need to be developed before all students across the nation can work on computers to take a test, all working at roughly the same time of year. The biggest price tag of the planned assessments, however, will be evident once the scores are in. Some have projected that if American students today were tested to determine whether their work was at the level established by the CCSS, almost three-quarters of them would be shown to be working below standards; many would be working far below the ambitious standards of the Common Core. Students who fail will need remedial education. Providing those services to a large percentage of our student population would be costly indeed. Given the present economic situation, it's hard not to question whether states will actually have the financial resources necessary to adopt these assessments.

For now, educators must wait to see what will come from the effort to create new Common Core–aligned assessments. We cannot move forward with crystal-clear knowledge of what we will encounter around the next bend. We will want to keep ears to the ground; we suggest you bookmark the web pages for the two consortia, and especially the one to which your state belongs. PARCC's address is www.parcconline.org, and SMARTER Balanced's is www.smarterbalanced.org.

Of course, it's never wise to judge the work of an organization only by its website. There are many understandable reasons why a website would not feature a full picture of an organization's work. However, in trying to understand the assessment pictures painted by PARCC and by SMARTER Balanced, it would be foolish to ignore the picture the websites do paint. It is easy to read both websites quickly and decide that there is no real difference between the two organizations; at first pass, the two consortia seem to make similar claims about their goals and the work they are taking up. It appears, at first, that the only difference to grab hold of is that SMARTER Balanced is planning for an adaptive computer-based assessment, rather than the static one PARCC intends. (The veneer of likeness is perpetuated somewhat by the webinars they offer up jointly to the public—both PARCC and SMARTER Balanced present comparable condensed PowerPoint slides, making analogous points. The archived, free webinars are easy to access through a web search.) On the other hand, if you were to devote several hours exploring the two sites, as they stand at the date of this publication, here are some of the observations you would probably make:

Content Availability

+ SMARTER Balanced's website is extremely content rich. It is clearly devoted to the purposes of orienting the reader to the assessment task they've taken up and to the considerations and complexities involved in making sound, research-based decisions. They've posted dozens of reports and articles to help visitors to the site understand their goals and the reasons for the choices they are making to attain those goals.

+ PARCC's website has content as well, though not as much and not in the same categories or with the same depth. The website has a slight public relations or marketing feel to it, with categories such as "Hot Topics" and with a light-reading newsletter that calls on readers to submit testimonials about PARCC's work to date.

Transparency and Authority Base

+ SMARTER Balanced has posted information about itself that anticipates questions readers should, and have a right to, ask about the consortium's authority and research base. The descriptions of the team and the evolution of the work have been written with the awareness that the education world is often populated, nowadays, with businesspeople who have little or no experience with school and children and teachers. The consortium is careful to describe the in-depth education experience of its members and careful to describe the research upon which the assessment is being constructed.

✦ While it does not mean that the PARCC team is not equally qualified, the same depth of transparency of process and participants is not provided on their site. The site does not seemed designed to anticipate questions and critiques from the field about the foundations upon which this work is built and the claim to authority that its participants hold.

✦ SMARTER Balanced has, in its top leadership posts, well-established educators and leaders in the field of education, in addition to the state-by-state representatives. Linda Darling-Hammond, for example, is a well-recognized education researcher and policy advisor at Stanford—she was a top contender for the post of Secretary of Education for the Obama administration. Laura Benson is formerly of PEBC, a leading teacher professional development organization based in Colorado. They have also paired with WestEd, the California-based, highly respected, deeply embedded research-centered organization.

✦ PARCC membership, while representative of the states, does not visibly draw on the preexisting teacher and administrator professional development organizations prominent in the field in the last decade. Further research might reveal that those connections exist, however.

Assessment or Curriculum?

✦ Perhaps the most important observation one might make, however, is that SMARTER Balanced posts materials about assessments and assessment design. The document entitled "English Language Arts and Literacy Draft Content Specifications," in particular, is a seventy-four-page document of carefully and neatly laid out explanations of the individual talks, the decision-making process, the research foundations, and the caveats inherent in the development of the assessment.

- ✦ PARCC, in contrast, has posted "Model Content Frameworks for ELA and Literacy" as the bulk of the material available to the public. As stated in the document, these frameworks are "to serve as a bridge between the Common Core State Standards and the PARCC assessments." The document goes on to say that the Model Content Frameworks are to help curriculum developers and teachers as they work to implement the standards in their states and districts. In other words, the consortium seems to have taken on a task beyond that of the CCSS and beyond that of developing assessments—they have selected methods and curricula for teachers. On what foundations do they base the decisions they've made about how to teach to the standards? Does their advice and do their frameworks lead students to the CCSS? Those are very good questions, and ones to which we have no answers. In fact, it is hard to imagine how one could have an answer, since there is much research to suggest that their frameworks are not grounded in best practice, and they have not had the time to pilot this work and match it to the standards in order to create new research. A cynic might infer that PARCC is approaching this task with a stance of "cornering the market" and wooing additional states through appealing to busy teachers with free, "CCSS–aligned" teaching materials.

During this time of assessment uncertainty, the most important thing you can do is focus on the work that lies before you—becoming the strongest teacher you can become, working to turn your school into a place where teachers help each other become stronger together than anyone could be alone. Research by Michael Pressley has shown that students in the classrooms of the most effective teachers learn in six months what children in an average classroom learn in a year. The real work of implementing the Common Core, then, is nothing short than the work of improving teaching and learning.

CREATE, REVISE, AND CRITIQUE PRESENT ASSESSMENTS TO FUEL WHOLE-SCHOOL REFORM

If there is a magical solution to reforming schools in line with the CCSS— and we think there is—that magic will come from an increased attention to formative assessments in the richest and best sense of the word, and from instruction that is increasingly assessment based.

But let's be clear: There is no guarantee that formative assessments will be forces for the good. They often aren't. Often, in the name of assessments, teachers spend countless hours weighing and measuring for no real purpose except that they have been told to do so, making spreadsheets and data charts, all designed to package and market and defend one's teaching or to please some external inspector. Sometimes schools link student achievement on formative assessments to teacher evaluations, and it is almost inevitable, then, that those assessments become toxic, pitting teacher against teacher, creating competition, antagonism, mistrust. So when we say that formative assessments have the potential to be powerfully good, it is important to also acknowledge that they have the potential to be powerfully bad.

But our experience has shown us that there are ways to use performance assessments that can help teachers be much more clear with themselves and with students about what constitutes good work, and those assessments (and the conversations around them) can help teachers provide students with more informative, instructive, and enabling feedback. This feedback, in turn, allows learners to progress in ways that are visible to themselves and to others; that visible progress allows both students and teachers to see that hard work actually produces concrete, observable results.

This system of continual improvement can start with teachers developing easy-to-deliver, homespun, low-stakes performance assessments, designed to gauge students' progress on skills that the teachers decide are front and center in a particular unit of study.

We and our colleagues at the Teachers College Reading and Writing Project have developed a set of formative assessments, approved by PARCC and used across New York City in a citywide effort to roll out the CCSS. These are available for no charge, along with samples of student responses, on our website (www.readingandwritingproject.com).

As you and your school team create, revise, and critique assessments, keep the following points in mind.

If you assess skills from reading standards beyond standard 1, then you may need to assess the skills named in the earlier standards, too. If you assess standard 2 of informational reading (determining central ideas), for example, but you don't assess standard 1 (reading literally), and the child you're assessing doesn't reach standard 2 well, you won't know if that is because she couldn't determine the central idea or if she could not read the text.

The CCSS apply to both print and digital informational texts, so if you're assessing skills related to the reading standards, you could assess them on a digital text. Although it is possible to assess a skill using a digital text, our piloting has shown that digital texts have many detractors and it is not necessarily easier to perform high-level reading work on them than it is on print texts at similar levels of complexity.

If you assess a skill like reading standard 1 or 2 (restating or determining central ideas), you'll need to assess it at more than one text level. If you assess a skill on only one level of text, and the student doesn't demonstrate the skill, you still won't know if the child can actually do that skill. It could be he can do the skill, but not yet on that level of text. If you ask a student to perform the skill on a few text levels or on a level of text that you know the reader can handle, you will find out if he can do the skill (and if he can, you will find out at what level it breaks down).

If you assess a skill and want to know if a student is doing it independently, the assessment can't include parts the students do collaboratively. If any parts of the performance assessments are done with others, if the meaning is co-constructed, such as with partners talking through the text together, then the assessment won't measure what it is intended to measure. In that case, you are assessing an ability to make meaning collaboratively, which is a different skill. Many Common Core–aligned assessments we have reviewed to date have involved collaboration yet were designed to assess independence. Make sure to filter these two kinds of assessments—those that test independent skill use and those that test collaborative skill use—into separate categories, for accuracy.

If you want to assess any kind of writing, but the writing requires responding to a text, then what manifests itself as inability to do the writing skill might in fact be inability to do the reading skill. For accuracy when assessing a writing skill, you may first need to assess the writing skill separately from any reading, on a topic the student is clearly knowledgeable about, so you can know you are assessing the skill itself. Then, if you want to assess ability to do that same kind of writing in response to a text, you'll know whether the issue is the ability to construct an argument, for example, or the ability to first read and then construct an argument on that text.

If you want to assess any writing, but building the writing requires understanding of content-area information, then what manifests itself as inability to do the writing skill might in fact be inability to understand the content. The same issue arises with content-area information as arises in writing based on a reading. If you want to assess a writing skill, you'll first have to be sure the student is familiar with the content she'll be writing about.

Consider using the same assessment task for both the beginning and the end of a unit of study. Some object to using the same instrument twice as bookends for the instruction (students have already tried this task once), but we have not found a feasible, sound alternative. If these assessments are responsive to curriculum and children's needs, growing out of the field, it is highly unlikely that a teacher or a group of teachers can devise two entirely separate assessments, one to be used for the preassessment and one for the postassessment, that will be calibrated exactly to match each other. And, if the match is not exact, then how can you determine if the students have increased in skill? If the preassessment and postassessment are not calibrated, a teacher cannot see the effects of her teaching; changes in the students' responses may be due to changes in the assessment, not due to learning. Using the same assessment before and after a chunk of teaching makes it easy for teachers to see how teaching has affected students' abilities. When such assessments are used across the grade level, it will be apparent that some teachers' students have grown dramatically, and those teachers' methods of teaching will need to be studied.

Think carefully about the rubric associated with the assessment. If there is a rubric with the assessment, we advise that you avoid relying primarily on deficit language—describing children's absence of skill in terms like *sometimes*, *never*, and *rarely*. The most helpful rubrics describe exactly what one *does* see; they describe what learning a skill looks like even in the very earliest stages of its development. At best, a rubric for any one grade level will need also to show the progression of work that leads up to the goal, not just lump it all together. Rubrics are most helpful if they are grounded in a K–12 learning progression that links one grade to another, showing a progression of skill development. Examples are available on the Reading and Writing Project's website, www.readingandwritingproject.com.

■　■　■

When teachers across a grade level have agreed to try some shared performance assessments, either ones from our website, ones they have created, or ones they have critiqued and revised from another source, we have seen huge changes in the culture of the schools. For example, the teachers might have agreed to do a shared preassessment at the start of a unit of study and a shared postassessment toward the end of that unit, scoring both the preassessment and the postassessment collaboratively, with all the student work in one giant pile. This has often led to the realization that some teachers have been teaching in ways that yield pretty dramatic results. What a wonderful thing it is when teachers feel safe enough to be able to admire the results of each other's teaching and to say, "May I come learn from what you are doing?"

This can happen. We've seen it in scores of schools. If this time, the call for reform is finally, at long last, accompanied by research—real research into what conditions allow some schools to lift levels of teaching and learning in ways that make a visible difference—then it will be evident to all that, in fact, the Common Core State Standards themselves had it right when they said, from the start, that it must be teachers and principals who figure out methods for implementing these standards. For the process of figuring out how to implement the Common Core State Standards will, itself, be the pathway. When teachers pull together to study student work, to study their own teaching, to study what does and does not lead to increasing achievement and what does and does not support trajectories of progress, that process of studying and talking and reading and teaching and questioning and teaching again will, in fact, be the pathway to implementing the Common Core State Standards.

Achieve. 2011. *Rubrics for Evaluating Open Education Resource (OER) Objects.* Washington, DC: Achieve.

Allington, Richard. 2002. "You Can't Learn Much from Books You Can't Read." *Association for Supervision and Curriculum Development* 60 (3): 16–19.

———. 2005. *What Really Matters for Struggling Readers: Designing Research Based Programs.* 2d ed. Boston: Allyn and Bacon.

Allington, Richard, and Peter Johnston. 2002. *Reading to Learn: Lessons from Exemplary Fourth-Grade Classrooms.* New York: Guilford Press.

Anderson, Carl. 2000. *How's It Going? A Practical Guide to Conferring with Student Writers.* Portsmouth, NH: Heinemann.

———. 2005. *Assessing Writers.* Portsmouth, NH: Heinemann.

Beers, Kylene. 2003. *When Kids Can't Read, What Teachers Can Do: A Guide for Teachers, 6–12.* Portsmouth, NH: Heinemann.

Booker, Cory. 2011. Williams College commencement speech, Williamstown, MA, June 5.

Bransford, John D., Ann L. Brown, and Rodney R. Cocking, eds. 1999. *How People Learn: Brain, Mind, Experience, and School.* Washington, DC: National Academy Press.

Bruner, Jerome S. 1963. *The Process of Education.* New York: Vintage Books.

Calkins, Lucy, et al. 2006. *Units of Study for Teaching Writing, Grades 3–5.* Portsmouth, NH: Heinemann.

———. 2010. *Units of Study for Teaching Reading: A Curriculum for the Reading Workshop, Grades 3–5.* Portsmouth, NH: Heinemann.

Campbell, Donald T. 1976. "Assessing the Impact of Planned Social Change." In *Social Research and Public Policies,* edited by Gene M. Lyons, 3–45. Hanover, NH: University Press of New England.

Chall, Jeanne S., Glenda L. Bissex, Sue S. Conard, and Susan Harris-Sharples. 1996. *Qualitative Assessment of Text Difficulty: A Practical Guide for Teachers and Writers.* Cambridge, MA: Brookline Books.

Coleman, David, and Susan Pimentel. 2011. "Publishers' Criteria for the Common Core State Standards in English Language Arts and Literacy, Grades 3–12." Available at www.sde.ct.gov/sde/cwp/view.asp?a=2618&q=322592.

Corcoran, Tom, Frederic A. Mosher, and Aaron Rogat. 2009. *Learning Progressions in Science: An Evidence-Based Approach to Reform.* Philadelphia: Consortium for Policy Research in Education.

Daniels, Harvey. 2002. *Literature Circles: Voice and Choice in Book Clubs and Reading Groups.* Portland, ME: Stenhouse.

Darling-Hammond, Linda, Brigid Barron, P. David Pearson, and Alan H. Schoenfeld. 2008. *Powerful Learning: What We Know About Teaching for Understanding.* San Francisco: Jossey-Bass.

Deutschman, Alan. 2007. *Change or Die: The Three Keys to Change at Work and in Life.* New York: HarperBusiness.

Donahue, Patricia L., Kristin E. Voelkl, Jay R. Campbell, and John Mazzeo. 1999. *NAEP 1998 Reading Report Card for the Nation and the States.* Washington, DC: U.S. Department of Education.

Ehrenworth, Mary, and Vicki Vinton. 2005. *The Power of Grammar: Unconventional Approaches to the Conventions of Language.* Portsmouth, NH: Heinemann.

Elmore, Richard F. 1995. "Teaching, Learning, and School Organization: Principles of Practice and the Regularities of Schooling." *Educational Administration Quarterly* 31: 355–74.

———. 2004. "The Hollow Core of Leadership Practice in Education: And What to Do About It." Draft of article. Available at http://pc4p.com.au/images/Elmore_Hollow_Core.pdf.

Ericsson, K. Anders, Ralf T. Krampe, and Clemens Tesch-Römer. 1993. "The Role of Deliberate Practice in the Acquisition of Expert Performance." *Psychological Review* 100 (3): 363–406.

Fletcher, Ralph, and JoAnn Portalupi. 2001. *Writing Workshop: The Essential Guide.* Portsmouth, NH: Heinemann.

Fullan, Michael. 1993. *Change Forces: Probing the Depths of Educational Reform.* New York: Routledge.

———. 1999. *Changing Forces: The Sequel.* New York: Routledge.

———. 2007. *The New Meaning of Educational Change.* 4th ed. New York: Teachers College Press.

Gladwell, Malcolm. 2008. *Outliers: The Story of Success.* Boston: Little, Brown.

Goodman, Jesse. 1995. "Working with Teachers to Reform Schools: Issues of Power, Expertise, and Commitment." In *Critical Discourses on Teacher Development*, edited by John Smyth. London: Cassells Press.

Graff, Gerald. 2003. *Clueless in Academe.* New Haven: Yale University Press.

Graham, Steve, and Dolores Perin. 2007. *Writing Next: Effective Strategies to Improve Writing of Adolescents in Middle and High Schools.* Washington, DC: Alliance for Excellent Education.

Graves, Donald. 2003. *Writing: Teachers and Children at Work.* 20th anniversary ed. Portsmouth, NH: Heinemann.

Guthrie, John T. 2004. "Teaching for Literacy Engagement." *Journal of Literacy Research* 36 (1): 1–30.

Guthrie, John T., and Nicole Humenick M. 2004. "Motivating Students to Read: Evidence for Classroom Practices That Increase Reading Motivation and Achievement." In *The Voice of Evidence in Reading Research*, edited by Peggy McCardle and Vinita Chhabra, 329–54. Baltimore: Brookes Publishing.

Hardy, Barbara. 1977. "Narrative as a Primary Act of Mind." In *The Cool Web: The Patterns of Children's Reading*, edited by Margaret Meek, Aidan Warlow, and Griselda Barton, 12–23. London: Bodley Head.

Hattie, John. 2009. *Visible Learning: A Synthesis of Over 800 Meta-Analyses Relating to Achievement*. New York: Routledge.

Hiebert, Elfrieda H. 2012. "The Common Core's Staircase of Text Complexity: Getting the Size of the First Step Right." *Reading Today* (Dec. 2011/Jan. 2012): 26–27.

Krashen, Stephen D. 2004. *The Power of Reading: Insights from Research*. 2d ed. Westport, CT: Libraries Unlimited.

Martin, Guy. 2009. "Shoot-Out." *The New Yorker*, 22 June, 27.

Murray, Donald. 1990. *Shoptalk: Learning to Write with Writers*. Portsmouth, NH: Boynton/Cook.

———. 2003. *A Writer Teaches Writing*. Rev. 2d ed. Belmont, CA: Wadsworth.

National Assessment Governing Board. 2007. *Writing Framework and Specifications for the 2007 National Assessment of Educational Progress*. Washington, DC: U.S. Department of Education.

National Commission on Excellence in Education (NCEE). 1983. "A Nation at Risk: The Imperative for Educational Reform." A Report to the Nation and the Secretary of Education, United States Department of Education, by the National Commission on Excellence in Education. Washington, DC: National Commission on Excellence in Education.

National Governors Association Center for Best Practices (NGA Center) and Council of Chief State School Officers (CCSSO). 2010a. *Common Core State Standards for English Language Arts and Literacy in History/Social Studies, Science, and Technical Subjects*. Washington, DC: NGA Center and CCSSO.

———. 2010b. *Common Core State Standards for English Language Arts and Literacy in History/Social Studies, Science, and Technical Subjects: Appendix A: Research Supporting Key Elements of the Standards; Glossary of Key Terms*. Washington, DC: NGA Center and CCSSO.

———. 2010c. *Common Core State Standards for English Language Arts and Literacy in History/Social Studies, Science, and Technical Subjects: Appendix B: Text Exemplars and Sample Performance Tasks*. Washington, DC: NGA Center and CCSSO.

———. 2010d. *Common Core State Standards for English Language Arts and Literacy in History/Social Studies, Science, and Technical Subjects: Appendix C: Samples of Student Writing*. Washington, DC: NGA Center and CCSSO.

Nye, Barbara, Spyros Konstantopoulos, and Larry Hedges. 2004. "How Large Are Teacher Effects?" *Educational Evaluation and Policy Analysis* 26 (3; fall): 237–57.

OECD. 2010. *PISA 2009 Results: What Students Know and Can Do—Student Performance in Reading, Mathematics and Science* (Volume 1). Available at http://dx.doi.org/10.1787/9789264091450-en.

Partnership for Assessment of Readiness for College and Careers (PARCC). 2011. *Draft Model Content Frameworks for English Language Arts/Literacy.* Washington, DC: Achieve.

Piercy, Thomasina. 2011. "The Text Complexity 'Staircase' in the Common Core Standards." The Leadership and Learning Blog. Leadership and Learning Center. Available at www.leadandlearn.com/blog/2011/04/text-complexity-staircase-common-core-standards?utm_source=feedburner&utm_medium=feed&utm_campaign=Feed%3A+leadandlearn+%28The+Leadership+and+Learning+Blog%29.

Popham, W. James. 2007. "The Lowdown on Learning Progressions." *Educational Leadership* 64 (7): 83–84.

Pressley, Michael, Sara E. Dolezal Kersey, Lisa Raphael Bogaert, Lindsey Mohan, Alysia D. Roehrig, and Kristen Warzon. 2003. *Motivating Primary-Grade Students.* New York: Guilford Press.

Rasinski, Tim. 2010. *The Fluent Reader: Oral and Silent Reading Strategies for Building Fluency, Word Recognition, and Comprehension.* 2d ed. New York: Scholastic.

Reeves, Douglas B. 2000. "Standards Are Not Enough: Essential Transformations for School Success." *NASSP Bulletin* 84 (620): 5–19.

———. 2010. *Finding Your Leadership Focus: What Matters Most for Student Results.* New York: Teachers College Press.

Rosenblatt, Louise. 1938/1968/1976/1995. *Literature as Exploration.* New York: Modern Language Association.

Sarason, Seymour. 1996. *Revisiting "the Culture of the School and the Problem of Change."* New York: Teachers College Press.

Scholes, Robert. 1989. *Protocols of Reading.* New Haven: Yale University Press.

Tyack, David, and Larry Cuban. 1997. *Tinkering Toward Utopia: A Century of Public School Reform.* Cambridge, MA: Harvard University Press.